QUANTITATIVE ANALYSIS
FOR
INVESTMENT MANAGEMENT

Robert A. Taggart, Jr.
Professor of Finance
Boston College

PRENTICE HALL, Upper Saddle River, NJ 07458

Acquisition Editor: Paul Donnelly
Marketing Manager: Susan McLaughlin
Senior Project Manager: Alana Zdinak
Production Editor: Progressive Publishing Alternatives
Interior Design: Progressive Publishing Alternatives
Cover Design: Jayne Conte
Manufacturing Buyer: Vincent Scelta
Assistant Editor: Teresa Cohan
Editorial Assistant: Mary Beth Sanok
Production Coordinator: David Cotugno

Transferred to digital print on demand, 2002

Printed and bound by Antony Rowe Ltd, Eastbourne

10 9 8 7 6 5 4 3 2

ISBN   0-13-319690-9

Prentice-Hall International (UK) Limited,London
Prentice-Hall of Australia Pty. Limited, Sydney
Prentice-Hall Canada Inc., Toronto
Prentice-Hall Hispanoamericana, S.A., Mexico
Prentice-Hall of India Private Limited, New Delhi
Prentice-Hall of Japan, Inc., Tokyo
Pearson Education Asia Pte. Ltd., Singapore
Editora Prentice-Hall do Brasil, Ltda., Rio de Janeiro

Brief Contents

Contents

Preface

Quantitative analysis and models have rapidly pervaded financial markets and the investment management industry over the past quarter century. Without these tools, the explosive growth in the derivative and asset-backed securities markets, the introduction and refinement of portfolio management techniques, and the development of new trading strategies, all of which have revolutionized world financial markets, would hardly have been possible. Despite their widespread use, however, the tools of quantitative investment analysis are truly accessible to a relatively small number of market participants, and they are viewed as arcane and forbidding to many others.

The purpose of this book is to provide a concise overview of the quantitative tools and models that have been most widely used in investment management. These tools are primarily useful for the following: (a) measuring and managing the different dimensions of risk, (b) valuing securities of different types, (c) identifying arbitrage pricing relationships across securities markets, and (d) implementing portfolio strategies. It is the premise of the book that many of the most popular quantitative techniques have certain elements in common, and that if these elements can be understood, the reader can gain a working understanding of a wide variety of complex securities and portfolio management techniques.

To say that a working understanding can be gained is not to say that the reader will be transformed into an instant "rocket scientist." That would require a good deal of additional advanced study. Rather, the target audience for this book is current or aspiring capital market professionals who wish to have a better understanding of securities, financial services, and investment management techniques, even if they are not actively engaged in their design. As a rough benchmark, the reader of this book should acquire sufficient background to read articles in such practitioner-oriented publications as the *Financial Analysts Journal* or the *Journal of Portfolio Management* with understanding and an eye for their application.

The book emphasizes tools, models, and problem-solving. Since it devotes little space to the institutional details of financial markets and instruments, the reader should have some general background in the investments field. A knowledge of basic calculus and the rudiments of matrix algebra is useful for understanding derivations, but for the most part these have been placed in appendices. The end-of-chapter problems and text discussions rely primarily on algebra. At Boston College, the material in this book is taught in a one-semester course entitled Capital Market Theory. It is a required course for our Master of Science in Finance students, who take it after they have taken Investments and before they have taken a more advanced course on derivative securities. In addition, the course is taken as an advanced elective by M.B.A. students, and the material in the book is also suitable for advanced undergraduates in finance or economics. The book can be used as the basis for a stand-alone course, as it is at Boston College, but it is also suitable as a supplement for such courses as Money and Capital Markets, Fixed Income Securities, Derivative Securities, and Portfolio Management. The book is designed for use in company training programs in any of these areas as well.

Introduction

FINANCE AS A TECHNOLOGY

As it has in other areas, developing technology has wrought a revolution in the practice of finance over the past two decades. Advances in communications and computing technology have greatly facilitated global integration of capital markets, proliferation of new and increasingly complex securities, and the ability of capital market institutions to process growing transaction volumes. In addition to these rather apparent influences of technology, a hallmark of capital market developments since the 1970s has been that the entire field of finance has increasingly come to be recognized as a technology in its own right.

Technology has been defined as "the application of scientific knowledge, methods or research to practical purposes." This definition emphasizes the fact that academic research has interacted with capital market practice as it has in few other areas of management in recent years. The purpose of this book is to introduce some of the basic results from that research and show how those results can be used to gain insight into practical problems in investment management.

Joseph Grundfest, a former member of the United States Securities and Exchange Commission, has argued that there are four primary aspects to the "new technology of finance".[1] While other aspects might also be identified, these four afford a convenient guide to some of the major elements in this book.

The first aspect of the new technology is the enhanced ability of financial market professionals to define and reallocate risk. This book contains numerous examples of this aspect under such topics as measuring and managing interest rate risk, designing portfolio strategies, and using options and futures contracts to tailor a portfolio's risk profile.

A second and closely related aspect is the growth of portfolio thinking, which refers to assessing risk and return in terms of entire portfolios rather than individual securities. As illustrated in Part 2 on portfolio management, this aspect gives new insights into how to make use of security analysis and measure overall performance.

The third aspect is market efficiency, which refers to the tendency under competition for security prices to embody all relevant information. In particular, this book addresses efficiency across securities and across markets. The essence of the no-arbitrage principle, which appears in many guises throughout the book, is that perfect substitutes should sell at the same price. Thus, if we wish to price a given security, no matter how complex, and if we can create a perfect substitute for that security using different types of securities or similar securities from other markets, the pricing of the substitute securities provides relevant information as to how the original security should be priced. This insight has proven particularly useful in the pricing of bonds, options, and futures contracts.

The fourth aspect, which results from the other three and the explosion in information availability, is the increased premium on sophistication and specialization among capital market professionals. There are more markets, more securities, and more pricing relationships to keep track of. New theoretical work is often highly mathematical, and increasingly complex computer programs have come into use. As a result, the technical specialists can be seen as exerting a kind of tyranny over the rest of us, who may not have the expertise to follow their every step. However, a basic theme of this book is that many of even the most arcane elements of the new technology of finance rest on a few basic principles, such as the no-arbitrage principle, which appear over and over again in different forms. If these basic principles are firmly grasped, they can lead to an understanding of the essential features of a complex transaction, even if some of the steps along the way are too technical to follow. A primary objective of the book, then, is to help the capital market professional who does not necessarily aspire to be a technical specialist gain a working understanding of the new technology of finance.

OUTLINE OF TOPICS

The book's thirteen chapters are divided into two parts. Part I is devoted to the analysis and valuation of individual securities, while Part II considers portfolios of securities. The first three chapters discuss option-free fixed income securities, addressing such topics as price-yield relationships, measuring and managing interest rate risk, and the term structure of interest rates. Chapter 4 covers the discounted cash flow approach to equity valuation, while Chapter 5 considers option pricing, including both the binomial and Black-Scholes models. Chapters 6 and 7 use the principles of option pricing to analyze fixed income securities and equities with embedded options, which include callable bonds, mortgage-backed securities, and convertible bonds. Chapter 8 concludes the first section of the book with a discussion of futures and forward contracts.

The book's section on portfolio management begins in Chapter 9 with a discussion of investor preferences and attitudes toward risk. Chapter 10 then develops the mean-variance framework for portfolio selection and analyzes a number of generic portfolio problems, which form the basic building blocks for more complex portfolio strategies. When investors in the aggregate form portfolios according to the principles developed in Chapter 10, this practice has implications for security pricing, and Chapter 11 thus considers models of equilibrium security pricing in the capital markets. These models include the capital asset pricing model and the arbitrage pricing theory. Chapter 12 analyzes more complex variations on the generic portfolio problems, including tactical asset allocation and the use of futures and options to control various dimensions of portfolio risk. Finally, Chapter 13 discusses the problem of portfolio performance management as well as other facets of the administration of the portfolio management process.

Essential elements of the book are the numerical problems and spreadsheet exercises at the end of each chapter. This approach reflects a belief that the material is best learned if students work with it and try to apply the basic principles in a variety of different contexts. A number of ancillary topics are developed through problems, rather than being explicitly discussed in the text, and the problems also illustrate the properties of many of the concepts introduced in the text. To achieve the fullest understanding of the text material, then, it is essential to work through the problems. The specific details of financial instruments and services have constantly been changing and this pattern undoubtedly will continue, so no book in this field can hope to remain up-to-date on institutional details for very long. However, if students can develop problem-solving skills, they will be able to see the basic principles at work behind new instruments and products, and they will be able to analyze these developments on their own.

Footnotes

[1] See Joseph A. Grundfest, "The New Technology of Finance," *Financial Executive,* September/October 1987, pp. 44–47.

I

Analysis of
Individual Securities

1

Fixed Income Security Prices and Yields

I. OVERVIEW

Fixed income securities, as their name implies, stipulate a formula according to which the issuer is to make payments to the investor at specified future dates. In many cases, these payments are fixed in nominal terms at the time the securities are issued. Ignoring complexities such as call provisions and prepayment options, which are discussed in Chapter 6, this arrangement is true of most bonds and mortgages issued in the U.S. Other fixed income securities, however, stipulate future payments that are tied in some specified way to future economic conditions. Examples include floating rate and purchasing power bonds.

The initial discussion of fixed income securities is spread over three chapters, this first of which deals with prices and yields. The fundamental pricing principles for fixed income securities are relatively simple. However, different categories of fixed income securities are subject to different price quotation and yield conventions, and it is necessary for market professionals to be familiar with these conventions. In addition, the Introduction emphasized the importance throughout this book of arbitrage pricing relationships between complex securities and more fundamental building block securities. This chapter affords a first look at such arbitrage pricing in the relationship between coupon-bearing and zero-coupon bond prices. In the two subsequent chapters, these price and yield principles are applied to some classic problems in fixed income securities management. Chapter 2 is devoted to measuring and managing interest rate risk for option-free bonds, while Chapter 3 discusses the yield curve and different explanations for the term structure of interest rates.

II. THE STANDARD RELATIONSHIP BETWEEN BOND PRICES AND YIELDS

A bond's indenture stipulates the amount and timing of its cash flows (i.e., coupon and principal payments), and based on these, market transactions determine the bond's price. While the cash flows and price are the most fundamental features of any bond, it is also conventional to define a bond's yield to maturity, which links the two. The standard relationship between a bond's price and its yield defines yield through the following discounted cash flow expression:

$$P = \sum_{t=1}^{n} \frac{C}{(1 + y)^t} + \frac{F}{(1 + y)^n} \tag{1.1}$$

where P = the current market price of the bond,
n = the number of periods remaining until the bond matures,
C = the bond's promised, or contractual, coupon payment per period,
F = the bond's face value, or principal amount, and
y = the bond's yield to maturity.

This expression is useful for illustrating some fundamental properties of bond pricing (for example, when required market yields go up, bond prices go down; $P > F$, $= F$, and $< F$ correspond respectively to $C/F > y$, $= y$, $< y$). However, this standard equation doesn't account for several complexities in price-yield relationships that market professionals must be aware of.

III. COMPLEXITIES IN FIXED INCOME SECURITY PRICE-YIELD RELATIONSHIPS

A. Different Compounding Periods

In introductory textbook discussions, the length of the periods in Equation (1.1) is usually taken to be one year. This value is appropriate for the typical bond traded in the Eurobond market, which makes coupon payments once per year. Consider, for example, a Eurodollar bond with a 10% coupon rate and 10 years remaining to maturity. If the bond is currently selling in the market for $100.507 (per $100 of face value), we can use Equation (1.1) to compute the yield to maturity as 9.9178%.

For bonds issued and traded in the U.S., however, the typical convention is for coupon payments to be made semiannually. Such a bond would thus pay half the annual coupon amount every six months. In recognition of this fact, we can rewrite Equation (1.1) for a bond that pays coupons semiannually as follows:

$$P = \sum_{t=1}^{n} \frac{\dfrac{C}{2}}{\left(1 + \dfrac{y}{2}\right)^t} + \frac{F}{\left(1 + \dfrac{y}{2}\right)^n} \tag{1.2}$$

where n is now the number of semiannual periods remaining until the bond matures. With the price-yield relationship written in this form, when one solves Equation (1.2) for the yield using most financial calculators or spreadsheets, the result is a semiannual yield, $y/2$. Instead of leaving the answer in this form, it is common practice to "annualize" it by multiplying by 2, the number of semiannual periods in a year.

For example, consider a domestic U.S. bond with a 10% coupon rate and ten years remaining to maturity, which sells for $102 (again, per $100 face value). This bond will make 20 coupon payments of $5 each, plus a principal payment of $100 at the end of 10 years. If we use Equation (1.2) to solve for the bond's yield, the answer given by a financial calculator is $y/2 = 4.8417\%$. It is then standard practice to multiply by 2 and quote the bond's yield to maturity as $y = 9.6834\%$.

While this yield calculation for the domestic bond is perfectly correct, it is important to note that is not directly comparable to the yield calculated previously for the Eurodollar bond. This is because the two yield calculations are based on different compounding period assumptions. For the Eurodollar bond, which pays coupons annually, it is natural to calculate a yield based on annual compounding using Equation (1.1). For the domestic bond, on the other hand, it is more natural to calculate a semiannually compounded yield using Equation (1.2), which reflects the bond's actual pattern of cash payments.

It is important not to infer, however, that the Eurodollar bond, with a quoted yield of 9.9178%, is a better investment than the domestic bond with the same annual coupon rate but a quoted yield of only 9.6834%. If we wish to compare the two yields, we must use the same compounding period assumption, which will adjust for any differences in the two securities' cash flow patterns.

In the example at hand, we could convert the semiannual yield of 4.8417% on the domestic bond to an effective annual yield. This conversion is done by noting that, over one year, a bond that pays interest semiannually would compound twice (assuming that any coupons received could be reinvested at the same yield). Thus, a bond that paid interest only once would have a comparable yield, y_a, only if

$$(1.048417)^2 = (1 + y_a) \qquad (1.3)$$

Solving for y_a then gives an effective annual yield for the domestic bond of 9.9178%, which is identical to the yield on the Eurodollar bond.

Alternatively, we could convert the yield on the Eurodollar bond to an effective yield assuming semiannual compounding. This conversion entails finding the semiannual yield, y_s, that would produce the same total return over one year as the Eurodollar bond, or

$$(1.099178) = \left(1 + \frac{y_s}{2}\right)^2 \qquad (1.4)$$

The solution is $y_s = 9.6834\%$, which is identical to the semiannually compounded yield on the domestic bond.

To summarize, it can be misleading to compare yields to maturity that have been calculated using different compounding period assumptions. Because these different assumptions reflect different cash flow patterns, there is no reason why a difference in yields, even for bonds with the same maturity, represents a profit opportunity. In the example just given, the yields on the Eurodollar and domestic bonds differ when one is calculated assuming annual compounding while the other is calculated assuming semiannual compounding. This difference does not imply that the bonds are mispriced, however, since the bonds' yields are identical when both are calculated using the same assumed compounding period.

B. Zero-Coupon Bonds and Treasury Bills

Unlike the standard bonds just discussed, a zero-coupon bond makes no periodic coupon payments, but only a single payment at maturity. For the most part, such bonds present no pricing difficulties: Equations (1.1) or (1.2) can be used, setting $C = 0$, so that the price is simply the present discounted value of the principal payment, F. Since the sole return comes from earning this discount over the life of the bond, these securities are also referred to as pure discount bonds.

As with ordinary coupon-bearing bonds, the cash flow—in this case, the single payment at maturity—and the bond's price are its fundamental characteristics, but we can also define various yield measures. For U.S. domestic zero-coupon bonds, standard practice would call for using Equation (1.2) to calculate semiannually compounded yields, so that these can be compared with the yields on domestic coupon-bearing bonds. U.S. Treasury bills, on the other hand, follow different price-yield conventions.

Treasury bills are also pure discount or zero-coupon securities, is-sued with maturities of 3, 6, or 12 months. The bid and ask quotations appearing in the newspaper are actually bank discount yields, y_D, which are defined as follows:

$$y_D = \frac{D}{F} \times \frac{360}{t} \qquad (1.5)$$

where D = dollar discount, or difference between face value and price,
$\quad\quad\ F$ = face value,
$\quad\quad\ t$ = number of days remaining to maturity.

The dollar price, P, of a Treasury bill is then the difference between F and D, or $P = F - D$.

It is clear that the bank discount yield is not a good measure of re-turn on investment, since it compares the dollar discount with the face value, or principal amount, rather than the price. A measure that at-tempts to correct this deficiency is the bond-equivalent yield, y_{BEQ}, de-fined for bills with less than six months to maturity as follows:[1]

$$y_{BEQ} = \frac{365 y_D}{360 - t y_D} \qquad (1.6)$$

If we substitute the definition of y_D from (1.5) into (1.6), we can see how the bond-equivalent yield attempts to convert the bank discount into a more natural measure of yield, or percentage return on investment, as follows:

$$y_{BEQ} = \frac{365 \dfrac{D}{F} \times \dfrac{360}{t}}{360 - \dfrac{D}{F} 360} = \frac{D}{F - D} \times \frac{365}{t} \qquad (1.7)$$

Thus, the bond-equivalent yield takes the dollar discount, which is the implicit net return on the Treasury bill, expresses it as a percentage of the bill's initial price, $F - D$, and then annualizes this percentage re-turn. It is important to note, however, that this measure effectively as-sumes a compounding period of t days, because it carries out the annual-ization by multiplying by the number of t-day periods in a 365-day year. Thus, one cannot directly compare bond-equivalent yields for bills with different times remaining to maturity, since these will be based on dif-ferent compounding period assumptions.

Suppose, for example, that an investor wants to measure precisely the difference in yields between 3-day bills and 6-month bills. Suppose further that today's *Wall Street Journal* reports the ask yield (this is the bond-equivalent yield calculated using the bill's asked price) as 8.00% for a 3-day bill and 8.20% for a 180-day bill. Comparing these yields directly suggests that somewhat higher yields can be earned by investing for six months, rather than on a very short-term basis. However, the 3-day bill's yield has been calculated using a 3-day compounding period, while the 180-day bill's yield has been calculated using a 180-day compounding period. If we wish to convert the 3-day bill's yield into a 180-day equivalent, we find the effective 180-day yield, y_{180}, needed to give the same total return as the 3-day yield compounded sixty times, as follows:

$$\left[1 + \frac{3}{365}(.0800) \right]^{60} = \left(1 + \frac{180}{365} y_{180} \right) \tag{1.8}$$

The solution is $y_{180} = 8.157\%$, which suggests that, instead of earning an extra 20 basis points by going somewhat longer, the investor can actually earn only about 4 basis points more. While this may not seem like a huge difference relative to the reported bond-equivalent yield of 8.00%, it can be significant for an institutional investor managing large amounts of money. Thus a knowledge of how to make accurate yield comparisons can be essential.

C. Prices and Yields between Coupon Dates

A third complexity in bond pricing is that, on most days, the bond price reported in the newspaper is not the actual cash (or invoice) price that an investor must pay to buy the bond. This is because most days fall between two coupon dates, in which case the buyer must pay the seller the accrued interest, or that portion of the next coupon payment the seller has implicitly earned by holding the bond from the last coupon date until now.

Consider, for example, a Treasury note with an $8\frac{1}{8}\%$ coupon that matures in February of 1998. Coupons are payable on February 15 and August 15 of each year. The *Wall Street Journal* of June 10, 1994, reported that the asking price of the bond for trading occurring June 9 was 105:29, or 105 and $\frac{29}{32}$, or 105.90625 per $100 face value. It is standard practice to quote U.S. Treasury bond prices on a skip-day settlement basis, which means that a trade occurring on June 9 was settled on the second business day after the trade, or on June 13. June 13 was in turn 118 days from the previous coupon date, while the entire coupon period, from February 15 to August 15 lasted 181 days. Thus, in addi-

TABLE 1.1   Numbers corresponding to days of the year

DAY OF MO.	JAN.	FEB.	MAR.	APR.	MAY	JUNE	JULY	AUG.	SEP.	OCT.	NOV.	DEC.
1	1	32	60	91	121	152	182	213	244	274	305	335
2	2	33	61	92	122	153	183	214	245	275	306	336
3	3	34	62	93	123	154	184	215	246	276	307	337
4	4	35	63	94	124	155	185	216	247	277	308	338
5	5	36	64	95	125	156	186	217	248	278	309	339
6	6	37	65	96	126	157	187	218	249	279	310	340
7	7	38	66	97	127	158	188	219	250	280	311	341
8	8	39	67	98	128	159	189	220	251	281	312	342
9	9	40	68	99	129	160	190	221	252	282	313	343
10	10	41	69	100	130	161	191	222	253	283	314	344
11	11	42	70	101	131	162	192	223	254	284	315	345
12	12	43	71	102	132	163	193	224	255	285	316	346
13	13	44	72	103	133	164	194	225	256	286	317	347
14	14	45	73	104	134	165	195	226	257	287	318	348
15	15	46	74	105	135	166	196	227	258	288	319	349
16	16	47	75	106	136	167	197	228	259	289	320	350
17	17	48	76	107	137	168	198	229	260	290	321	351
18	18	49	77	108	138	169	199	230	261	291	322	352
19	19	50	78	109	139	170	200	231	262	292	323	353
20	20	51	79	110	140	171	201	232	263	293	324	354
21	21	52	80	111	141	172	202	233	264	294	325	355
22	22	53	81	112	142	173	203	234	265	295	326	356
23	23	54	82	113	143	174	204	235	266	296	327	357
24	24	55	83	114	144	175	205	236	267	297	328	358
25	25	56	84	115	145	176	206	237	268	298	329	359
26	26	57	85	116	146	177	207	238	269	299	330	360
27	27	58	86	117	147	178	208	239	270	300	331	361
28	28	59	87	118	148	179	209	240	271	301	332	362
29	29	a	88	119	149	180	210	241	272	302	333	363
30	30		89	120	150	181	211	242	273	303	334	364
31	31		90		151		212	243		304		365

a In leap years, add 1 to the number shown in the table for all dates after February 28.

tion to the quoted price, the bond buyer had to pay the seller $\frac{118}{181}$ of a coupon payment. The invoice price of the bond was then \$105.90625 + $\left(\frac{118}{181}\right)(4.0625) = \$108.55473$. In making such accrued interest calculations, Table 1.1 can help to determine the number of days elapsed between particular dates.

For days between coupon dates, the calculation of yields to maturity is also affected by the accrued interest and by the fact that the number of periods remaining to maturity is not an integer, as is assumed in Equations (1.1) and (1.2). Instead, the yield between coupon dates for a bond that pays coupons semiannually is calculated from the following:

$$P = \sum_{t=1}^{n} \frac{\dfrac{C}{2}}{\left(1 + \dfrac{y}{2}\right)^{v}\left(1 + \dfrac{y}{2}\right)^{t-1}} + \frac{F}{\left(1 + \dfrac{y}{2}\right)^{v}\left(1 + \dfrac{y}{2}\right)^{n-1}} \qquad (1.9)$$

where $v = \dfrac{\text{number of days between settlement and next coupon}}{\text{number of days in coupon period}}$

Note that P in (1.9) denotes the full invoice of the price of the bond, including accrued interest, not the price quoted in the newspaper. In addition, n denotes the number of coupon dates remaining through maturity, so it includes both whole periods and the initial fractional period.

The $8\frac{1}{8}\%$ notes of February 1998 that we just priced provide an example of the use of Equation (1.9). The ask yield on these notes was quoted as 6.30%, given the \$105.55473 ask price of June 9, 1994. If we take this yield, convert it to its semiannual equivalent of 3.15%, and discount the bond's cash flows using Equation (1.9), with $v = 1 - \left(\frac{118}{181}\right) = .3481$, we calculate a present value of 108.5376, which checks with our calculated price (up to a rounding error in the quoted yield).

IV. ARBITRAGE RELATIONSHIPS BETWEEN WHOLE BONDS AND ZERO-COUPON BONDS

A. Coupon Stripping

The arbitrage relationship between U.S. Treasury bonds and Treasury strips affords a good application of the pricing principles discussed in Section II. Consider, for example, the same $8\frac{1}{8}\%$ notes of February 1998 that we examined in Section IIC. We determined there that these bonds could be purchased on June 9, 1994, at a price of 108.55473, payable on June 13. If it were possible to buy these notes, immediately separate them into their component pieces, and sell the pieces for more than we paid for the whole bonds, an arbitrage opportunity would clearly exist.

Exactly this opportunity has already been exploited by many securities firms engaging in coupon-stripping activities. In effect, coupon stripping entails taking a conventional bond and selling each of the cash payments as a separate security. Since each of the separate coupon payments and the principal payment then represent securities with a single payment at maturity, they trade as if they were zero-coupon bonds. Prices for these pieces of whole bonds are quoted under the heading U.S. Treasury Strips in the *Wall Street Journal*.

To see if the $8\frac{1}{8}\%$ notes of February 1998 afforded an arbitrage op-

TABLE 1.2 Proceeds from selling stripped $8\frac{1}{8}$s of February 1998
on June 9, 1994

DATE OF PAYMENT	AMOUNT	BID PRICE PER $ OF PAYMENT	PROCEEDS
Aug. 1994	4.0625	.993125	4.03457
Feb. 1995	4.0625	.9690625	3.93682
Aug. 1995	4.0625	.9421875	3.82764
Feb. 1996	4.0625	.910625	3.69941
Aug. 1996	4.0625	.8815625	3.58135
Feb. 1997	4.0625	.8515625	3.45947
Aug. 1997	4.0625	.821875	3.33887
Feb. 1998	4.0625	.79375 (Coup.)	3.22461
Feb. 1998	100.00	.7940625 (Prin.)	79.40625
		Total	108.50898
		Whole Bond Ask Price	108.55473
		Arbitrage Profit	−0.04575

portunity, we can use the Treasury strip prices from June 9, 1994, to see if we could have sold the pieces for more than the whole. Since we are selling these pieces, we should use bid instead of ask price quotations. The total proceeds from selling these pieces is shown in Table 1.2. The calculations indicate not only that the prices of the notes and strips were very close, but that a trader who bought the notes and stripped them would actually have lost about 4 cents per $100 face value. What about going in the other direction? If you would lose money by buying notes and selling strips, perhaps it would have paid to reconstitute the notes by buying strips and selling notes. In that case, however, we would have had to sell notes at the bid price and buy strips at the ask prices. Going through identical calculations to those in Table 1.2, but using the prices on the other side of the dealer's spread, as quoted for June 9, indicates that the strips would have cost 108.6192 per $100 of underlying face value, while selling the notes would have brought in only $108.4922. For these particular notes, therefore, there was no arbitrage opportunity from either stripping or reconstituting. While the prices of the notes and the strips were not identical, transaction costs (in the form of the dealers' bid-ask spreads) were such that one could not have exploited the small price differentials in either direction.

B. Using a Sequence of Bonds of Different Maturity to Determine Prices of Zeros

Coupon-stripping activities suggest that any coupon-bearing bond can be thought of as a portfolio of zeros, with each separate payment on the whole bond representing a zero-coupon bond. This approach in turn suggests that a sequence of whole bonds, of successively longer maturity, can be used to determine zero-coupon bond prices, even if we do not actually strip the whole bonds. In particular, for any bond with invoice price P, maturing n, and coupon rate C/F, the price of the whole bond can be represented as follows:

$$P = \sum_{t=1}^{n} \left(\frac{C}{2} \right) z_t + F z_n \qquad (1.10)$$

where z_t = current price of a zero-coupon security with a \$1 face value and a maturity date t periods from now.

Clearly, if we have a one-period bond, with any coupon rate, we can solve for z_1 if we know the price of the bond. Knowing z_1, we can solve for z_2 if we know in turn the price of a two-period bond with any coupon rate. Proceeding sequentially, we can thus solve for as many zero-coupon bond prices as we have coupon-bearing bond prices of successively longer maturity. This process is illustrated in Problem 6 at the end of this chapter. Note also that once we have determined these zero-coupon bond prices, we can check for arbitrage opportunities by seeing if the price of any given bond is consistent, through Equation (1.10), with these calculated zero-coupon prices. An example appears in Problem 7 at the end of the chapter.

C. Creating Zero-Coupon Bonds from Two Whole Bonds with the Same Maturity

Another way to create a synthetic zero-coupon bond is to combine long and short positions in two coupon-bearing bonds with the same maturity but different coupon rates. Consider again our $8\frac{1}{8}$% Treasury notes of February 1998. These notes make coupon payments of 4.0625 per \$100 face value every August 15 and February 15 and a final payment of 104.0625 on February 15, 1998. There is another Treasury note issue outstanding that also matures on February 15, 1998, but has a coupon rate of $5\frac{1}{8}$%. These notes make coupon payments of 2.5625 per \$100 face value each August 15 and February 15 plus a payment of \$102.5625 at maturity. The ratio of the coupon payments on the two note issues is $4.0625/2.5625 = 1.5854$.

Suppose, then, that we purchased 1.584 of the $5\frac{1}{8}$% notes for every one of the $8\frac{1}{8}$% notes that we sold. Our sale of the $8\frac{1}{8}$s entails a cash outflow (either actual or in an opportunity cost sense) of 4.0625 on each coupon date up to maturity, while the long position in the $5\frac{1}{8}$s entails a cash inflow of $1.5854(2.5625) = 4.0625$ on each of the same dates. Thus the net cash flow is zero on each of the coupon dates prior to maturity. On February 15, 1998, the short position entails a cash outflow of 104.0625 while the long position entails a cash inflow of 1.5854(102.5625) = 162.5991. In effect, then, we have created a zero-coupon bond with a net cash inflow at maturity of 162.5991 − 104.0625 = 58.53659. The net cost of creating this synthetic zero was 1.5854 times the ask price of the $5\frac{5}{8}$s (which was 97.67058 on June 9, 1994, including accrued interest) minus the bid price of the $8\frac{1}{8}$s (which was 108.4922 on June 9, including accrued interest). Thus it cost 1.5854(97.67058) − 108.4922 = 46.3514 on June 9, 1994 to create a zero that promised a payment of 58.53659 on February 15, 1998, which is equivalent to a price of .79184 on June 9, 1994, for every $1 to be received on February 15, 1998. This price compared with a price of .79375 per $1 of face value for selling Treasury strips directly that mature on the same date. Thus there was an arbitrage opportunity (equal to about one quarter of one percent) in buying synthetic zeros and simultaneously selling strips.

A trader should be careful in the face of such apparent opportunities, however. First, no transaction costs other than the dealers' bid-ask spreads have been incorporated in this calculation. In addition, the prices used are only newspaper quotations rather than actual contemporaneous dealer quotes. The *Wall Street Journal,* for example, obtains its Treasury bond price quotations from a Federal Reserve Bank of New York survey of government bond dealers taken each day at about 3:00 PM. The dealers surveyed are not committing themselves to trade at these prices, and thus, especially in the case of bonds for which actual trading is light, these quotations can give a misleading idea of the prices at which trades could be made.[2] In order for a real arbitrage opportunity to exist, it is necessary for the trader to have price quotations available at which simultaneous transactions could be conducted.

V. SUMMARY

While many essential features of bond pricing can be summarized in the simple price-yield relationship of Equation (1.1), bond prices and yields also have a number of peculiar institutional features that market participants need to know about. These include the following: (1) the fact that yields on different fixed income securities, as quoted according to conventional practice, may not be directly comparable because of differences in compounding-period assumptions; (2) the peculiar conventions of the Treasury bill market that surround bank-discount yields and bond-equivalent yields; and (3) the need to calculate accrued interest to arrive at the invoice price for a bond that is traded between coupon dates.

Arbitrage relationships between coupon-bearing and zero-coupon bonds provide an important application of some of these pricing principles. Among these are (1) the relationship between whole bond prices and strips; (2) the use of a sequence of coupon-bearing bonds of different maturity to derive synthetic zero-coupon prices that can be compared with market strip prices; and (3) the combination of long and short positions in coupon-bearing bonds of the same maturity but different coupon rates to create synthetic zeros whose prices can be compared with existing market strips.

SUGGESTIONS FOR FURTHER READING

Additional material on the details of prices and yields for bonds and money market instruments can be found in the following:

1. Daskin, Alan J., and Vivek Kulkarni, "The Curious Case of the Treasury's Callable Bonds of August, 1988–93," *Financial Analysts Journal,* 49 (March/April 1993), pp. 78–82.

2. Daskin, Alan J., and Donald J. Smith, "Using Implied Forward Rates in the Selection of a CD Maturity," *Financial Practice and Education,* 1 (Fall/Winter 1991), pp. 49–54.

3. Fabozzi, Frank J., *Bond Markets, Analysis and Strategies* (2nd ed.). Englewood Cliffs, N.J.: Prentice Hall, 1993.

4. Fabozzi, Frank J., and Irving M. Pollack, eds., *The Handbook of Fixed Income Securities* (2nd ed.). Homewood, Ill.: Dow Jones-Irwin, 1987.

5. Gregory, Deborah W., and Miles Livingston, "Development of the Market for U.S. Treasury STRIPS," *Financial Analysts Journal,* 48 (March/April 1992), pp. 68–74.

6. Stigum, Marcia (in collaboration with John Mann), *Money Market Calculations: Yields, Break-Evens and Arbitrage.* Homewood, Ill.: Dow Jones-Irwin, 1981.

PROBLEMS AND QUESTIONS

1. Find a U.S. Treasury bill that matures approximately three months from now. Using current newspaper quotations, find the price you would have to pay to buy this bill today. What is the bill's quoted yield? What is the implicit compounding period assumed in calculating this yield? How would you adjust this yield if you wanted to compare it with the quoted yield on an $8\frac{1}{8}\%$ U.S. Treasury note which matures February 15, 1998?

2. There is a U.S. Treasury note issue outstanding with a 7% coupon rate and a maturity date of April 15, 1999. What price would you have to pay to buy this bond? (Use current quotations from the newspaper.)

3. **Spreadsheet Exercise:** Construct a spreadsheet into which you can enter quoted Treasury bond and strip prices from the newspaper. Your spreadsheet should be set up so that it converts 32s to decimals for bonds and strips and so that it adds accrued interest to quoted bond prices. (Spreadsheets assign serial numbers to specific dates, and you will find this feature useful in calculating accrued interest.) Be careful to distinguish between bid and ask prices, and set up your spreadsheet so that it can check for arbitrage opportunities between whole bond prices and series of strip prices.

4. What would it cost to duplicate the $5\frac{1}{2}$% February 1999 note by buying Treasury strips? (Again, use current price quotations.) Given current prices, is there any arbitrage opportunity in this bond?

5. There is also a U.S. Treasury note maturing on February 15, 1999, with an $8\frac{7}{8}$% coupon rate. Explain how you could use the $5\frac{1}{2}$% and the $8\frac{7}{8}$% notes simultaneously to create a synthetic zero coupon bond that matures on February 15, 1999. What is the cost of purchasing this synthetic zero? Using current quoted Treasury strip prices, explain whether there is any arbitrage opportunity between the two Treasury notes and the strip that matures on February 15, 1999.

6. Look up the prices of Treasury notes that mature in May and November for the next three years. Use these note prices to derive implied prices for strips maturing on the same six dates as the notes. How do these implied strip prices compare with actual quoted strip prices for the same day?

7. Consider three Eurobonds (which pay coupons annually). Their times to maturity, coupon rates, and yields to maturity (based on current market prices) are as follows:

BOND	MATURITY	COUPON RATE	YIELD
A	1 year	8%	10%
B	2 years	10%	12%
C	3 years	12%	9%

a) If arbitrage opportunities are driven out of the market, what should be the current prices of one-, two-, and three-year zero coupon bonds?

b) What should be the yields to maturity on one-, two-, and three-year zero coupon bonds? Briefly explain why they differ from the yields on the coupon bonds listed in (a).

c) Suppose now that a quote for a fourth bond flashes across your trading screen. This bond matures in three years, has a 14% coupon rate, and is priced to yield 8.9%. Is this bond mispriced? If so, by how much?

Footnotes

[1] For bills with more than six months to maturity, the bond-equivalent yield is given by

$$y_{BEQ} = \frac{-\dfrac{2t}{365} + 2\left[\left(\dfrac{t}{365}\right)^2 + \left(\dfrac{2t}{365} - 1\right)\left(\dfrac{ty_D}{360 - ty_D}\right)\right]^{1/2}}{\dfrac{2t}{365} - 1}$$

In both bond-equivalent yield definitions, a 366-day year would be used during a leap year.

[2] For a detailed example of misleading newspaper quotes, see Alan J. Daskin and Vivek Kulkarni, "The Curious Case of the Treasury's Callable Bonds of August, 1988–93," *Financial Analysts Journal,* (March/April 1993), pp. 78–82.

2

Option-Free Bonds:
Measuring and Managing
Interest Rate Risk

I. THE PROBLEM OF INTEREST RATE RISK

One of the primary risks facing bondholders is that of a change in prevailing market interest rates. This risk can manifest itself in at least two ways. First, fluctuations in interest rates can affect the value of the investor's portfolio immediately. The typical bond promises a fixed stream of cash payments over its life, so as changes occur in investors' required returns, a standard bond's price must adjust to allow its yield to move to the new required level. Second, interest rate fluctuations can affect an investor who is trying to provide some particular amount of money on a specified future date. In this case, changes in interest rates affect both the value of the portfolio's bonds on the horizon date and also the rates at which coupons received along the way can be reinvested.

In the next section, we will discuss the measurement of a bond's immediate price sensitivity to market interest rate changes. In Section III, we will consider the problem of an investor who is trying to guard against the effects of interest rate fluctuations on his or her horizon date wealth. In both cases, in order to concentrate on general market interest rates, as opposed to firm-specific factors, we will confine our attention to bonds that are free of default risk. For the time being, we will also analyze only those bonds that contain no attached options, such as call provisions. To avoid unnecessary complication, we will ignore bonds that are between coupon dates, and we will assume annual coupon payments. This approach implies that Equation (1.1) in Chapter 1 is an adequate description of the price-yield relationship.

II. DURATION AND CONVEXITY

A. Duration as a Measure of Interest Sensitivity

The prices of long-term bonds are generally thought to be more sensitive to interest rate fluctuations than those of short-term bonds. While there is some validity to this notion on average, however, a bond's interest rate sensitivity depends on other factors, and maturity alone is not a good indicator of risk. Consider, for example, three bonds: (1) a perpetuity with an annual coupon rate of 10%; (2) a zero-coupon bond, maturing in 15 years; and (3) a bond maturing in 15 years that pays a 15% annual coupon. Suppose that all three bonds are currently selling to yield 10%.

Given this yield, the current prices of the three bonds, calculated from Equation (1.1), are shown in Table 2.1. Also shown are the prices that the bonds would have if market yields were suddenly to fall by 100 basis points to 9% or rise by 100 basis points to 11%. The Table indicates that if market yield levels fall, the value of the perpetuity would rise by about 11.1%, while the values of the zero and the 15% 15-year bond would increase by about 14.7% and 7.5%, respectively. If market yield levels rise, the value of the perpetuity would fall by about 9.1%, while the values of the zero and the 15%, 15-year bond would fall by about 12.7% and 6.7%, respectively. This example suggests that the bond with the longest maturity, the perpetuity, doesn't necessarily fluctuate in value the most for given changes in market yields. It also indicates that two bonds of the same maturity, such as the zero and the 15% coupon bond, can have quite different sensitivities to interest rate fluctuations. Thus, maturity by itself is not an adequate measure of a bond's interest rate sensitivity.

We can derive such a measure directly if we differentiate Equation (1.1) with respect to $(1 + y)$ and calculate an elasticity of bond price with respect to $1 + y$ (that is, the percentage change in bond price given a

TABLE 2.1 Prices for three bonds at three different market yield levels

	MARKET YIELD LEVEL		
BOND	9%	10%	11%
10% Coupon Perpetual Bond	111.11	100.00	90.91
Zero-Coupon 15-Year Bond	27.45	23.94	20.90
15% Coupon 15-Year Bond	148.39	138.03	128.76

percentage change in $(1 + y)$,[1] which gives the Macaulay duration expression, D_{Mac}, as follows:

$$-\frac{\dfrac{dP}{P}}{\dfrac{d(1 + y)}{1 + y}} = D_{Mac} = \frac{\displaystyle\sum_{t=1}^{n} \frac{tC}{(1 + y)^t} + \frac{nF}{(1 + y)^n}}{P} \tag{2.1}$$

The Macaulay duration expression, which measures the percentage changes in a bond's price given a change in market yields, is a weighted average of the times at which cash payments are received from the bond, with the present values of each cash payment relative to the present value of the entire bond serving as weights. Since cash payments must be repriced, or reinvested at current market yields when they are received, duration can also be interpreted as a weighted average time to repricing.

To gain further insight into the properties of duration, multiply Equation (2.1) by P and then subtract PD_{Mac} from both sides. We can write the bond's price as $P = \sum_{t=1}^{n} [C/(1 + y)^t] + [F/(1 + y)^n]$, which gives the following:

$$0 = \sum_{t=1}^{n} \frac{(t - D_{Mac})C}{(1 + y)^t} + \frac{(n - D_{Mac})F}{(1 + y)^n} \tag{2.2}$$

Expressed in this form, D_{Mac} can be seen as a center of gravity. This is illustrated in Figure 2.1, in which a plank with equally-spaced weights just balances when the fulcrum is placed at D_{Mac}. The weights are the present values of the bond's cash payments, so the present values of the coupon payments are smaller the further they are in the future. The final payment has a larger present value, however, because it includes the principal payment.

Consider now what would happen to the center of gravity if we made various changes. For example, an increase in the coupon rate, holding the yield constant, will add more weight to the left-hand side of the plank than to the right, because the coupon payments received earlier will have larger present values. This change in turn necessitates moving the fulcrum to the left to maintain balance, which implies that an increase in the coupon rate, other things being equal, shortens a bond's duration.

Alternatively, consider an increase in market yields, holding the coupon rate constant. This change will reduce the present values of the payments that are further in the future by more than it will those pay-

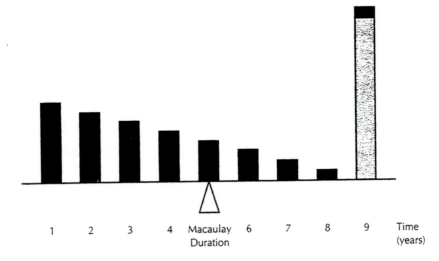

FIGURE 2.1 Macaulay duration as a center of gravity. (Dark shaded areas = coupon payments; Light shaded areas = principal payment.)

ments received earlier. Again, the fulcrum must be moved leftward to maintain balance, so the increase in yields shortens the bond's duration.

Finally, consider an increase in the bond's maturity. In this case, the effect is ambiguous. Lengthening the maturity by one year will add an extra coupon payment, and it also moves the final payment farther to the right of the fulcrum's existing position. Both of these effects tend toward increasing the center of gravity. At the same time, however, the final payment of coupon plus principal is moved further into the future, which lowers its present value and thus reduces the weight on the right-hand side. Whether duration is lengthened or shortened by an increase in maturity, then, depends on which of these effects predominates. It turns out that, for zero-coupon bonds and for coupon-bearing bonds selling at par or above, duration and maturity are always positively related. For coupon bonds selling at a discount, however, duration and maturity can be negatively related for long maturities and high yields.[2] The way in which duration changes with yield and maturity is illustrated in Problem 3 at the end of the chapter.

To gain some additional insights into the concept of duration, we can use some properties of geometric series, as shown in the Appendix to Chapter 2, to derive the following alternative form for duration:

$$D_{Mac} = \frac{1 + y}{y} - \frac{1 + y + n\left(\frac{C}{F} - y\right)}{\frac{C}{F}\left[(1 + y)^n - 1\right] + y} \qquad (2.3)$$

Bond durations can be calculated easily with this form using a financial calculator.[3] In addition, this form, and the steps leading up to it, can be used to derive duration expressions for a number of special cases of fixed income securities. These are summarized in Table 2.2, with details of the derivations given in the Appendix to this chapter.

We can use Equation (2.1) plus the special-case formulas in Table 2.2 to calculate Macaulay durations for the three bonds in the numerical example at the beginning of this section. The perpetuity has a duration of 11.0 years, while the zero has a duration of 15 years and the 15% 15-year bond has a duration of 7.79 years. Thus the duration measure is able to predict correctly that the zero will have the greatest sensitivity to interest rate fluctuations, while the perpetuity and the 15% coupon bond will rank second and third, respectively, on this dimension. Additional examples of the durations of special-case bonds appear in Problem 1 at the end of the chapter.

One other special case of duration that is worth noting is that of a floating rate bond. If we think of duration as a measure of time to repricing, then a floating rate bond, even one of long maturity, should have a relatively short duration, since the stream of coupon payments is repriced, or marked to market, at every coupon reset date. In effect, we can think of the borrower as repaying the principal at each reset date and then immediately taking out a new loan at the going market interest rate. The limiting case would be a floater whose coupon payments were reset continuously. Since such a bond would always sell at par, it would have no sensitivity to interest rate changes, and its duration would be zero.

Finally, it should be noted that there are alternative ways to define and calculate duration. The Macaulay duration is relatively easy to calculate and work with, but it is difficult to gain an intuitive understanding of its numerical value; it is more natural to think of the percentage

TABLE 2.2 Special cases of Macaulay duration for n-period fixed income securities

SECURITY	EXPRESSION FOR MACAULAY DURATION
Zero-Coupon Bond	n
Par Bond	$(1 + y) \dfrac{1}{y} \left(1 - \dfrac{1}{(1 + y)^n}\right) = (1 + y)A_n$
Annuity	$\dfrac{1 + y}{y} - \dfrac{n}{(1 + y)^n - 1}$
Perpetuity	$\dfrac{1 + y}{y}$

change in a bond's price given a percentage change in the yield, rather than in one plus the yield. To correct this deficiency, market professionals often find it easier to work with the modified duration measure, D_{mod}, where

$$D_{mod} = \frac{-\dfrac{dP}{P}}{dy} \tag{2.4}$$

As shown in the Appendix to this chapter, the relationship between the Macaulay and the modified duration measures is $D_{mod} = D_{Mac}/(1 + y)$.

An additional limitation of the Macaulay duration measure is its use of the bond's yield to maturity to calculate the present value weights that are applied to the times at which payments are received in the numerator of Equation (2.1). As will be discussed in detail in Chapter 3, yields often differ for different maturities, so discounting all cash flows at the same yield, regardless of their maturity, will not give the true present value of each cash flow individually. An alternative duration measure, called *Fisher duration*, values each cash flow instead using the prices of zero-coupon bonds that mature at the time the cash flow is received. This measure can be especially useful in assessing the durations of bond portfolios. As illustrated in Problem 6 at the end of this chapter, the Macaulay duration of a bond portfolio is equal to the weighted average of the durations of the individual bonds, but only if all of the bonds have the same yield. For the Fisher duration, on the other hand, portfolio duration equals the weighted average of the individual bond durations regardless of the individual bond yields.

B. Convexity

For a standard option-free bond, the relationship between price and yield is as depicted by the curve in Figure 2.2. Duration measures, which incorporate the first derivative of this relationship, are essentially measures of the slope of the price-yield relationship at a given point, such as (y^*, P^*). As the diagram makes clear, however, the slope changes continuously because of the curvature of the price-yield relationship. Thus, if we were to use a duration measure to predict how much a standard bond's price would change for a given change in yield, we would overestimate the true price change for increases in yield and underestimate it for yield decreases. Moreover, the error in our prediction would become larger as the change in yield became larger.

A bond's convexity, which is a measure of the degree of curvature in its price-yield relationship, can be used to try to correct for these types of prediction errors. If we denote the functional relationship be-

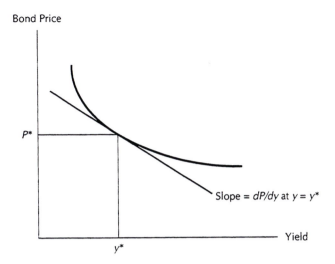

FIGURE 2.2   Relationship between bond price and bond yield.

tween price and yield by $P(y)$, a commonly-used convexity measure is defined as:

$$\text{Convexity} = \frac{1}{P} \frac{d^2P}{dy^2} \qquad (2.5)$$

As shown in the Appendix to this chapter, the convexity measure can be used as a supplement to the duration measure when predicting how a given bond's price will change with a given change in yield. For example, the percentage change in a bond's price, given a change in yield Δy, can be approximated using both modified duration and convexity as:

$$\frac{\Delta P}{P} \cong (-\text{Duration})\Delta y + \frac{1}{2}(\text{Convexity})\Delta y^2 \qquad (2.6)$$

If convexity is positive, then its effect is to increase the price change predicted from duration alone when yields fall and to reduce the predicted price reduction when yields rise.

Take, for example, a perpetual bond with an annual coupon payment of 5 and a yield to maturity of 5%. The current price of the bond is $5/.05 = 100$. If the yield were to rise to 6%, we can calculate directly that the bond's price would fall to $5/.06 = 83.33$. Similarly, if the yield fell to 4%, the bond's price would rise to $5/.04 = 125$. If, instead of calculating these price changes directly, we tried to predict them using modified duration alone, Equation (2.6) tells us that we would predict the percentage change in the price of the bond as $(-\text{Duration})\Delta y$. From Table 2.2, the modified duration of the perpetual bond is $1/y = 20$. Thus our prediction of the bond's percentage price change is $(-20)(\pm.01) = \pm.20$, and we would guess that the bond's price would fall to 80 if the yield rose to 6% or rise to 120 if the yield fell to 4%.

Alternatively, we could make more accurate price change predictions if we used convexity in addition to duration. Expressing the current price of the perpetual bond as $5/y$, the second derivative is $10/y^3 = 80,000$ and convexity equals $80,000/100 = 800$. From Equation (2.6), if we use both duration and convexity to predict the bond's percentage price change, our prediction is $(-20)(\pm.01) + 400(.0001) = \pm.20 + .04$. Thus we would predict that the bond's price would fall to 84 if the yield rose to 6% and rise to 124 if the yield fell to 4%. In both cases, we have achieved a better prediction of the bond's price change by taking into account the degree of curvature of the price-yield relationship.

The degree of convexity also tells us something about a bond's qualitative properties. A greater degree of convexity is thought of as desirable in a bond, since it implies that yield changes will work in the investor's favor to a greater degree. That is, when yields are decreasing and bond prices are increasing, a bond with greater convexity will exhibit larger price increases for a given decrease in yield. Conversely, when yields are rising and bond prices are falling, the price of a bond with greater convexity will fall by less. While it can be seen intuitively that convexity is a desirable property, there is little in the way of empirical evidence to suggest that bond portfolios that are managed with an emphasis on convexity will outperform other bond portfolios.[4] This fact does not imply, however, that convexity is unimportant. Rather, it may suggest that, because convexity is important to investors, it is efficiently captured in security prices so that bonds with greater convexity cannot be expected, on average, to outperform bonds with less.

The convexity measure can be computed the most readily for any given bond if we start with Expression (1.1) for a bond's price in terms of its cash flows and yield, and differentiate twice with respect to the yield. As shown in the Appendix to this chapter, this results in:

Convexity $=$

$$\frac{1}{P}\left\{\frac{2C}{y^3}\left[1 - \frac{1}{(1+y)^n}\right] - \frac{2Cn}{y^2(1+y)^{n+1}} + \frac{n(n+1)\left(F - \dfrac{C}{y}\right)}{(1+y)^{n+2}}\right\} \qquad (2.7)$$

Despite its messy appearance, Expression (2.7) can be rather easily entered in a spreadsheet for convenient calculation for any bond, including such special cases as zero coupon bonds ($C = 0$), par bonds ($P = F$) and annuities ($F = 0$).[5] To illustrate, Expression (2.7) has been used to calcu-

TABLE 2.3   Convexities for three bonds at three different market yield levels

	MARKET YIELD LEVEL		
BOND	9%	10%	11%
10% Coupon Perpetual Bond	246.91	200	165.29
Zero-Coupon 15-Year Bond	202.00	198.35	194.79
15% Coupon 15-Year Bond	81.99	77.16	72.58

late convexities for the three bonds and three different yield levels that were used to illustrate the duration concept. The results are shown in Table 2.3, and they illustrate some standard properties of convexity for option-free bonds.[6] First, all of the values are positive, which implies that duration declines as yields rise. In Chapter 6, by contrast, we will see some examples of bonds with options attached that exhibit negative convexity. Second, for all three bonds, convexity falls as yields rise. Thus, the effect of convexity on a bond's sensitivity to interest rate movements is more important at low yield levels than at high. Finally, the strip has greater convexity than the 15-year coupon bond. In general, for bonds of the same maturity, the lower the coupon rate, the greater the convexity. The properties of convexity and its relative importance in explaining bond price changes are further illustrated in Problems 4 and 5 at the end of this chapter.

III. IMMUNIZATION

We now turn our attention to the second aspect of interest rate risk: How do interest rate changes affect the value of a bond portfolio on a specific future date? The portfolio strategy known as immunization has been widely used to deal with this aspect of interest rate risk. The basic idea behind this strategy is to construct a portfolio whose projected total value as of a future horizon date will be unchanged if current market yields change. As demonstrated in the Appendix to this chapter, this goal can be accomplished if we set the portfolio's Macaulay duration equal to the investment horizon.

This strategy can be seen most clearly if we consider zero-coupon bonds. If we have an investment horizon of H years, the immunization rule calls for buying zero-coupon bonds that mature in H years. Between now and year H, the value of the portfolio will, of course, fluctuate with changes in market yields. As long as there is no default risk, however, the bonds will be worth par at maturity, which coincides with the horizon date. Thus the portfolio's projected value *as of the horizon date* is invariant to any changes in yield that may occur between now and then.

The immunization rule implies that the same principle can also work with coupon bonds, because two forces can offset one another if the bonds' durations equal the investment horizon. If the duration equals the investment horizon for a coupon-bearing bond, the maturity will exceed the investment horizon. This fact implies, on the one hand, that an increase in interest rates will reduce the bond's horizon value. At the same time, however, reinvested coupons will earn a higher rate of return, so as long as the two effects offset one another, the portfolio will be immunized.

It is important to note, however, that the immunization rule is subject to some severe limitations. First, as indicated in the Appendix, yields on instruments of all maturities are assumed to be the same. That is, the yield curve is assumed to be flat. Second, if yields do change, the portfolio will be immunized only against a one-time shift to a new, flat yield curve. The reason, as we have seen earlier in this chapter, is that bonds' durations change as yields change, and except for zero-coupon bonds, there is no guarantee that a portfolio's duration will still coincide with the investment horizon once a shift in yields has occurred. Following a discussion of the yield curve in Chapter 3, Problem 5 at the end of that chapter illustrates the effects on an immunization strategy of non-parallel yield curve shifts.

Unless an investor resorts to zeros, implementation of an immunization strategy requires frequent portfolio rebalancing, which in turn entails transaction costs. This fact helps explain the popularity of zero-coupon bonds in portfolio immunization. It also helps explain the development of alternative strategies, such as contingent immunization, which are aimed at reducing the transaction costs incurred through portfolio rebalancing.

IV. SUMMARY

A first step in understanding and managing the interest rate risk of fixed income securities is to derive a measure of interest sensitivity. The Macaulay and modified duration measures have proved useful for this purpose. These measures can be interpreted as elasticities (that is, the percentage change in a bond's price, given a percentage change in one plus the yield, or in the yield itself in the case of the modified duration) or as weighted average times to repricing. In general, duration varies with coupon rate and yield in addition to maturity, so except for zero-coupon bonds, term to maturity by itself can be a misleading indicator of interest sensitivity.

Duration emphasizes the slope of a bond's price-yield relationship, but does not take its curvature into account. The curvature in the price-yield relationship implies that a bond's duration will change with yields. Thus, duration may not be very useful in predicting how a bond's price will change with yield if the yield changes by very much. Convexity, which measures the degree of price-yield curvature, can thus be a useful supplement to duration in predicting bond price changes.

A common technique for managing interest rate risk is immunization, which entails setting the duration of the portfolio equal to the investment horizon to ensure that the portfolio's projected total value on a specified horizon date will be unaffected by changes in market yields. Unless one immunizes using zero-coupon bonds, however, this strategy can require frequent and costly portfolio rebalancing.

SUGGESTIONS FOR FURTHER READING

Additional discussion and extensions of the concepts of duration, convexity, and immunization may be found in the following:

1. Bierwag, Gerald O., Charles J. Corrado, and George C. Kaufman, "Computing Durations for Bond Portfolios," *Journal of Portfolio Management,* 17 (Fall 1990), pp. 51–55.

2. Brooks, Robert, and Miles Livingston, "Relative Impact of Duration and Convexity on Bond Price Changes," *Financial Practice and Education,* 2 (Spring/Summer 1992), pp. 93–99.

3. Fabozzi, Frank J., *Bond Markets, Analysis and Strategies* (2nd ed.). Englewood Cliffs, N.J.: Prentice Hall, 1993.

4. Fabozzi, Frank J., and Irving M. Pollack, eds., *The Handbook of Fixed Income Securities* (2nd ed.). Homewood, Ill.: Dow Jones-Irwin, 1987.

5. Hiller, Ronald S., and Christian Schaack, "A Classification of Structured Bond Portfolio Management Techniques," *Journal of Portfolio Management,* 17 (Fall 1990), pp. 37–48.

6. Kritzman, Mark, "What Practitioners Need to Know About Duration and Convexity," *Financial Analysts Journal,* 48 (November/December 1990), pp. 17–20.

7. Leibowitz, Martin L., William S. Krasker, and Ardavan Nozari, "Spread Duration: A New Tool for Bond Portfolio Management," *Journal of Portfolio Management,* 16 (Spring 1990), pp. 40–45.

8. Reitano, Robert R., "Non-Parallel Yield Curve Shifts and Immunization," *Journal of Portfolio Management,* 18 (Spring 1992), pp. 36–43.

9. Smith, Donald J., "The Duration of a Bond as a Price Elasticity and a Fulcrum," *Journal of Financial Education*, (Fall 1988), pp. 26–38.

PROBLEMS AND QUESTIONS

1. a) Calculate the durations of the following:
      (1) Canadian Pacific's 4% coupon perpetual bond issue, priced to yield 8%;
      (2) A 30-year monthly-payment mortgage, which is priced to yield 8%;
      (3) A 15-year zero-coupon bond, priced to yield 8%.
   b) Briefly explain, in light of your answers to (a), why term to maturity is not a good index of an instrument's susceptibility to interest rate risk.

2. Consider the following three bonds:
   a) A stripped (zero-coupon) U.S. Treasury bond, maturing in nine years and priced to yield 8.00%.
   b) An AT&T bond with a $7\frac{1}{8}$% coupon rate, maturing in twelve years and priced to yield 8.42%.
   c) An RJR Nabisco bond with a $17\frac{3}{8}$% coupon rate, maturing in 18 years and priced to yield 9.92%.
      (1) Calculate the Macaulay durations of the three bonds.
      (2) Explain why the three calculated durations differ. Why is the number of years to maturity not a reliable measure of the bonds' relative durations?
      (3) What do the calculated durations tell us about the relative risks of these three bonds? Does the duration measure capture all relevant dimensions of bond risk?

3. **Spreadsheet Exercise:** Take a base-case 25-year bond with a 5% coupon rate, coupons payable semiannually, and an annualized yield to maturity of 5% per year.
   a) Calculate the base-case bond's Macaulay duration. Show how this duration will vary as the bond's semiannual yield goes from 1% to 10% in increments of $\frac{1}{2}$% (that is, .01, .015, .02, .025, etc.) and as the maturity goes from 5 years to 30 years in increments of $2\frac{1}{2}$ years (that is, 10 semiannual periods, 15 periods, 20 periods, etc.). Note: Since there are 19 different yields within this range and 11 different maturities, your table should contain $19 \times 11 = 209$ different duration values.
   b) What is the shortest duration in your table? To what yield and maturity does it correspond? What is the longest duration in your table? To what yield and maturity level does it correspond? For

what bonds, if any, in your table does duration become shorter as maturity lengthens (holding yield constant)? How can you explain this relationship?

4. **Spreadsheet Exercise:** Consider a base-case bond with 20 years to maturity, a coupon rate of 8% per year, coupons payable semiannually, and an annualized yield to maturity of 9%. Assume a face value of $100.

a) What are the price, Macaulay duration (in years), and annualized convexity of this base-case bond?

b) Show how duration and convexity vary with yield as the semiannual yield goes from .01 to .10 in increments of .005 (that is, the annualized yield goes from .02 to .20 in increments of .01). Briefly interpret your results.

c) Show how duration and convexity vary with the coupon rate (holding yield constant at the base-case annualized figure of 9%) as the semiannual coupon goes from $0 to $10 per $100 face value in increments of $0.5 (that is, the annual coupon rate goes from 0 to 20% in increments of 1%). Briefly interpret your results.

5. **Spreadsheet Exercise:** From Equation (2.6), the relative importance, R, of convexity and modified duration in explaining a bond's percentage price change resulting from a given change in yield, Δy, can be expressed as

$$R = \frac{\frac{1}{2}(\text{Convexity})\Delta y^2}{(-\text{Duration})\Delta y}$$

a) Take a base-case zero-coupon bond with 10 years to maturity, an annualized yield (assuming semiannual compounding) of 9%, and a face value of 100. Calculate the bond's modified duration and convexity and, for a decline in the annualized yield of 0.1% (that is, $\Delta y = -.001$), the value of R as defined by the equation.

b) How does the value of R change as the maturity increases from two years (four semiannual periods) to 20 years in increments of two years at the same time that the semiannual coupon rate goes from 0 to 10% in increments of 0.5%? Note: The bond's annualized yield remains at 9% while $\Delta y = -.001$ throughout.

c) How does the value of R change as the maturity increases from two years (four semiannual periods) to 20 years in increments of two years at the same time that the change in the annualized yield goes from $-.001$ to $-.025$ in increments of $-.001$? Note: The bond's annualized yield remains at 9% while the coupon rate remains at zero throughout.

d) What conclusions can you draw from your analysis in (b) and (c) above? How might these conclusions be useful to a bond investor?

6. a) Suppose that a portfolio consists of two assets, A and B. The proportion of the portfolio invested in A is w_A, the proportion invested in B is w_B, and $w_A + w_B = 1$. In any period t, the cash flow from the portfolio is equal to $C_{At} + C_{Bt}$, where C_{At} and C_{Bt} are the cash flows from A and B, respectively. Show that, if assets A and B both have the same yield, the Macaulay duration of the portfolio, D_p, is given by

$$D_p = w_A D_A + w_B D_B,$$

where D_A and D_B are the Macaulay durations of assets A and B, respectively.

b) In similar fashion, any company's equity, E, can be thought of as a portfolio of assets, A, and liabilities, L, governed by the balance sheet identity, $E = A - L$. Express the Macaulay duration of the firm's equity in terms of the Macaulay durations of its assets and liabilities. If a company wants to immunize the value of its equity against interest rate changes, explain why, using the duration expression you have just derived, it will generally not be sufficient to set the duration of its assets equal to the duration of its liabilities.

c) Suppose that a thrift institution has assets of 100, deposits of 90 and equity of 10. The duration of its assets is 7 years. What would the duration of its liabilities have to be to set the duration of its equity equal to zero (that is, to immunize its equity)?

Footnotes

[1] A derivation of (2.1) is provided in the Appendix to Chapter 2.

[2] See Donald J. Smith, "The Duration of a Bond as a Price Elasticity and a Fulcrum," *Journal of Financial Education*, (Fall 1988), 26–38.

[3] For bonds that pay coupons semiannually, using the semiannual yield and measuring n as the number of semiannual coupon periods gives a duration measure in semiannual periods. While it is more accurate to calculate duration using periods that correspond to the length of coupon periods, it is common practice to report the result in years by simply taking duration measured in semiannual periods and dividing by 2. For bonds that are between coupon periods, it can be shown that duration declines linearly from one coupon date to the next. If we let 0 denote the beginning of the coupon period and 1 the end, then D_v, the bond's Macaulay duration when there is a fraction v of the current coupon period remaining, is given by $D_v = D_0 - (1 - v)$. That is, simply calculate the bond's duration, given the number of coupon payments left, as if

each of these periods were a whole period and then subtract $(1 - v)$. For a derivation of this property, see Guilford C. Babcock, "On the Linearity of Duration," *Financial Analysts Journal,* 42, (September/October 1986), 75–77.

[4] See, for example, Ronald N. Kahn and Roland Lochoff, "Convexity and Exceptional Return," *Journal of Portfolio Management,* 16, (Winter 1990), 43–47; and Nelson J. Lacey and Sanjay K. Nawalkha, "Convexity, Risk and Returns," *Journal of Fixed Income,* 3, (December 1993), 72–79.

[5] Convexity expressions for bonds that are between coupon dates, as well as for special-case bonds, are derived in Sanjay K. Nawalkha and Nelson J. Lacey, "Convexity for Bonds with Special Cash Flow Streams," *Financial Analysts Journal,* 47, (January/February 1991), 80–82.

[6] Because all of the bonds in this example pay coupons annually, the convexity figures in Table 2.3 are measured in years. For bonds that pay coupons semiannually, if we calculate convexity letting n be the number of semiannual coupon periods remaining (and letting y be the semiannual yield), the result will measure convexity in semiannual periods. To express the result in years, we need to divide by 4 (the square of the number of coupon periods in a year).

Appendix to Chapter 2

I. DERIVATION OF MACAULAY AND MODIFIED DURATION MEASURES FOR OPTION-FREE BONDS

A. Macaulay Duration as an Elasticity

First, rewrite Equation (1.1) as follows:

$$P = C(1 + y)^{-1} + C(1 + y)^{-2} + \cdots + C(1 + y)^{-n} + F(1 + y)^{-n} \quad (2A.1)$$

Differentiating (2A.1) with respect to $(1 + y)$,

$$\frac{dP}{d(1 + y)} = -C(1 + y)^{-2} - 2C(1 + y)^{-3} \quad (2A.2)$$
$$- \cdots - nC(1 + y)^{-(n+1)} - nF(1 + y)^{-(n+1)}$$

Multiplying by -1, factoring out $(1 + y)^{-1}$, and re-expressing the discounted cash flow terms in fractional form,

$$-\frac{dP}{d(1 + y)}$$
$$= \frac{1}{1 + y} \left[\frac{C}{(1 + y)} + \frac{2C}{(1 + y)^2} + \cdots + \frac{nC}{(1 + y)^n} + \frac{nF}{(1 + y)^n} \right] \quad (2A.3)$$

Finally, multiplying (2A.3) by $(1 + y)$ and dividing by P gives the Macaulay duration expression, D_{Mac};

$$-\frac{\dfrac{dP}{P}}{\dfrac{d(1+y)}{1+y}} = D_{Mac}$$

$$= \frac{\dfrac{C}{(1+y)} + \dfrac{2C}{(1+y)^2} + \cdots + \dfrac{nC}{(1+y)^n} + \dfrac{nF}{(1+y)^n}}{P}$$

$$= \frac{\displaystyle\sum_{t=1}^{n} \dfrac{tC}{(1+y)^t} + \dfrac{nF}{(1+y)^n}}{P} \tag{2A.4}$$

B. Closed-Form Equation for Macaulay Duration

Equation (2A.4) can be expressed in a form that lends itself more readily to calculation using financial calculators if we make use of two properties of finite geometric series. The first is the expression for the present value of an annuity, which we will use to value the stream of coupon payments on the bond:

$$\sum_{t=1}^{n} \frac{C}{(1+y)^t} = \frac{C}{y}\left[1 - \frac{1}{(1+y)^n}\right] \tag{2A.5}$$

The second property is less well-known, so we will derive it. Consider the sum of the series S, where

$$S = \sum_{t=1}^{n} \frac{tC}{(1+y)^t} = \frac{C}{(1+y)} + \frac{2C}{(1+y)^2} + \cdots + \frac{nC}{(1+y)^n}$$

Dividing S by $(1+y)$ and subtracting from S,

$$S - \frac{S}{1+y} = \frac{C}{(1+y)} + \frac{C}{(1+y)^2} + \cdots + \frac{C}{(1+y)^n} - \frac{nC}{(1+y)^{n+1}}$$

$$= \frac{C}{y}\left[1 - \frac{1}{(1+y)^n}\right] - \frac{nC}{(1+y)^{n+1}}$$

We can then solve for S by multiplying both sides of the equation by $(1+y)/y$:

$$S = \frac{(1+y)C}{y^2}\left[1 - \frac{1}{(1+y)^n}\right] - \frac{nC}{y(1+y)^n} \tag{2A.6}$$

If we then substitute (1.1), (2A.5) and (2A.6) into (2A.4), we can express D_{Mac} as:

$$D_{Mac} = \frac{\dfrac{(1+y)C}{y^2}\left[1 - \dfrac{1}{(1+y)^n}\right] - \dfrac{nC}{y(1+y)^n} + \dfrac{nF}{(1+y)^n}}{\dfrac{C}{y}\left[1 - \dfrac{1}{(1+y)^n}\right] + \dfrac{F}{(1+y)^n}} \qquad (2A.7)$$

Multiplying both numerator and denominator of (2A.7) by $y(1+y)^n$,

$$D_{Mac} = \frac{\dfrac{1+y}{y}C[(1+y)^n - 1] - nC + ynF}{C[(1+y)^n - 1] + yF} \qquad (2A.8)$$

Adding and subtracting $(1+y)F$ to the numerator of (2A.8),

$$D_{Mac} = \frac{\dfrac{1+y}{y}\{C[(1+y)^n - 1] + yF\} - (1+y)F - nC + ynF}{C[(1+y)^n - 1] + yF} \qquad (2A.9)$$

$$= \frac{1+y}{y} - \frac{(1+y)F + nC - ynF}{C[(1+y)^n - 1] + yF}$$

Finally, dividing the numerator and denominator of the second term in (2A.9) by F and rearranging gives (2.3).

The Macaulay durations of particular types of bonds can be derived using Equation (2.3). For example, a zero-coupon bond has $C/F = 0$, in which case (2.3) reduces to $D_{Mac} = n$. Zero-coupon bonds are the only bonds for which duration and maturity always coincide, a fact that will prove useful when we study the term structure of interest rates in Chapter 3.

For a bond that sells at par, $C/F = y$, so

$$D_{Mac} = \frac{1+y}{y} - \frac{1+y}{y[(1+y)^n - 1] + y}$$

$$= (1+y)\frac{1}{y}\left(1 - \frac{1}{(1+y)^n}\right) = (1+y)A_n \qquad (2A.10)$$

where A_n is present value factor for an n-period annuity with a discount rate of y. Thus the durations of par bonds can easily be calculated using standard financial tables.

To calculate the duration of an annuity, a stream of n equal payments of $\$C$ each, note first that, for an annuity, Equation (2A.4) can be combined with (2A.5) and (2A.6) to give:

$$D_{Mac} = \frac{\sum_{t=1}^{n} \frac{tC}{(1+y)^t}}{P} = \frac{\frac{(1+y)C}{y^2}\left[1 - \frac{1}{(1+y)^n}\right] - \frac{nC}{y(1+y)^n}}{\frac{C}{y}\left[1 - \frac{1}{(1+y)^n}\right]}$$

$$= \frac{1+y}{y} - \frac{n}{(1+y)^n - 1}$$

(2A.11)

Note that the duration of an annuity does not depend on the size of the annual payment but only on the yield and the maturity. Finally, note that the denominator of the second term in Equation (2A.11) increases faster than the numerator increases as n grows larger. For a perpetuity, therefore, the second term disappears, and thus the duration of a perpetuity is given by the following:

$$D_{Mac} = \frac{1+y}{y}$$

(2A.12)

C. Modified Duration

The modified duration measure is defined as follows:

$$D_{mod} = \frac{-\frac{dP}{P}}{dy}$$

(2A.13)

Noting, however, that when a bond's price, P, can be represented in terms of a sum of cash flows that are discounted in discrete time, $dP/dy = dP/d(1 + y)$. Thus, comparing (2A.13) with (2A.4),

$$D_{mod} = \frac{-\frac{dP}{P}}{dy} = \frac{-\frac{dP}{P}}{d(1+y)} = \frac{D_{Mac}}{1+y}$$

(2A.14)

D. Convexity

If we express a bond's price-yield relationship as $P = P(y)$, Taylor's theorem tells us that we can express the function P in the vicinity of $y = y^*$ as follows:

$$P(y) = P(y^*) + \frac{dP}{dy}(y - y^*) + \frac{d^2P}{dy^2}\frac{(y - y^*)^2}{2!}$$
$$+ \frac{d^3P}{dy^3}\frac{(y - y^*)^3}{3!} + \cdots + \frac{d^nP}{dy^n}\frac{(y - y^*)^n}{n!}$$

(2A.15)

If we denote $P(y) - P(y^*)$ as ΔP, $y - y^*$ as Δy, and divide both sides by P, (2A.15) can in turn be expressed as follows:

$$\frac{\Delta P}{P} = \left(\frac{1}{P}\frac{dP}{dy}\right)\Delta y + \left(\frac{1}{2}\frac{1}{P}\frac{d^2P}{dy^2}\right)\Delta y^2$$
$$+ \left(\frac{1}{6}\frac{1}{P}\frac{d^3P}{dy^3}\right)\Delta y^3 + \cdots$$

(2A.16)

Equation (2A.16) says that we can use a Taylor series expansion to predict the percentage change in a bond's price given a yield change from $y = y^*$ by the amount Δy. The accuracy of the prediction increases with the number of terms included in the expansion. Note further that, except for its sign, the coefficient of Δy in (2A.16) is the bond's modified duration. Thus, the entire first term on the right-hand side of (2A.16) is the percentage change in price that we would predict using only the duration measure to make our prediction. The coefficient of Δy^2 in (2A.16) is one-half the bond's convexity, a measure of the curvature in $P(y)$ that we can use to improve upon the price-change prediction we would make using duration alone. Since the second derivative of $P(y)$ is positive, the convexity term tells us to (1) increase the prediction we would make using duration alone when bond yields decrease and (2) reduce our predicted price change when bond yields increase.

E. Closed-Form Expression for Convexity

We can derive Expression (2.7), which is useful in calculating convexity by substituting (2A.5) into (1.1) to express a bond's price as follows:

$$P = \frac{C}{y}\left[1 - \frac{1}{(1 + y)^n}\right] + \frac{F}{(1 + y)^n}$$

(2A.17)

Differentiating (2A.17) twice with respect to y gives

$$\frac{dP}{dy} = -\frac{C}{y^2}\left[1 - \frac{1}{(1+y)^n}\right] + \frac{n\left(F - \dfrac{C}{y}\right)}{(1+y)^{n+1}}$$

$$\frac{d^2P}{dy^2} = \frac{2C}{y^3}\left[1 - \frac{1}{(1+y)^n}\right] - \frac{2nC}{y^2(1+y)^{n+1}} \qquad \text{(2A.18)}$$

$$+ \frac{n(n+1)\left(F - \dfrac{C}{y}\right)}{(1+y)^{n+2}}$$

Dividing (2A.18) by P then gives Expression (2.7) in the text.

II. IMMUNIZATION

Suppose your investment horizon is H years. That is, you wish to invest your portfolio so as to provide a particular amount of wealth H years from now (for example, for retirement). Suppose further that your entire portfolio will be invested in a standard option-free, coupon-bearing bond that matures n years from now. Finally, suppose that the current market yield on an instrument of any maturity is equal to y.

In year H, your total wealth will consist of the value at that time of our n-period bond plus the value of all reinvested coupons that will be received between now and year H. Using (2A.17), the value, $P(y, H)$, of our n-period bond in year H is given by

$$P(y, H) = \frac{C}{y}\left[1 - \frac{1}{(1-y)^{n-H}}\right] + \frac{F}{(1+y)^{n-H}} \qquad \text{(2A.19)}$$

Multiplying (2A.5) by $(1 + y)^H$ to get the future value of an annuity, we can express the value of all reinvested coupons, $R(y, H)$, as of year H as follows:

$$R(y, H) = \frac{C}{y}[(1 + y)^H - 1] \qquad \text{(2A.20)}$$

Total wealth in year H, $V(y, H)$, is then given by

$$V(y, H) = P(y, H) + R(y, H)$$

$$= \frac{C}{y}(1 + y)^H + \frac{1}{(1+y)^{n-H}}\left(F - \frac{C}{y}\right) \qquad \text{(2A.21)}$$

Then, if we wish to protect, or immunize, our total wealth in year H

against changes in market yields, we wish to set $\partial V/\partial y = 0$. Differentiating (2A.21) with respect to y,

$$\frac{\partial V(y, H)}{\partial y} = \frac{C}{y} H(1 + y)^{H-1} - \frac{C}{y^2}(1 + y)^H$$

$$- \frac{(n - H)\left(F - \dfrac{C}{y}\right)}{(1 + y)^{n-H+1}} + \frac{C}{y^2}\frac{1}{(1 + y)^{n-H}} = 0 \qquad (2A.22)$$

Dividing each term by $C(1 + y)^{H-1}$,

$$H = \frac{1 + y}{y} + \frac{n\left(y - \dfrac{C}{F}\right)}{\dfrac{C}{F}(1 + y)^n} - \frac{H\left(y - \dfrac{C}{F}\right)}{\dfrac{C}{F}(1 + y)^n} - \frac{1 + y}{y(1 + y)^n} \qquad (2A.23)$$

Grouping terms containing H,

$$\frac{H\left\{\dfrac{C}{F}[(1 + y)^n - 1] + y\right\}}{\dfrac{C}{F}(1 + y)^n} = \frac{1 + y}{y}\left[\frac{(1 + y)^n - 1}{(1 + y)^n}\right]$$

$$+ \frac{n\left(y - \dfrac{C}{F}\right)}{\dfrac{C}{F}(1 + y)^n} \qquad (2A.24)$$

Multiplying through by the denominator of the left-hand side of (2A.24),

$$H\left(\frac{C}{F}[(1 + y)^n - 1] + y\right) = \frac{(1 + y)}{y}\frac{C}{F}[(1 + y)^n - 1]$$

$$+ n\left(y - \frac{C}{F}\right) \qquad (2A.25)$$

Finally, adding and subtracting $(1 + y)$ from the right side of (2A.25) and solving for H,

$$H = \frac{1 + y}{y} - \frac{1 + y + n\left(\dfrac{C}{F} - y\right)}{\dfrac{C}{F}[(1 + y)^n - 1] + y} = D_{Mac} \qquad (2A.26)$$

Thus, we will be immunized against interest rate changes if we set our portfolio's Macaulay duration equal to our investment horizon.

3

The Term Structure
of Interest Rates

I. THE YIELD CURVE

As we saw in Chapter 2, bonds of different duration subject investors to different degrees of interest rate risk. Moreover, as the immunization principle suggests, investors with different horizons may assess the riskiness of the same bond in different ways. Market prices (and hence yields) for various bonds will be determined by investor trading activity, but because of differences in investor preferences and in the risk characteristics of different bonds, there is no inherent reason why market yields on instruments of different duration or maturity must be the same. The configuration of yields for different maturities is referred to as the yield curve, or the term structure of interest rates, and this curve can take on different shapes at different times. The subject of this chapter is the various theories that have been advanced to explain the term structure of interest rates. These theories attempt to uncover the economic reasons why the yield curve takes on the shape it does at a given time and why this shape changes periodically.

A. Measuring the Yield Curve: Spot and Forward Rates

Before we can explain the yield curve, we must be able to describe it accurately. For this purpose, zero-coupon bond prices are extremely useful, since we can think of them as pure securities of a particular maturity. Since there are no intermediate coupon or principal payments prior to maturity, there is no ambiguity about the length of time for which in-

40

vestors have committed their funds. As we saw in Chapter 1, any other option-free bond with a contractually fixed stream of coupon and principal payments can be thought of as a package of these pure securities, or building blocks. However, even coupon-bearing bonds of identical maturity can represent different packages of zeros if they differ in terms of coupon rate or principal repayment pattern, and this difference will manifest itself in different yields to maturity. Thus, there is no unique relationship between yield and maturity date for coupon-bearing bonds, whereas there is a unique relationship for zeros. Additionally, as we saw in Chapter 2, zeros are the only securities whose duration is equal to their maturity, so distinctions need not be made between interest sensitivities and maturities.

The first step, then, is to assemble zero-coupon yields for a variety of maturities. This step can be done directly, using Treasury strip prices from the newspaper. If shorter maturities are desired, Treasury bill yields can be used, although it is important to quote them on a semiannually compounded basis to facilitate comparison with the strip yields. If bill and strip prices are not available, implicit zero-coupon yields can be constructed from coupon-bearing bond prices using the arbitrage relationships described in Sections IV.B and IV.C of Chapter 1. If we wish to focus on the term structure of interest rates, as opposed to the credit risk structure, it is also important to confine our analysis to bonds that are free of default risk to ensure that differences in yield are attributable purely to differences in maturity.

Suppose we have calculated the yields, $y_1, y_2, \ldots, y_n$, for zero-coupon bonds with maturities of one, two, . . . , and n periods, respectively. These yields are referred to as spot rates, since they are the rates applying to transactions that could be immediately executed (on the spot) in the market. We can in turn use spot rates of different maturity to define forward rates. A two-period loan, for example, can be thought of as equivalent to a one-period loan made now at the going one-period rate plus a second forward one-period loan to be made one period from now (maturing at time 2) at a forward rate, f_2, that the parties to the loan agree upon now. Thus we can define the forward rate that is implicit in a two-period spot rate through the following relationship:

$$(1 + y_2)^2 = (1 + y_1)(1 + f_2)$$

which implies

$$f_2 = \frac{(1 + y_2)^2}{(1 + y_1)} - 1 \qquad (3.1)$$

For example, if the current one-period rate is 4% and the current two-period rate is 5%, the forward rate for the second period is

$$f_2 = \frac{(1.05)^2}{1.04} - 1 = .0601$$

Equivalently, if $P_1 = 1/(1 + y_1)$ and $P_2 = 1/(1 + y_2)^2$ are the prices of one- and two-period zeros, the forward rate for the second period is $f_2 = P_1/P_2 - 1$. To illustrate, on March 17, 1995, the price of a Treasury strip maturing on August 15, 1995, was $97{:}22 = 97.6875$. On the same day the price of a strip maturing February 15, 1996, was $94{:}17 = 94.53125$. Thus the forward rate, as of March 17, 1995, on a loan covering the period August 15, 1995, to February 15, 1996, was $97.6875/94.53125 - 1 = .033388$, or 6.678% on an annualized basis. Note that when using prices in this fashion, the periods covered by the two strips need not be the same. The calculation of forward rates for a variety of fixed income instruments is further illustrated in Problems 1 to 4 at the end of this chapter.

More generally, the forward rate for a one-period loan to be made n periods from now is defined as follows:

$$f_n = \frac{(1 + y_n)^n}{(1 + y_{n-1})^{n-1}} - 1 \qquad (3.2)$$

We can also define forward rates for loans of more than one period analogously to the forward one-period loans. For example, given the spot rates y_7 and y_4 for seven and four-period loans, respectively, we can define the forward rate, $_3f_7$, for a three-period loan that matures at time 7 through the relationship

$$(1 + y_7)^7 = (1 + y_4)^4(1 + {}_3f_7)^3$$

The time scheme for the spot and forward rates is illustrated in Figure 3.1.

These implied forward rates can be useful in checking arbitrage relationships among prices in different markets. As we will see in Chapter 8, for example, the yields on current six-month and three-month Treasury bills implicitly define a three-month forward bill rate for a transaction to take place three months from now. However, there is also an explicit forward yield for a three-month bill to be delivered three months from now that is determined by trading in the Treasury bill futures market. If this forward rate from the futures market and the implicit forward rate based on spot yields are not the same, an arbitrage opportunity is available. Such arbitrage pricing relationships tell us nothing, however, about what determines forward rates, or in case the two rates are different, which one more accurately reflects market fundamentals. That is the task of the different theories of the term structure of interest rates.

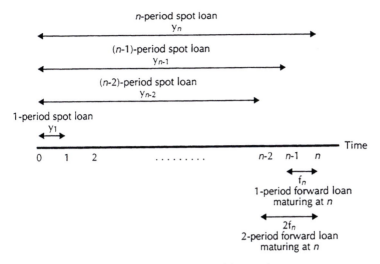

FIGURE 3.1 Time scheme for spot and forward rates

II. THEORIES OF THE TERM STRUCTURE OF INTEREST RATES

A. The Arbitrage Pricing Principle

Up to this point, the only theory of bond pricing that we have seen has been based on arbitrage relationships. The underlying principle implicit in this theory is that, in a competitive securities market, investors will keep exploiting any arbitrage opportunities until they no longer exist. An arbitrage opportunity exists if there is a way to combine securities or portfolios so as to create two perfect substitutes that sell at different prices. We can exploit such an opportunity by selling the high-priced securities package and buying the low-priced one until the differential has been eliminated. When equilibrium has been established, therefore, any perfect substitutes should sell at the same price. This principle in turn should enforce certain pricing relationships among different securities. We saw in Section IV of Chapter 1, for example, that this principle implies several relationships between the prices of zero-coupon and coupon-bearing bonds, based on the insight that any coupon-bearing bond can be decomposed into an equivalent package of zeros. Similarly, in the preceding section of this chapter, we saw that the arbitrage principle implies a relationship between bond prices and futures or forward market prices.

The arbitrage pricing principle has proved extremely useful in finance, and we will see numerous examples of it throughout this book.

However, it also has its limitations. The arbitrage principle tells us about the relative prices of securities, for example, but it tells us nothing about how these prices are linked to economic fundamentals. Given a change in these fundamentals (that is, a change in productive capacity, a shift in demand, or a change in the inflation rate), the arbitrage principle offers no guidance for predicting how security prices will change. It tells us only how the prices of two securities should line up after the change has taken place.

To go further, we must make some assumptions about investors' preferences. Thus we can distinguish between arbitrage-based pricing relationships and utility-based relationships. The former assume only that investors like profits and that they will exploit any arbitrage opportunity. The three primary theories of the term structure of interest rates, on the other hand, are utility-based theories, and they are distinguished primarily by the different assumptions thay make about investors' willingness to substitute bonds of one maturity for another.

B. The Pure Expectations Theory

The basic assumption behind the pure expectations theory is that investors view securities of any maturity as perfect substitutes for one another, as long as their expected holding-period returns are equal. Suppose, for example, that investors have a two-period horizon. They can provide income over this horizon by buying either a two-period zero-coupon security or a one-period zero now and rolling over the proceeds at maturity into another one-period zero, one period from now. Let $_2\tilde{y}_1$ denote the one-period spot rate that will prevail on a loan maturing at time 2 (note that as of now, time 0, this rate is a random variable), and let E denote the expectations operator. Then, in order for investors to be indifferent between these two strategies for providing income in the second period, securities must be priced so that

$$(1 + y_2)^2 = E[(1 + y_1)(1 + {}_2\tilde{y}_1)] = (1 + y_1)E(1 + {}_2\tilde{y}_1)$$
$$= (1 + y_1)[1 + E({}_2\tilde{y}_1)] \tag{3.3}$$

Solving Equation (3.3) for $E({}_2\tilde{y}_1)$,

$$E({}_2\tilde{y}_1) = \frac{(1 + y_2)^2}{(1 + y_1)} - 1 \tag{3.4}$$

Note, however, that the right-hand side of (3.4) is identical to that of (3.1), which implies that, in equilibrium, $E({}_2\tilde{y}_1) = f_2$. More generally, the pure expectations theory can be characterized as implying that securities will be priced so that the forward rates implicit in long-term secu-

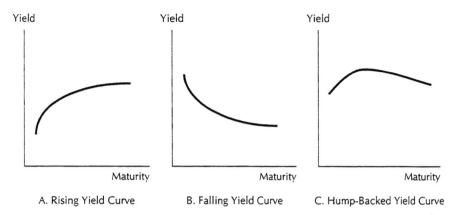

A. Rising Yield Curve   B. Falling Yield Curve   C. Hump-Backed Yield Curve

FIGURE 3.2   Common yield curve shapes

rities are equal to the expected furture spot rates on short-term securities. Since these forward rates are completely determined by investors' expectations of future rates, moreover, the pure expectations theory asserts that these expectations are the sole economic fundamental determining the shape of the yield curve.

To gain further insight into this point, consider the three common yield curve shapes depicted in Figure 3.2. If the yield curve is rising, as in curve A, the expectations theory offers the explanation that investors must be expecting future short rates to be higher than current levels. To see why, suppose that the yield curve were flat, but that investors expected future short rates to rise. If current long-term securities offered no higher return than short-term securities, investors would prefer to invest short now and then roll over the proceeds at the higher short rates that they expected to prevail in the future. But if investors are buying short-term securities and selling long-term securities, this will drive down prices on longs relative to shorts, and thus the yields on long-term securities must rise to higher levels than on short-term securities. In a similar manner, the expectations theory would explain a falling yield curve (curve B) in terms of investor expectations of a decline in future short rates and a hump-backed yield curve (curve C) in terms of investor expectations that future short rates will first rise and then fall.

The expectations theory has been widely used, since it offers a simple, yet intuitively reasonable explanation for the shape of the yield curve. It can also be used to estimate market consensus interest rate forecasts, since implied forward rates are nothing more than expected future short rates under the expectations theory. For all of its appeal, however, the expectations theory suffers from at least two shortcomings.

First, as shown in the Appendix to this chapter, expected holding-period yields cannot be equated for all holding periods. Thus the analyst must choose a particular investor horizon over which expected returns are to be assumed equal in equilibrium. Second, many analysts are skeptical about the assumption of perfect substitutability between short- and long-term bonds. The two primary competing theories do not deny an important role for expectations in determining the shape of the yield curve, but they assert that securities of different maturity are not perfect substitutes in investors' minds. They imply that other factors, especially relative security supplies, play a role in determining relative yields.

C. Competitors to the Pure Expectations Theory

The liquidity preference theory asserts that investors prefer liquidity, or short-term securities, other things being equal. This theory could be rationalized, for example, by asserting that all investors have a very short investment horizon, in which case holding long-term securities would expose them to a greater degree of interest rate risk. The only way bond issuers could coax investors to hold long-term securities, then, would be to offer premium yields relative to short-term securities. If we designate a two-period security as long-term and a one-period security as short-term, then the principal implication of the liquidity preference theory is

$$E(_2\tilde{y}_1) < f_2 \qquad (3.5)$$

The amount by which the forward rate exceeds the expected future spot rate in (3.5) is called a liquidity premium, and it represents the extra reward that issuers must offer investors to get them to hold long-term securities.

The preferred habitat theory, by contrast, attempts to generalize upon the liquidity preference theory by asserting that different groups of investors may have different horizons. Some, as the liquidity preference theory suggests, might have short horizons, but others, such as pension funds and life insurance companies, might have quite long horizons. Still others may be investing with an eye toward some intermediate horizon. If these investors wish to minimize their exposure to interest rate risk, the immunization principle suggests that they equate the durations of their portfolios to their investment horizons. Thus, risk-averse investors in different groups may have different preferred maturities, or habitats, in which they would like to concentrate their portfolios. Again, these investors can be coaxed out of the maturity that would minimize their interest rate risk, but only if they are offered premium yields. Like the liquidity preference theory, then, the preferred habitat theory asserts that implied forward rates will differ from expected future spot rates. In the case of the preferred habitat theory, however, these differences can be either positive or negative, depending on the amounts of investment funds seeking particular habitats relative to the amounts issuers wish to raise in different maturities.

The essential difference between the pure expectations theory and these competitor theories can be further illustrated with supply and demand diagrams. For simplicity, we will assume that there are only two types of bonds, longs and shorts. In Figures 3.3 and 3.4, issuers are assumed to be willing to issue more of either long or short bonds as yields decline. The difference between the two diagrams lies in the demand curves. Under the pure expectations theory, shorts and longs are perfect substitutes as long as the yields line up in such a way that the implied forward rate in the long market is equal to the expected future short rate. Thus demands in both the long and short markets are perfectly elastic, as illustrated in Figure 3.3, and the market comes into equilibium with amounts S^* and L^* of long and short bonds being issued and bought at yields of $y(S^*)$ and $y(L^*)$, respectively. The perfectly elastic demand curves imply that, if the long rate rose even one iota from $y(L^*)$, investors would completely abandon the short market and put all their money in longs. Conversely, if the long rate fell by even one iota, investors would completely abandon the long market.

Under the preferred habitat theory, by contrast, longs and shorts are not perfect substitutes, and thus the demand curves in both the long and short markets are imperfectly elastic, as illustrated in Figure 3.4.[1]

FIGURE 3.3   Equilibrium in the short- and long-term bond markets under the pure expectations hypothesis

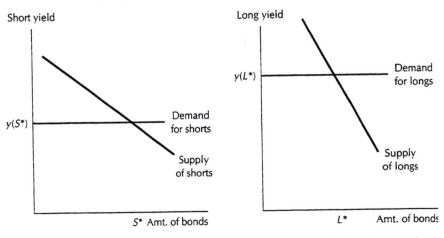

A. Market for Short-Term Bonds

B. Market for Long-Term Bonds

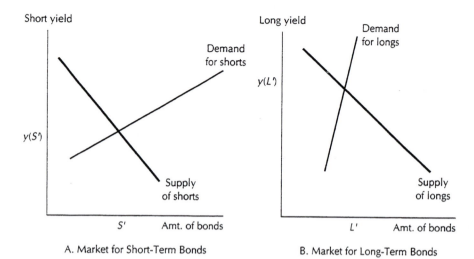

A. Market for Short-Term Bonds   B. Market for Long-Term Bonds

FIGURE 3.4   Equilibrium in the short- and long-term bond markets under the preferred habitat hypothesis

In this case, the market comes into equilibrium with amounts S' and L' of shorts and longs being issued and bought at yields of $y(S')$ and $y(L')$, respectively.

Now suppose that issuers decide they want to issue more long bonds and fewer short bonds at all yield levels. This means that the supply curve shifts outward in the long market and inward in the short market. The effect of this shift on relative yields depends on whether one believes the pure expectations or the preferred habitat theory.

As illustrated in Figure 3.5, the shift in relative supplies has no effect on relative yields under the pure expectations theory. The reason is that investors are prefectly willing to substitute long bonds for short in their portfolios, as long as yields continue to line up so as to equate the implied forward rate with the expected future spot rate. Issuers need not offer investors any inducement to get them to rearrange their portfolios. As shown in Figure 3.5, the shifts in supply result in an increase in long bonds from L^* to L^{**} and a decrease in short bonds from S^* to S^{**}, but there is no change in yields. Under the pure expectations theory, therefore, the shape of the yield curve is determined solely by expectations of future short rates and is unaffected by shifts in relative security supplies.

Under the preferred habitat theory, on the other hand, longs and shorts are not perfect substitutes, and investors are not willing to rebalance their portfolios at the same yields. As shown in Figure 3.6, the outward shift in the supply of longs results in an increase from L' to L'' in

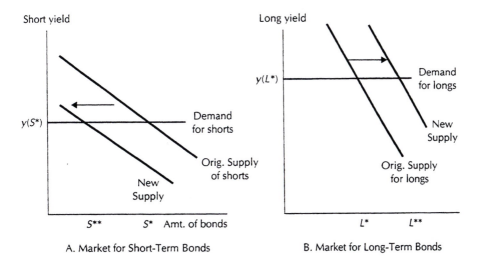

FIGURE 3.5   Effect of increased relative supply of long bonds under the pure expectations hypothesis

the amount of long bonds sold, but it also results in an increase in the long yield from $y(L')$ to $y(L'')$. Conversely, the amount of short bonds is reduced from S' to S'', and at the same time the short yield falls from $y(S')$ to $y(S'')$. It has taken an increase in the yield spread to coax additional investors out of their preferred short maturity, and thus the pre-

FIGURE 3.6   Effects of increased relative supply of long bonds under the preferred habitat hypothesis

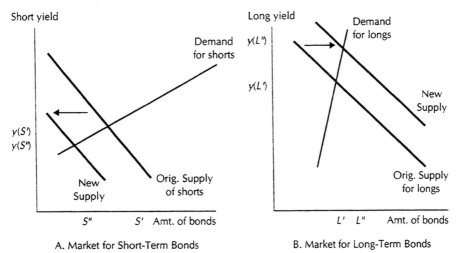

ferred habitat theory implies that the shape of the yield curve is influenced not only by interest rate expectations but also by relative security supplies.

Ideally, empirical studies would be able to distinguish between these two types of theories and identify the significant determinants of the term structure. Unfortunately, it has been difficult to design powerful empirical tests, partly because researchers need a theory of expectations formation to model the influence of expected future rates. Thus, if empirical results fail to support one of the term structure theories, it is never clear whether the reason is that the term structure theory is incorrect or because expectations have been measured improperly. By the same token, it is difficult to isolate the pure effect of a change in relative security supplies, holding interest rate expectations constant, because a shift in supplies may signal something to investors about bond issuers' expectations and thus may induce investors to revise their own expectations.

While it may be difficult to pin down the one correct theory, the analysis just presented is at least useful in explaining why both expectations and relative security supplies can play a potential role in yield curve determination, and it is clear that market participants look closely at both of these factors. Regular perusal of the Credit Markets column of the *Wall Street Journal,* for example, reveals numerous instances in which supply and demand factors for different financial institutions, government and corporate issuers, and other investors are invoked to help explain the relative movements of long-term and short-term interest rates. The theories of the term structure can be useful as we read such articles by helping to identify the types of assumptions about investor behavior that these analysts are implicitly making.

III. SUMMARY

The yield curve, or term structure of interest rates, depicts the relationship among yields on instruments of different duration. If we measure the yield curve using zero-coupon bond yields, there is no confusion between maturity and duration, and we can think of the yield curve as depicting the spot rates on single-payment loans of different maturity. These spot rates can also be used to calculate implied forward rates, or the implicit yields that are determined now on short-term loans for future delivery.

Theories of the term structure of interest rates attempt to identify those economic factors that influence the shape of the yield curve. This approach is different from the arbitrage approach to security pricing, which seeks only to identify relationships among securities combinations that are perfect substitutes for one another. The arbitrage approach is incapable of linking these security prices to underlying economic fundamentals.

Uncovering such linkages requires some assumptions about investor preferences. For example, the pure expectations theory assumes that investors view bonds of different maturity as perfect substitutes for one another as long as their expected returns are the same over a given holding period. These returns will in turn be equated as long as the forward rates implicit in long-term bond yields are equal to investors' expected future spot rates on short-term bonds. The pure expectations theory further implies that the shape of the yield curve is determined solely by investors' interest rate expectations.

Two competing theories differ by assuming that investors do not view short and long-term bonds as perfect substitutes because, over a particular investment horizon, they expose investors to different degrees of interest rate risk. The liquidity preference theory assumes that investors have short-term investment horizons and that, other things being equal, they must be offered a premium yield to hold long-term bonds. The preferred habitat theory is more general in recognizing that different investors may have a variety of investment horizons. Thus the amount of the premium yields required to equate supply and demand at various points on the yield curve depends on investor preferences relative to security supplies. For both of these competing theories, an important feature distinguishing them from the expectations theory is that securities of different maturity are not perfect substitutes, so shifts in relative security supplies can influence the shape of the yield curve.

SUGGESTIONS FOR FURTHER READING

More on yield curve analysis, theories of the term structure, and the ability of the expectations inherent in the term structure to forecast future values of such economic variables as inflation can be found in the following:

1. Abken, Peter A., "Inflation and the Yield Curve," Federal Reserve Bank of Atlanta *Economic Review*, 78 (May/June 1993), pp. 13–31.

2. Fabozzi, Frank J., *Bond Markets, Analysis and Strategies* (2nd ed.). Englewood Cliffs, N.J.: Prentice-Hall, 1993.

3. Fabozzi, Frank J., and Irving M. Pollack, eds., *The Handbook of Fixed Income Securities* (2nd ed.). Homewood, Ill.: Dow Jones-Irwin, 1987.

4. Grieves, Robin, and Alan J. Marcus, "Riding the Yield Curve: Reprise," *Journal of Portfolio Management*, 18 (Summer 1992), pp. 67–76.

5. Kritzman, Mark, "What Practitioners Need to Know About the Term Structure of Interest Rates," *Financial Analysts Journal,* 49 (July/August 1993), pp. 14–18.

PROBLEMS AND QUESTIONS

1. Suppose that the asked discounts (y_D) on Treasury bills maturing exactly 10, 20, and 30 weeks from today are 5.38%, 5.48%, and 5.58%, respectively.
   a) What are the spot rates for loans to the government of 10 weeks, 20 weeks, and 30 weeks, respectively?
   b) What are the implicit forward rates for a 10-week loan starting 10 weeks from today and a 10-week loan starting 20 weeks from today?

2. Suppose that the asked discounts (y_D) on Treasury bills maturing exactly 8, 16, and 24 weeks from today are 6.26%, 6.54%, and 6.44%, respectively.
   a) What are the spot rates for loans to the government of 8 weeks, 16 weeks, and 24 weeks, respectively?
   b) What is the implicit forward rate for an 8-week loan starting 8 weeks from today?
   c) What is the implicit forward rate for an 8-week loan starting 16 weeks from today?

3. Assume that the current one-year interest rate is 5%. The forward rate for a one-year loan one year from now is 6%. The forward rate for a one-year loan two years from now is 7%. The forward rate for a two-year loan two years from now is 6%. The forward rate for a two-year loan three years from now is 5%.
   a) Given the data above, what are the points you could identify on the yield curve?
   b) What possible explanations can you offer for the shape of this yield curve?

4. You have current price information on the following 6 instruments:
   a) A Treasury bill with exactly 6 months remaining from settlement to maturity is selling at an asked discount of 3% (for simplicity in calculating a bond-equivalent yield, assume that the bill thus has 182.5 days remaining to maturity);
   b) An $8\frac{1}{4}$% Treasury note, with exactly one year to maturity is selling for 104.527 (prices are quoted here in decimals, rather than 32nds);
   c) A $7\frac{1}{2}$% Treasury note, with exactly 18 months to maturity, is selling for 105.047;

d) A 6% Eurobond, which pays coupons annually, has no default risk, and exactly two years to maturity, is selling for 101.86;

e) A $7\frac{1}{8}$% Treasury note, with exactly 30 months to maturity, is selling for 106.142;

f) A $3\frac{1}{2}$% Treasury note, with exactly 3 years to maturity, is selling for 98.60.

   (1) What should be the prices of zero-coupon bonds with maturities of $\frac{1}{2}$, 1, $1\frac{1}{2}$, 2, $2\frac{1}{2}$, and 3 years to maturity, respectively?

   (2) Construct the theoretical spot rate curve for maturities out to 3 years. What explanations can you offer for its shape?

   (3) What is the forward rate for a 6-month loan (with no default risk), where the loan is to start one year from now? What is the forward rate for a one-year loan (with no default risk), where the loan is to start two years from now?

5. Your investment horizon is 8 years. You wish to purchase a portfolio that will be immunized against interest rate changes, as nearly as possible, at the end of this horizon. The only asset you are considering buying is an annuity that pays $100 per year. The yield curve is flat at 8%, so you can buy annuities that mature any number of years from now (fractional-year maturities are not available, however), and each of these annuities carries an 8% yield to maturity (this yield is calculated using annual compounding).

   a) If you are going to buy just one annuity, which maturity should you choose most closely to immunize your portfolio? What is the duration of your chosen annuity?

   b) Given this annuity, what total wealth (including the reinvested value of any annuity payments received plus the value of any remaining annuity payments) do you expect to have at the end of 8 years?

   c) If the yield curve were suddenly to make a parallel downward shift so that the yield for all maturities was now 7.95% instead of 8%, what would happen to your expected wealth at the end of 8 years?

   d) If the yield curve were suddenly to make a parallel downward shift so that the yield for all maturities was now 4% instead of 8%, what would happen to your expected wealth at the end of 8 years?

   e) Suppose the yield curve suddenly shifted in a non-parallel fashion. In particular, suppose the yields to maturity for bonds of varying maturity are now as follows:

Maturity (years):	1	2	3	4	5	6	7	8
Yield (%)	4	4.5	5	5.5	6	6.5	7	7.5

For all maturities of 8 years and more, the yield curve is flat at 7.5%. Given this yield curve shift, what would happen to your expected wealth at the end of 8 years?

f) What insights do you gain about the immunization strategy from your answers to parts (c), (d), and (e)?

6. You have current price information on the following four instruments:

a) A Treasury bill with exactly 6 months remaining from settlement to maturity is selling at an asked discount of 2.8% (for simplicity in calculating a bond-equivalent yield, assume that the bill thus has 182.5 days remaining to maturity);

b) A Treasury strip, maturing exactly one year from today, is selling at a yield of 3.6%;

c) A Treasury strip with exactly 18 months to maturity is selling to yield 3.8%;

d) A $10\frac{1}{2}$% coupon Treasury note, maturing 18 months from today, is selling to yield 4%.

   (1) What prices for zero-coupon bonds with maturities of $\frac{1}{2}$, 1, and $1\frac{1}{2}$ years to maturity, respectively, are implied by the yield information for instruments (a), (b) and (c) above? (For convenience, assume a $1 face value for the zero-coupon bonds.)

   (2) What price for a zero-coupon bond with a $1\frac{1}{2}$ year maturity is implied by the yield information for instruments (a), (b) and (d) above?

   (3) How could you set up an arbitrage transaction to exploit the price discrepancy between $1\frac{1}{2}$ year zeros from instruments (c) and (d) above? (Note that you may use any of the four available instruments in setting up your arbitrage transaction). You should set up your transaction so that it allows you to take out an immediate profit without incurring any net future obligations. How much profit could you earn on this transaction per $1 of gross investment (that is, measure your arbitrage profit relative to $1 of securities purchased)?

   (4) What two forward rates for a 6-month loan, starting one year from today, are implied by the $1\frac{1}{2}$-year zero prices you have calculated from instruments (c) and (d) above?

   (5) Can you say whether it is instrument (c) or instrument (d) that is mispriced? Suppose you knew that investors expected short-term interest rates to rise over the next two or three years. Does this help you decide whether it is instrument (c) or instrument (d) that is mispriced? Briefly explain.

7. Municipal bonds (bonds issued by state and local governments) are exempt from income taxes. Thus, the holder of a municipal bond

(subject to some minor qualifications that we will ignore here) pays no income tax on the interest income received from the bond, which in turn has implications for how municipal bonds are priced relative to ordinary taxable bonds. At least three theories have been advanced to try to explain this pricing relationship. They can be briefly characterized as follows:

a) Although individual investors are generally forbidden to borrow and deduct their interest payments from their taxable income for the purpose of purchasing municipal bonds, corporations are not. Thus, the relationship between R_M, the municipal bond interest rate, and R_T, the taxable bond interest rate (for a given maturity and credit quality) must be $R_M = R_T(1 - T_c)$, where T_c is the corporate tax rate. If the relationship were anything otherwise, corporations would have an incentive to either issue taxable debt (deducting the interest payments from their own tax bill) and buy municipal bonds or sell municipal bonds and buy taxable bonds.

b) For liquidity management and balance sheet hedging reasons, corporations tend to hold primarily short-term municipal bonds. Therefore, the relationship $R_M = R_T(1 - T_c)$ should hold for short-term municipal bonds, but a different relationship may hold for long-term municipals. The exact relationship at the long-term end will depend on the supply of long-term municipals relative to the demand.

c) There is always a possibility that Congress will repeal the tax exemption from municipal bonds. Because investors will demand a premium to compensate them for the uncertainty inherent in the tax exemption feature, municipal bonds will have higher yields than they would if the tax exemption were absolutely certain.

(1) For each of these theories, briefly explain whether it is an arbitrage-based pricing theory or a utility-based pricing theory and why.

(2) Two primary facts are known about municipal bond interest rates: (1) Municipal bond interest rates are lower than taxable interest rates given the same maturity and credit quality; (2) The yield curve for municipal bonds is more frequently upward-sloping than the taxable bond yield curve; in addition, when the taxable bond yield curve is upward-sloping, the municipal bond yield curve tends to be even more steeply upward-sloping. Assess the ability of the three outlined theories to explain these two facts.

(3) In the light of your previous anwers, briefly explain what you think are the relative merits of arbitrage-based and utility-based theories of asset pricing.

Footnotes

[1] These diagrams are not well-suited to illustrating differences between the preferred habitat and liquidity preference theories, so no attempt is made to do so here. In terms of distinguishing between these theories and the pure expectations hypothesis, the essential feature of either the liquidity preference or preferred habitat theories is that they imply imperfectly elastic demand curves for long and short securities because of their imperfect substitutability.

Appendix to Chapter 3

I. THE EXPECTATIONS THEORY
AND JENSEN'S INEQUALITY

We saw in Section II.B of Chapter 3 that equality of holding-period returns for one- and two-period securities over a two-period horizon implies $E(_2\tilde{y}_1) = f_2$. Suppose, on the other hand, that investors have only a one-period horizon. In that case, they could invest in one-period securities and earn the total return $(1 + y_1)$. Alternatively, an investor could buy a two-period security and hold it for one period. The cost today of this one-period security is $1/(1 + y_2)^2$. One period from now, the two-period security will effectively be a one-period security, so it will be priced to yield the prevailing one-period rate. That is, one period from now, the one-period security will be worth $1/(1 + _2y_1)$. As of now, however, $_2y_1$ is not yet known. Thus we must equate the certain one-period return from the one-period security with the expected one-period return from the two-period security as follows:

$$1 + y_1 = \frac{E\left(\dfrac{1}{1 + _2\tilde{y}_1}\right)}{\dfrac{1}{(1 + y_2)^2}} \qquad (3A.1)$$

which implies

$$E\left(\frac{1}{1 + _2\tilde{y}_1}\right) = \frac{1 + y_1}{(1 + y_2)^2} \qquad (3A.2)$$

However, Equation (3.3) in the text implies that

$$\frac{1 + y_1}{(1 + y_2)^2} = \frac{1}{E(1 + {}_2\tilde{y}_1)} \tag{3A.3}$$

so if we are simultaneously to equate holding-period returns for horizons of both one and two periods, it must be the case that

$$E\left(\frac{1}{1 + {}_2\tilde{y}_1}\right) = \frac{1}{E(1 + {}_2\tilde{y}_1)} \tag{3A.4}$$

Unfortunately, the mathematical principle known as Jensen's inequality stipulates that, if $\tilde{X}$ is a random variable,

$$E\left(\frac{1}{\tilde{X}}\right) > \frac{1}{E(\tilde{X})} \tag{3A.5}$$

Thus, (3A.4) cannot hold, and, in the face of uncertainty, we cannot characterize the expectations theory as implying that expected returns are equated across securities of different maturity for all different holding periods. This difficulty can be avoided only by choosing a particular holding period over which expected returns are to be equated. Most analysts choose the shortest possible holding period (the next instant) for this purpose.

4

Equities: The Discounted Cash Flow Approach

There are two commonly-used approaches to equity valuation: the dividend discount model approach and the capital asset pricing model approach. The former starts from the position that the market price of a share of common stock stems from the company's value as a stand-alone enterprise, and it emphasizes analysis of the company's economic fundamentals. The latter, by contrast, starts from the position that a share in one company is usually held in a portfolio along with many other companies' shares, and it emphasizes the way in which one company's value depends on the interaction between its own risk and return characteristics with those of other companies. In keeping with Part I's focus on individual securities, this chapter's emphasis is on the dividend discount approach to equity valuation. The portfolio approach is presented in Chapters 10 and 11.

I. THE DIVIDEND DISCOUNT MODEL

A. The Basic Model

As with option-free bonds, the most widely used approach to valuing common equity securities is a relatively simple discounted cash flow model. For example, if we expect a share of common stock to pay a dividend of D_1 per share in the upcoming period, if we expect to sell the share at a price P_1 at the end of the period, and if the required rate of return on securities of comparable risk is r, we can express the current price, P_0, of the share as follows:

$$P_0 = \frac{D_1 + P_1}{1 + r} \tag{4.1}$$

Even if we ignore for the time being the question of how to find the proper discount rate, this formulation begs the question of what the price will be at the end of the period. However, we can use the same logic to assert that whoever buys the share from us at the end of the period will also hold it for a period and then sell it, so the new investor will be willing to pay a price such that

$$P_1 = \frac{D_2 + P_2}{1 + r} \tag{4.2}$$

We can substitute (4.2) into (4.1) and continue applying this same logic successively into the future, which results in the following:

$$P_0 = \frac{D_1}{1 + r} + \frac{D_2}{(1 + r)^2} + \frac{D_3}{(1 + r)^3} + \cdots = \sum_{t=1}^{\infty} \frac{D_t}{(1 + r)^t} \tag{4.3}$$

Expression (4.3) and variations of it are known as dividend discount models (DDM), because they express the current price of a common share as the discounted stream of all future dividends on the stock. Expression (4.3) is quite widely applicable. Note, for example, that it is not necessary for the company to be paying a dividend right now. Dividend values of zero can be accommodated for a large number of periods into the future, as long as the analyst can predict when the dividend stream will commence and how large it will be. Unfortunately, projecting future dividends throughout an unlimited horizon is no mean feat. Hence, most variations on the basic dividend discount model (4.3) are distinguished by the assumptions they make in an attempt to simplify the task of projecting the dividend stream.

B. The Constant Growth DDM

One of the most popular variations makes the assumption that dividends grow perpetually at a constant rate, g, per period, which implies that

$$P_0 = \frac{D_1}{1 + r} + \frac{D_1(1 + g)}{(1 + r)^2} + \frac{D_1(1 + g)^2}{(1 + r)^3} + \cdots$$

$$= \sum_{t=1}^{\infty} \frac{D_1(1 + g)^{t-1}}{(1 + r)^t} \tag{4.4}$$

Using the basic properties of infinite geometric series, the equation can be simplified to

$$P_0 = \frac{D_1}{r - g} \qquad (4.5)$$

which expresses the current stock price as a relatively simple function of its initial dividend, the growth rate, and the discount rate.[1] As is consistent with intuition, Equation (4.5) suggests that a stock's value increases with the initial dividend and growth rate and decreases with the discount rate.

It is also possible to link the growth in dividends to the amount and profitability of the firm's investment each period. Suppose, for example, that a firm starts with assets A_0. We will simplify the analysis by assuming that the firm is entirely equity financed, although debt financing could be incorporated rather easily. The firm earns a rate of return ROE (return on equity) on both its existing assets and on all future assets in which it invests. We will ignore taxes, although these could be included by making ROE an after-tax return. Suppose further that, each period, the firm retains the fraction b of that period's earnings and reinvests it in assets that will earn a perpetual return of ROE per period. It pays out the remaining fraction, $(1 - b)$, as a dividend to shareholders. Under these assumptions, the firm will evolve through time as shown in Table 4.1.

The entries in Table 4.1 reveal several insights into the constant growth DDM. First, the growth rate in dividends is equal to ROEb, or the return on equity times the firm's retention, or plowback, ratio. This product is often referred to as the firm's sustainable growth rate. Given the firm's dividend policy and the profitability of its investments, this is the rate of growth the firm can sustain, year in and year out, without having to resort to external financing.[2] The sustainable growth rate also reveals that the firm's growth depends positively not only on the size of its investment opportunities (as measured by the fraction of earnings plowed back) but also on their profitability.

Second, Table 4.1 shows that, in the constant growth DDM, not just dividends but everything else grows at the same rate, g. This rate applies to the firm's investment, assets, earnings, and even the stock price. In that sense, g can also be interpreted as the annual rate of capital gains an investor can expect from this stock. The remainder of the investor's return comes in the form of dividend yield.

Third, the model allows us to distinguish between a firm that is growing in a mechanical sense and a firm that is growing in such a way as to add value. From the stock price column in Table 4.1, we see that the stock's current price, P_0, can be represented as $(1 - b)E_1/(r - \text{ROE}b)$. If $r = \text{ROE}$—that is, if the firm is investing so as to just earn investors' required rate of return—this expression reduces to $P_0 = E_1/r$. But this is the same value the firm would have if it paid out all of its

TABLE 4.1 Constant growth DDM: The link between dividends and the firm's investment

YEAR	BEGINNING ASSETS	EARNINGS	INVESTMENT	ENDING ASSETS	DIVIDENDS	STOCK PRICE
0	0	0	A_0	A_0	0	$\dfrac{(1-b)E_1}{r - \text{ROE}b}$
1	A_0	$\text{ROE}(A_0) = E_1$	$b\text{ROE}(A_0)$	$A_0(1 + \text{ROE}b)$	$(1-b)E_1$	$\dfrac{(1-b)E_2}{r - \text{ROE}b}$
2	$A_0(1 + \text{ROE}b)$	$E_1(1 + \text{ROE}b) = E_2$	$bE_1(1 + \text{ROE}b)$	$A_0(1 + \text{ROE}b)^2$	$(1-b)E_2 = D_1(1 + \text{ROE}b)$	$\dfrac{(1-b)E_3}{r - \text{ROE}b}$
3	$A_0(1 + \text{ROE}b)^2$	$E_1(1 + \text{ROE}b)^2 = E_3$	$bE_1(1 + \text{ROE}b)^2$	$A_0(1 + \text{ROE}b)^3$	$(1-b)E_3 = D_1(1 + \text{ROE}b)^2$	$\dfrac{(1-b)E_4}{r - \text{ROE}b}$

earnings as dividends and never reinvested a dime. What that implies is that, since the firm can earn only its investors' opportunity cost on funds reinvested, investors will be indifferent between whether the firm retains and reinvests or whether it pays out all funds to its shareholders who can then invest so as to earn the same return themselves.

To illustrate, suppose E_1 = $5, r = .20, ROE = .20 and b = .5. The firm's stock price is then $25 and it is growing at the relatively substantial rate of 10% per year. However, if the firm were to cut its retention ratio to zero, the stock price would still be $25. The growing firm is worth no more than an otherwise identical firm that doesn't grow at all, so its investment plan is adding no value for shareholders. The firm can always grow faster in a mechanical sense by reinvesting a greater fraction of its earnings, but if its investments earn only the cost of capital, this approach will not increase the value of its shares. All that the growing firm has accomplished is to rearrange investors' return so that they earn 10% in dividend yield and 10% in capital gains, as opposed to the 20% dividend yield earned by the shareholders of the firm that is not growing.

As we will discuss in more detail later, the secret to growth that adds value is investment opportunities that can be expected to earn more than the required rate of return. This lesson was brought home painfully to many investors during the conglomerate merger boom of the 1960s in the U.S. These investors were attracted to firms that bought earnings growth by merging with other firms. In many cases, however, the mergers generated mechanical growth but did not generate sufficiently high returns to add lasting value. The relationship between earnings retention, return on equity, and share value is further illustrated in Problem 1 at the end of this chapter.

II. DDM WITH VARIABLE GROWTH RATES

A. Two- and Three-Stage Growth Models

The constant growth DDM is appealingly simple, but it is highly susceptible to its constant growth assumption. Maintaining constant growth in perpetuity is really a rather rigid assumption, and it can lead to large swings in the stock price for what may seem like small changes in the growth rate. Suppose, for example, that we have a firm with a 10% discount rate, a 6% growth rate, and an expected dividend per share next year of $1. According to the model, the stock price should be $25. If the growth rate were to increase to 8%, however, with the dividend and discount rate remaining the same, the stock price would soar to $50. Intuitively, that seems like a large increase in the stock price for a somewhat modest increase in the growth rate.

The problem is that a two percentage point increase in the growth rate really is a large increase if it is expected to last forever, particularly if it raises the growth rate close to the discount rate. It is easy to imagine that a firm might grow at a rate that is two percentage points faster than normal for a limited period of time, but more difficult to imagine that an increase of that magnitude could be sustained indefinitely.

To remedy that difficulty, analysts have generalized the constant growth DDM to accommodate growth that takes place in two stages, three stages, and more, each with a different growth rate. In each case, the objective is to add the value stemming from one or more stages before constant growth is attained to the value from a later period after constant growth is attained. In a two-stage model, for example, growth might occur at the rate g_a for a period of A years, after which the growth rate would settle back to the normal long-run growth rate, g_n, in perpetuity. In this case, we can represent the current stock price as follows:

$$P_0 = \sum_{t=1}^{A} \frac{D_1(1 + g_a)^{t-1}}{(1 + r)^t} + D_A \sum_{t=A+1}^{\infty} \frac{(1 + g_n)^{t-A}}{(1 + r)^t} \qquad (4.6)$$

where $D_A = D_1(1 + g_a)^A$. As shown in the Appendix to this chapter, we can calculate (4.6) by taking limits of the geometric series as follows:

$$P_0 = \left(\frac{D_1}{r - g_a}\right)\left[1 - \left(\frac{1 + g_a}{1 + r}\right)^{A-1}\left(\frac{g_a - g_n}{r - g_n}\right)\right] \qquad (4.7)$$

While this two-stage growth model allows for a period of exceptional growth, followed by long-run growth at a more normal rate, it does seem somewhat unrealistic that growth would suddenly switch from one rate to another in a single, discrete jump. To remedy this deficiency, a three-stage growth model has been proposed, in which growth proceeds at the rate g_a for some initial period, after which it declines linearly, year by year, during an intermediate period. At the end of the intermediate period, the growth rate has reached the long-run normal rate, g_n, which the firm then maintains in perpetuity. The firm's stock price can thus be expressed in this three-stage model as follows:

$$P_0 = \sum_{t=1}^{A} \frac{D_1(1 + g_a)^{t-1}}{(1 + r)^t} + \sum_{t=A+1}^{B} \frac{D_{t-1}(1 + g_t)}{(1 + r)^t} + \frac{D_B(1 + g_n)}{(1 + r)^B(r - g_n)} \qquad (4.8)$$

where

$$g_t = g_a - (g_a - g_n)\frac{t - A}{B - A}$$

during the period $(A + 1) \le t \le B$.

The model embodied in (4.8) allows for a smoother transition from high initial growth to long-run normal growth, which is more flexible and probably more realistic than either the constant perpetual growth model or the two-stage model. Nonetheless, while the calculations required for using the three-stage model can be programmed into a calculator or computer, the process is still somewhat complex and cumbersome.[3]

B. The H-Model

A simplified alternative to the three-stage model described above is the H-model, developed by Fuller and Hsia.[4] The H-model allows for an initial high growth rate, g_a, a linear transition to a normal growth rate, g_n, over a period of $2H$ years and subsequent long-run growth at the rate g_n. It differs from the three-stage model in that there is no initial period of constant growth at the rate g_a. Rather, the transition from high growth to normal growth begins immediately. Under these circumstances, as is shown in the Appendix to this chapter, the value of a common share can be approximated as

$$P_0 = \frac{D_0}{r - g_n}[(1 + g_n) + H(g_a - g_n)] \tag{4.9}$$

where D_0 is the firm's current (as opposed to immediate future) dividend per share.

To illustrate, suppose we have a firm that is growing initially at a rate of 10%. This high growth rate is expected to last for three years, after which the growth rate will decline in linear fashion over a period of 6 years. By the ninth year, the firm will have reached its long-run growth rate of 4%, which it will maintain forever thereafter. Assume further that the initial dividend level is $1 per share and the discount rate is 20%.

If we calculate share price using the three-stage growth model in (4.8), we get a value of $8.17 per share. Using the H-model, on the other hand, with a value of $H = 4$ (that is, the period of exceptional growth lasts 8 years; by the ninth year the long-run normal growth rate has been reached), results in a value of $8.00. In this example, the H-model underestimates value slightly, because of its implicit assumption that the decline in growth begins immediately rather than after the third year. However, the approximation is quite close. More to the point, if we assume that the three-stage model correctly captures the pattern of actual growth, the H-model comes much closer to reflecting this pattern than do cruder growth model alternatives. For example, if we ignored any staged growth and simply assumed constant perpetual growth at either the initial or the normal rate, we would get share values ranging from $10 to $6.25, respectively. Alternatively, if we used a two-stage growth model, assuming a three-year initial growth period at the rate of 10% per year, followed by an immediate drop to the long-run normal growth rate of 4%, Equation (4.7) yields a share value estimate of $6.85.

III. GROWTH OPPORTUNITIES AND STOCK PRICES

A. The General Growth Opportunities Model

The models described in Section II of this chapter allow for more flexible and realistic growth patterns than the simple constant growth model, but they do not, of themselves, provide a link between the firm's growth rate pattern and its underlying investment opportunities. We saw, in our discussion of the constant growth model, that the kind of growth that adds value depends on both the size and profitability of a firm's investment opportunities. It would be desirable if we could establish a similar link between more general versions of the DDM and the characteristics of the firm's future investments.

We can get some insight into such a relationship if we consider first the simplified case of a firm with assets in place that are expected to generate a constant, perpetual earnings per share stream equal to E_1 per year. Suppose further that this firm has exactly one future investment opportunity, which it will undertake in the first year. Specifically, the firm can retain the fraction b of its first year's earnings and invest this amount in a project that will generate earnings at the perpetual expected rate of return of ROE per year, beginning in the second year. Since the firm plans to invest the amount bE_1 in the first year, the additional earnings generated by the project, beginning in year 2 and lasting forever, are thus equal to $\text{ROE}bE_1$. If the firm pays out the fraction $(1 - b)$ of its first-year earnings as a dividend and 100% of its earnings in each subsequent year, we can then express the current stock price in terms of discounted future dividend stream as follows:

$$P_0 = \frac{(1 - b)E_1}{1 + r} + \frac{E_1 + \text{ROE}bE_1}{(1 + r)^2} + \frac{E_1 + \text{ROE}bE_1}{(1 + r)^3} + \cdots \quad (4.10)$$

Separating the terms that pertain to the earnings stream from the assets in place from those that are associated with the new investment in the first year, we can rewrite (4.10) as

$$P_0 = \left(\frac{E_1}{1+r} + \frac{E_1}{(1+r)^2} + \frac{E_1}{(1+r)^3} + \cdots \right)$$
$$+ \left(\frac{-bE_1}{1+r} + \frac{\text{ROE}bE_1}{(1+r)^2} + \frac{\text{ROE}bE_1}{(1+r)^3} + \cdots \right) \quad (4.11)$$
$$= \frac{E_1}{r} + \frac{1}{1+r} \left(\frac{\text{ROE}bE_1}{r} - bE_1 \right)$$

Since investment per share in year 1 is $I_1 = bE_1$, and since the net present value, NPV_1, of this investment is equal to the present value of future cash inflows minus the initial investment outlay, (4.11) may in turn be expressed as

$$P_0 = \frac{E_1}{r} + \frac{1}{1+r} \left(\frac{\text{ROE}(I_1)}{r} - I_1 \right) = \frac{E_1}{r} + \frac{\text{NPV}_1}{1+r} \quad (4.12)$$

Equation (4.12) reveals an important and useful decomposition of share value. It says that the firm's current share price is equal to the value of the earnings stream from its assets in place plus the discounted net present value of the firm's future investment opportunity. Moreover, this principle is quite general. The same logic used to derive (4.12) can be used to show that, regardless of the number of future investment opportunities a firm may have, and regardless of the patterns of cash flows generated by these investments, the current share price can always be expressed as follows:[5]

$$P_0 = \frac{E_1}{r} + \sum_{t=1}^{\infty} \frac{\text{NPV}_t}{(1+r)^t} \quad (4.13)$$

Equation (4.13) reveals clearly the link between share price and the profitability of a firm's investment opportunities. If a firm has no opportunities to invest in positive net present value projects in the future, its share price cannot exceed the value of assets in place, no matter how much the firm may be investing each year nor how fast it may be growing. Conversely, the only source of the kind of growth that adds value is profitable future investments.

This consideration suggests that, instead of concentrating on trying to estimate growth rates per se, a security analyst's time might be better spent trying to assess the size and profitability of the firm's investment opportunities, as well as the length of time over which these opportunities can be expected to last. This approach in turn forces the analyst to try to identify as specifically as possible any advantages the firm in question may have over its rivals, such as cost advantages, brand recognition, or other barriers to entry. If no such advantage can be identified, the analyst should be exceedingly suspicious of any valuation estimates that significantly exceed the value of assets in place. There is also a link between this growth opportunities model and the staged growth models described in the preceding sections. Many barriers to entry and other competitive advantages tend to erode over time. For example, patent protection can expire or an early technological lead can be overcome by rivals' innovation or their ability to ride up the learning curve. The length of time that it takes for this to occur will determine the length of the transition period from exceptional growth to normal, long-run growth.

One special case of the growth opportunities model is that in which all new investments earn the same rate of return, ROE, and all new projects continue to do so forever. In that case, we can write the NPVs in (4.13) in terms of ROE, r, and the amount, I_t, invested in year t as:

$$P_0 = \frac{E_1}{r} + \sum_{t=1}^{\infty} \frac{1}{(1+r)^t} \left(\frac{ROE}{r} - 1 \right) I_t \qquad (4.14)$$

In this case, we can separate the size of each year's investment, I_t, from the net present value per dollar invested, $ROE/r - 1$.

Another special case is that in which growth occurs at a constant rate forever. Since Table 4.1 indicates that everything grows at the same rate, $g = ROEb$, in this case, the net present values of succeeding years' investment are no exception. Thus, we can express the firm's stock price as

$$P_0 = \frac{E_1}{r} + \frac{NPV_1}{r - g} \qquad (4.15)$$

where

$$NPV_1 = \left(\frac{ROE}{r} - 1 \right) bE_1$$

B. The Franchise Factor Model

A variation on the growth opportunities model that has gained recent attention is the franchise factor model.[6] This model describes the relationship between a firm's price-earnings (PE) ratio, its cost of capital, and both the size and profitability of its investment opportunities. As shown in the Appendix to this chapter, the franchise factor model can be expressed as follows:

$$\frac{P_0}{E_1} = \frac{1}{r} + (\text{FF})G \tag{4.16}$$

where

$$\text{FF} = \frac{\text{ROE} - r}{\text{ROE}r} \tag{4.17}$$

represents the firm's franchise factor, or the PE ratio impact of the firm's ability to make investments that earn more than the cost of capital, while

$$G = \frac{g}{r - g} \tag{4.18}$$

is the present value growth equivalent, or the present value of all future investment outlays per dollar of assets in place.

Like the general growth opportunities model, the franchise factor model emphasizes the fact that extraordinary investment quality benchmarks can be achieved only if the firm has extraordinary investment opportunities. The first term in Equation (4.16) represents the base PE. A firm that earns a competitive rate of return but has no unique market franchise relative to its competitors will exhibit a PE ratio equal to the base PE, or the reciprocal of the cost of capital. A PE ratio above the base level can be achieved only if the firm has such a unique franchise, or competitive advantage, which in turn has two components: (1) the ability to earn above-market returns on a given dollar of investment, as measured by the franchise factor, FF; and (2) the magnitude of total future investment opportunities, as measured by G in present value terms.

To illustrate, consider Firm A, which can annually retain 40% of its earnings and reinvest this amount in projects that promise a 20% perpetual annual return. If the firm's cost of capital, r, is 14%, the base-case PE is 7.14. However, Firm A has a franchise. Its franchise factor is 2.14, which tells us that for every time the firm can invest (in present value terms) an amount equal to the book value of its existing assets, it will be able to raise its PE ratio by 2.14. In addition, noting that the growth rate is ROEb, or 8%, the growth equivalent, G, is 1.33. This value says that Firm A has opportunities to make future investments that are equivalent, in present value terms, to one- and-one-third times the book value of its existing agents. Taken together, these two measures imply that Firm A's PE ratio will exceed the base PE by (2.14)(1.33) or 2.85, making for a firm PE of 10.0.

By contrast, suppose Firm B also has a 14% cost of capital but opportunities to invest 80% of each year's earnings. However, these investments promise to earn only a 14% annual return. Firm B's growth equivalent is 4.0, so the magnitude of its investment opportunities is considerably larger than that of Firm A. Nevertheless, B's franchise factor is zero. Despite its opportunities to invest large amounts relative to the current size of the firm, B's PE ratio will be equal only to the base PE of 7.14, because its investment returns do not exceed the cost of capital.

It is also worth noting that the basic concepts of the franchise factor model do not depend on the assumption of constant, perpetual growth. Whatever the pattern of a firm's future growth, we can measure its franchise as the present value growth equivalent times a franchise factor multiplier. An illustration of the use of the franchise factor model is provided in Problem 8 at the end of the chapter.

IV. INTEREST SENSITIVITY OF COMMON STOCKS

A. Duration and Convexity in the Constant Growth DDM

A number of financial institutions, such as life insurance companies and pension funds, have liabilities whose market values are sensitive to interest rate fluctuations. To the extent that such institutions hold equities in their investment portfolios, they will be concerned with the interest sensitivity of these equities. Certainly there are many other sources of fluctuations in common stock value besides interest rate changes. For at least some classes of investors, however, the susceptibility of equity values to interest rate changes will be an important consideration.

It has been suggested that the duration and convexity concepts, which we found useful in analyzing the interest sensitivity of fixed income securities, may also be applied to equities for this purpose. If we use the simple constant growth DDM, for example, modified duration and convexity can be readily calculated by taking the first and second derivatives of (4.5) with respect to the discount rate r and then using Equations (2.4) and (2.5) from Chapter 2, which results in the following:

$$D_{Mod} = \frac{1}{r - g} \tag{4.19}$$

and

$$\text{Convexity} = \frac{2}{(r - g)^2} \tag{4.20}$$

A quick inspection of (4.19) and (4.20) suggests that a common stock's duration, as well as its convexity, increases as the growth rate increases. The duration result, in particular, appears to make sense, since an increase in the growth rate pushes a greater proportion of the cash flows from holding a common stock further into the future. If we think in terms of the growth opportunities model, this reasoning further suggests that the larger the proportion of a common stock's value that is accounted for by growth opportunities, as opposed to assets in place, the longer is its duration.

However, this logic does not appear entirely consistent with certain empirical findings. For example, if a given stock has a 10% discount rate and a 6% growth rate, (4.19) tells us that its modified duration is 25 years. In contrast, we can calculate an empirical duration by simply measuring observed percentages changes in stock prices and comparing these changes with contemporaneous changes in interest rates. Leibowitz and Kogelman, among others, have found that this procedure results in duration measures that typically fall in the range of two to six years.[7] Even if the discount and growth rates used in this hypothetical example are not typical, the wide discrepancy between the theoretical and empirical duration measures suggests that other factors, not reflected in the simple constant growth DDM, may be important in determining equity duration.

B. Analyzing Different Sources of Interest Rate Changes

One possibility is that the simple DDM does not account for possible interactions between the discount rate and the growth rate. For example, a common cause of changes in the discount rate would be changes in the rate of expected inflation. To the extent that changes in inflation flow through to project cash flows, however, it may be that project ROE, and hence the growth rate in the cash flows, is affected by inflation in a way that at least partially offsets the effect of the increase in nominal discount rates.

In the Appendix to this chapter, it is shown that if changes in inflation flow through completely to future project cash flows, the duration of the value of future growth opportunities with respect to an inflation-induced increase in interest rates falls to zero. It is possible, then, that the relationship between equity duration and growth opportunities is the opposite of that predicted by the simple constant-growth DDM. Suppose, for example, that assets in place lack the flexibility to flow through increases in inflation. If their cash flows are relatively invariant to inflation, these assets may behave much like fixed nominal bonds with respect to inflation-induced changes in interest rates, and their durations may be rather long. To the extent that future projects have greater flexibility, because their design and implementation have not yet been fixed, future growth opportunities may actually have lower durations with respect to inflation-induced changes in rates than do assets in place. Thus, a common stock whose value is disproportionately accounted for by growth opportunities may exhibit a lower duration than one whose value is primarily accounted for by assets in place. These various possibilities should also serve to caution the reader against quick acceptance of general statements, such as, "Common stocks are an inflation hedge." The relationship between inflation and stock prices can be complex and quite dependent on the particular circumstances faced by individual firms.

Of course, there are other possible causes of discount rate changes besides expected inflation. We might think of equity discount rates as being composed of a real risk-free discount rate, an inflation premium, and an equity risk premium. A change in the overall discount rate can result from a change in any of these three components, and more than one component may change at a given time, exerting different effects on the values of assets in place and growth opportunities.[8]

As we will see in Chapter 7, it is also possible to view a firm's growth opportunities as options, since before the fact the firm always has a choice as to whether to undertake these opportunities or not. Options can react to interest rate changes in different ways from other assets, which further expands the range of possible effects of interest rate changes on common stock prices.

In the final analysis, the interest sensitivity of common stocks is a complex issue. The models of common stock valuation presented in this chapter can help the analyst sort through the different channels of influence, but careful consideration must still be given not only to the pattern of a company's future cash flows, but also to the potential sources of discount rate changes.

V. SUMMARY

In this chapter, we have explored the discounted cash flow approach to common stock valuation. One of the most popular variations of this approach is the dividend discount model (DDM), in which the stock's value is expressed as the present discounted value of the entire future dividend stream.

Because of the difficulty of forecasting future dividends far into the future, a variety of shortcuts have been employed to do so. One of the most widely used of these shortcuts is the constant growth DDM, in which it is simply assumed that dividends grow at a constant rate in perpetuity. This model also reveals that, when the firm maintains a constant dividend payout ratio and earns a constant rate of return on all funds reinvested, everything grows at the same constant rate, including earnings, assets, investment, and the firm's stock price. In addition, the model reveals that the firm's return on equity must exceed its cost of capital in order for growth to contribute to firm value.

Because it assumes that growth continues at the same pace forever, the constant growth DDM yields stock price predictions that are extremely sensitive to the assumed growth rate. In an attempt to remedy this deficiency, two- and three-stage growth models, as well as the more manageable H-model, have been developed to allow for a transition from an initial high-growth period to a lower long-run growth rate.

Other models place their primary emphasis on the firm's future investment opportunities. These include the growth opportunities and franchise factor models, which are quite flexible in terms of the types of growth and investment patterns they can accommodate. Both models focus the analyst's attention on the size and profitability of a firm's investment opportunities as well as the length of time over which these opportunities last. Both models also underscore the key message that only opportunities to earn a return that exceeds the cost of capital can add value to the firm.

All of these models can also be used to analyze the interest sensitivity of common stock. Caution must be used with the simpler models, such as the constant growth DDM, however. That model predicts that higher growth rates should be associated with longer equity durations, and that a firm with a greater proportion of its value represented by future investment opportunities will exhibit a longer equity duration than one whose value is predominantly reflected in assets in place. But these predictions do not distinguish between different sources of interest rate changes. If an increase in interest rates is induced entirely by an increase in expected inflation, for example, it may be that the firm's future investments will be better able to pass along price increases than will assets in place. In such an event a firm with a greater proportion of value tied up in growth opportunities in place may actually exhibit a shorter equity duration, at least with respect to inflation-induced changes in interest rates.

SUGGESTIONS FOR FURTHER READING

Further material on the discounted cash flow approach to equity valuation, on the development of the H- and franchise factor models, and on duration and convexity for equity securities can be found in the following:

1. Damodaran, Aswath, *Damodaran on Valuation: Security Analysis for Investment and Corporate Finance.* New York: John Wiley & Sons, 1994.

2. Fuller, Russell J., and Chi-Cheng Hsia, "A Simplified Common Stock Valuation Model," *Financial Analysts Journal,* 40 (September/October 1984), pp. 49–56.

3. Johnson, Lewis D., "The Role of Convexity in Equity Pricing," *Financial Analysts Journal,* 48 (September/October 1992), pp. 69–74.

4. Leibowitz, Martin L., and Stanley Kogelman, "Inside the P/E Ratio: The Franchise Factor," *Financial Analysts Journal,* 46 (November/December 1990), pp. 17–35.

5. Leibowitz, Martin L., and Stanley Kogelman, "Resolving the Equity Duration Paradox," *Financial Analysts Journal,* 49 (January/February 1993), pp. 51–64.

6. Leibowitz, Martin L., Eric H. Sorensen, Robert D. Arnott, and H. Nicholas Hanson, "A Total Differential Approach to Equity Duration," *Financial Analysts Journal,* 45 (September/October 1989), pp. 30–37.

PROBLEMS AND QUESTIONS

1. **Spreadsheet Exercise.** Enter the equation $P_0 = (1 - b)E_1(r - \text{ROE}b)$ in a spreadsheet. Create a two-dimensional table showing how stock price varies as the retention ratio varies from 0 to .65 in increments of .05 and as the return on equity goes from .10 to .21 in increments of .01. Graph the numbers in your table. What conclusions can you draw about the ways in which reinvestment of earnings affects firm value?

2. Growcorp, Inc., has 20 million shares outstanding and no debt. The shares are currently selling at $50 per share. The company expects earnings per share of $9 in the upcoming year (that is, one year from now). In addition, the company has a policy of retaining $\frac{1}{3}$ of each year's earnings and reinvesting these funds internally. The retained earnings are invested so as to earn a constant return on equity. The remainder of each year's earnings is paid out in dividends. It is estimated that the present value of the company's growth opportunities is $100 million.
   a) What rate of return do Growcorp's shareholders require?
   b) What rate of return (the ROE) does the firm expect to earn on the retained earnings that are reinvested in the business?

c) What is the net present value of the investment that the firm plans to make in the upcoming year (that is, one year from now)?

d) If an investor buys Growcorp's stock now at $50, what will he or she expect the stock price to be one year from now? What is the total rate of return that this investor can expect over the next year from dividends and capital gains? How much of this return is expected to come in the form of dividends and how much in the form of capital gains?

3. The stock of Company X is currently selling for $10 per share. Earnings per share in the coming year are expected to be $2 per share. The company has a policy of paying out 60% of its earnings each year as dividends. The rest is retained and reinvested in projects that are expected to earn an ROE of 20% per year.

a) What rate of return do Company X's shareholders require?

b) What is Company X's PVGO?

c) What level do you think investors can expect Company X's stock price to attain one year from now? How is their expected rate of return over the next year divided between dividend yield and percentage capital gains?

d) Now suppose that the company can reinvest funds so as to earn an ROE of 25%, rather than 20%. There is no change in risk, so investors' required rate of return is unaffected. Earnings per share in the coming year are still expected to be $2 per share, and the company still expects to pay out 60% of its earnings as dividends each year, while retaining and reinvesting the remaining 40%. What will the current stock price be under these circumstances? What is Company X's PVGO now? What level do you think investors can now expect Company X's stock price to attain one year from now? How is their expected rate of return over the next year now divided between dividend yield and percentage capital gains?

4. Titanic Corporation has 10 million shares outstanding, selling currently at a price of $50 per share. The company expects earnings per share next year to be $7.50. The company retains one-third of each year's earnings and reinvests these funds in projects with an expected return of 15%.

a) What rate of return do Titanic's shareholders require?

b) Suppose that, unexpectedly, the company announces plans to retain an additional $3 per share for the next ten years. These additional funds would be invested in ten separate perpetual projects, each with an expected rate of return of 9%. The required rate of return on the new projects would be the same as shareholders' current required rate of return. Calculate the effect of this announcement on Titanic's stock price.

c) Do you think Titanic is more of a growth company before or after this announcement? Briefly explain.

5. Fallingstar Co. has, in the recent past, been retaining and reinvesting 40% of its annual earnings per share in projects that have been generating a 25% return on equity. Fallingstar's cost of equity capital is 15%. Its most recent dividend, which was just paid out, was up to $2.40 per share. However, it is now expected that Fallingstar's period of rapid growth is coming to an end. Security analysts forecast that, over the next 10 years, Fallingstar's growth rate will steadily decline. By the end of this 10-year period, Fallingstar will have settled into a long-run normal growth phase, in which it will retain 20% of its annual earnings and reinvest these in projects that earn a 15% return on equity. Use the H-model to estimate Fallingstar's current share price.

6. ABC Corp.'s 1995 and projected 1996 end-of-year balance sheets (expressed in book value terms) are as follows:

1995 ($MILLIONS)		1996 ($MILLIONS)	
	Debt 213.4		Debt 226.6
Assets 426.8		Assets 453.2	
	Equity 213.4		Equity 226.6

The 1996 projected income statement is as follows:

Sales ($millions)	880.0
Expenses	828.0
Interest	22.0
Pre-Tax Profit	30.0
After-Tax Profit	19.8
Dividend	6.6

The company has 10 million shares outstanding. The shares are currently selling for $8.25 per share (consider the current time to be the end of the year, 1995). The company expects all the standard book value financial ratios (e.g., ROE, asset turnover, debt ratio, payout ratio, etc.) to remain stable for the foreseeable future.

a) What is ABC's sustainable growth rate?

b) What rate of return do investors require on ABC's equity?

c) What is ABC's present value of growth opportunities?

d) Do you think that ABC is following the best possible dividend policy? If so, why? If not, how do you think the dividend policy could be improved and why?

7. **Spreadsheet Exercise.** Expando Corp. expects earnings *before interest* next year (year 1) to be $1.0 MM. Expando currently has assets (at book value) of $5.0 MM and debt of $1.0 MM. The debt is perpetual, so no principal payments need be made, but interest at the rate of 8% must be paid on the beginning-of-year balance outstanding each year. Expando has unusual investment opportunities that it expects to occur in each of the next four years. Specifically, Expando believes it can invest twice the amount of each year's earnings *before interest* in projects that will earn a yearly rate of return of 20%. Starting in year 5, and forever after that, Expando anticipates that it will be able to invest only 25% of each year's earnings before interest in new projects (these new projects will also earn 20% per year). Expando pays no dividends, so its entire net income is available for new investments. In addition, if investment opportunities exceed net income, Expando issues debt to make up the difference. It never issues new equity. If investment opportunities are less than net income, Expando uses the excess retained earnings to pay down outstanding debt. For simplicity, assume that there are no taxes and no depreciation.

a) Use the information given to forecast Expando's earnings before interest, net income, retained earnings, new investment and new debt for years 1 to 6.

b) Estimate Expando's book value debt ratio for years 1 to 6 (measure this debt ratio as beginning-of-year book value of debt divided by beginning-of-year book value of assets).

c) Suppose the discount rate applicable to Expando's assets is 10%. The market value of these assets in any given year t can be estimated as the present value (@10%) of the constant, perpetual stream of earnings *before interest* that is generated by the firm's assets in place at the beginning of year t plus the present value of growth opportunities (PVGO). Estimate the market value of Expando's assets now and for the next five years.

d) Estimate a market value debt ratio for Expando by dividing the beginning-of-period book value of debt by the previous year's market value of assets. How will this ratio change over the next five years? Do you think that Expando management should be concerned about the amount of debt that the firm will be taking on over the next five years?

8. **Spreadsheet Exercise.** FF Corp. has assets in place of $4 per share and a cost of equity capital of 15%. Security analysts forecast that FF's earnings per share next year will be $.60. FF expects that it will have extraordinary investment opportunities, beginning next year and lasting for 10 years. During this period (years 1 to 10), FF will retain and reinvest 24% of its earnings annually, and the resulting investments will allow it to generate a sustainable growth rate of 6%. Following this ten-year period, FF will have no more investment opportunities, and it expects to pay out all of its earnings as dividends.

a) What is the value of FF's assets in place?

b) What are FF's franchise factor and growth equivalent?

c) What is the current value of FF's shares?

d) Suppose, in contrast to the facts given, that FF's investments over the next 10 years will generate a sustainable growth rate of 6%, but that this rate will result from the firm's retaining and reinvesting 40% of its annual earnings (as opposed to 24%). All other facts remain the same. What would FF's franchise factor be under these circumstances, and what would be the price of FF's shares?

Footnotes

[1] Note that it is necessary to have $r > g$ if (4.5) is to be a valid limit for the geometric series. As r approaches g, Equation (4.5) explodes.

[2] If we incorporate debt in the model, sustainable growth is the rate the firm can maintain without resorting to external equity and without increasing its debt ratio.

[3] Programming instructions for programmable financial calculators can be found in Russell Fuller, "Programming the Three-Phase Dividend Discount Model," *Journal of Portfolio Management*, 5, (Summer 1979), 28–34.

[4] See Russell J. Fuller and Chi-Cheng Hsia, "A Simplified Common Stock Valuation Model," *Financial Analysts Journal*, 40, (September/October 1984), 49–56.

[5] The phrase *present value of growth opportunities* (PVGO) has been coined by Brealey and Myers to label the second term in (4.13). Thus the current value of the firm can be thought of as the value of assets in place plus PVGO. See Richard A. Brealey and Stewart C. Myers, *Principles of Corporate Finance,* 4th ed. New York: McGraw-Hill, 1991, Chapter 4.

[6] See Martin L. Leibowitz and Stanley Kogelman, "Inside the P/E Ratio: The Franchise Factor," *Financial Analysts Journal*, 46, (November/December 1990), 17–35.

[7] See Martin L. Leibowitz and Stanley Kogelman, "Resolving the Equity

Duration Paradox," *Financial Analysts Journal,* 49, (January/February 1993), 51–64.

[8] For further analysis of this issue, see Martin L. Leibowitz, Eric H. Sorensen, Robert D. Arnott, and H. Nicholas Hanson, "A Total Differential Approach to Equity Duration," *Financial Analysts Journal,* 45, (September/October 1989), 30–37.

Appendix to Chapter 4

I. STAGED GROWTH MODELS

A. Closed-Form Solution for the Two-Stage Model

Starting with Equation (4.6), we can use the properties of growing geometric series to simplify the two terms. The first term, a finite series, can be expressed as the difference between an infinite growing series that starts one period from now and another infinite growing series that starts in period $A + 1$, as follows:

$$P_0 = \frac{D_1}{r - g_a} - \frac{D_1(1 + g_a)^A}{(1 + r)^A(r - g_a)} + \frac{D_1(1 + g_a)^{A-1}(1 + g_n)}{(1 + r)^A(r - g_n)} \quad (4A.1)$$

Factoring out $D_1/(r - g_a)$ and $[(1 + g_a)/(1 + r)]^{A-1}$, (4A.1) be expressed as follows:

$$P_0 = \left(\frac{D_1}{r - g_a}\right)\left\{1 - \left(\frac{1 + g_a}{1 + r}\right)^{A-1}\left[\frac{1 + g_a}{1 + r} - \frac{(1 + g_n)(r - g_a)}{(1 + r)(r - g_n)}\right]\right\} \quad (4A.2)$$

Putting the two fractions over a common denominator, the last term inside the square brackets can be simplified to

$$\frac{1 + g_a}{1 + r} - \frac{(1 + g_n)(r - g_a)}{(1 + r)(r - g_n)} = \frac{g_a - g_n}{r - g_n} \quad (4A.3)$$

Substituting this result into (4A.2) gives Equation (4.7) in the text.

B. The H-Model

Suppose we have a two-stage growth model in which the period of initial high growth lasts for just one period ($A = 1$). After that, the firm reverts

80

to normal growth at the annual rate g_n forever. We can express the firm's share value as the value it would have if growth occurred at the rate g_n forever, plus an upward adjustment to cover the fact that growth occurs at a faster rate for the first period. That is, we can express P_0 as follows:

$$P_0 = \frac{D_0}{r - g_n} + \frac{D_0(1 + g_a) - D_0(1 + g_n)}{r - g_n}$$

(4A.4)

$$= \frac{D_0}{r - g_n} [(1 + g_n) + (g_a - g_n)]$$

If the initial high-growth period lasts instead for A years, where $A > 1$, we can still approximate the stock price by making A adjustments to the constant normal growth perpetuity, similar to the one made in (4A.4), as follows:

$$P_0 = \frac{D_0}{r - g_n} [(1 + g_n) + A(g_a - g_n)]$$

This approximation errs by not considering the separate timing of the A adjustments, which should occur for successive years rather than all at once. However, if the period A does not last too long, the approximation will be tolerable.

In a similar vein, we could allow for an intermediate growth stage lasting $(B - A)$ years, in which growth occurs at the rate g_b. The same logic just used dictates that we can approximate the stock price in this case as follows:

$$P_0 = \frac{D_0}{r - g_n} [(1 + g_n) + A(g_a - g_n) + (B - A)(g_b - g_n)] \quad (4A.5)$$

Suppose, for example, that the intermediate growth rate, g_b, is halfway between g_a and g_n, or $g_b = (g_a + g_n)/2$. In this case, (4A.5) can be expressed as follows:

$$P_0 = \frac{D_0}{r - g_n} \left[(1 + g_n) + \frac{(A + B)}{2} (g_a - g_n) \right] \quad (4A.6)$$

More generally, if we let H represent half the length of the period of abnormal growth, where the growth rate declines linearly during this period from g_a to g_n, we can approximate the firm's stock price using Equation (4.9) in the text.

II. DERIVATION OF THE FRANCHISE FACTOR MODEL

From Table 4.1, we can write the firm's stock price for the case of constant, perpetual growth as follows:

$$P_0 = \frac{(1 - b)E_1}{r - g} \tag{4A.7}$$

Multiplying both the numerator and denominator of (4A.7) by r and adding and subtracting gE_1 from the numerator, the equation can be rewritten as follows:

$$P_0 = \frac{1}{r}\left[\frac{rE_1 - gE_1 + gE_1 - rbE_1}{r - g}\right] = \frac{1}{r}\left[E_1 + \frac{E_1(g - rb)}{r - g}\right] \tag{4A.8}$$

Noting that $E_1 = A_0 \text{ROE}$, we can then write (4A.8) as follows:

$$P_0 = \frac{E_1}{r} + \frac{gA_0}{r - g}\left(\text{ROE} - \frac{\text{ROE}rb}{g}\right)\left(\frac{1}{r}\right) \tag{4A.9}$$

Finally, noting that $g = \text{ROE}b$, we can simplify (4A.9) to

$$P_0 = \frac{E_1}{r} + A_0\left(\frac{g}{r - g}\right)\left(\frac{\text{ROE} - r}{r}\right) \tag{4A.10}$$

The second term in (4A.10) represents the present value of growth opportunities, which can in turn be separated into two components. The first of these, $A_0[g/(r - g)]$, represents the size of the firm's investment opportunities, measured relative to the book value of its assets in place. The second term $(\text{ROE} - r)/r$, represents the net present value per dollar invested in future projects.

Considering the first term in more detail, the firm's incremental investment in any year t can be represented as follows:

$$I_t = A_t - A_{t-1} = A_0(1 + g)^t - A_0(1 + g)^{t-1} = gA_0(1 + g)^{t-1}$$

The present value of all such future increments is then

$$\sum_{t=1}^{\infty} \frac{I_t}{(1 + r)^t} = \frac{gA_0}{(1 + r)} + \frac{gA_0(1 + g)}{(1 + r)^2} + \frac{gA_0(1 + g)^2}{(1 + r)^3} + \cdots$$

$$= \frac{gA_0}{1 + r}\left[1 + \frac{1 + g}{1 + r} + \frac{(1 + g)^2}{(1 + r)^2} + \cdots\right]$$

Using the fact that the series $\sum_{t=0}^{\infty} a_t$ converges to $1/(1 - a)$ for $a < 1$, we can in turn express the present value of all future investment as follows:

$$\sum_{t=1}^{\infty} \frac{I_t}{(1 + r)^t} = \frac{gA_0}{r - g}$$

Thus the term $g/(r - g)$ in (4A.10) represents the present value of all future investment outlays per dollar of assets in place.

Finally, noting that $E_1 = A_0 \text{ROE}$, and dividing both sides of (4A.10) by E_1 to express it in price-earnings ratio form, we have

$$\frac{P_0}{E_1} = \frac{E_1}{r} + \left(\frac{g}{r - g}\right)\left(\frac{\text{ROE} - r}{r\text{ROE}}\right) \qquad (4A.11)$$

which is equivalent to Equation (4.16) in the text.

III. SENSITIVITY OF COMMON STOCKS TO INFLATION-INDUCED INTEREST RATE CHANGES

Consider, for simplicity, a firm with assets in place plus one future investment opportunity, which occurs next year. Such a firm is described by Equation (4.11) in the text. If there is initially no inflation, the discount rate, r, and the return on equity, ROE, can be thought of as real rates of return, r_R and ROE_R, and we can write (4.11) as follows:

$$P_0 = \left(\frac{E_1}{1 + r_R} + \frac{E_1}{(1 + r_R)^2} + \frac{E_1}{(1 + r_R)^3} + \cdots\right)$$

$$+ \left(\frac{-I_1}{1 + r_R} + \frac{\text{ROE}_R I_1}{(1 + r_R)^2} + \frac{\text{ROE}_R I_1}{(1 + r_R)^3} + \cdots\right) \qquad (4A.12)$$

Now suppose that inflation is expected to occur at the rate i per year. Nominal discount rates will adjust to incorporate an inflation premium. Suppose further that the earnings stream, E_1, from assets in place is invariant to inflation, but that all cash flows (including the initial investment) associated with the future investment opportunity rise exactly in proportion to the inflation rate (that is, they exhibit a 100% flow through). We can then write (4A.12) as follows:

$$P_0 = \left[\frac{E_1}{(1 + r_R)(1 + i)} + \frac{E_1}{(1 + r_R)^2(1 + i)^2} + \frac{E_1}{(1 + r_R)^3(1 + i)^3} + \cdots \right]$$

$$+ \left[\frac{-I_1(1 + i)}{(1 + r_R)(1 + i)} + \frac{(1 + i)\text{ROE}_R I_1(1 + i)}{(1 + r_R)^2(1 + i)^2} \right.$$

$$\left. + \frac{(1 + i)^2\text{ROE}_R I_1(1 + i)}{(1 + r_R)^3(1 + i)^3} + \cdots \right] \tag{4A.13}$$

$$= \frac{E_1}{(1 + r_R)(1 + i) - 1} + \frac{I_1(1 + i)}{(1 + r_R)(1 + i)} \left(\frac{\text{ROE}_R I_1}{r_R} - 1 \right)$$

The first term in (4A.13), representing the value of assets in place, clearly declines as expected inflation increases. However, the second term, representing the present value of growth opportunities, is equivalent to the second term in (4.12) in the text. Thus the value of growth opportunities is invariant to inflation when inflation can be fully flowed through, which means that the growth opportunities component of common stock value has a duration of zero with respect to inflation-induced interest rate changes. The same logic can be used to show that this result holds for any number of future investment opportunities.

More generally, future projects (as well as assets in place) might exhibit inflation flow through factors that vary in value between 0 and 1. Suppose again, for simplicity, that we have a firm with a single investment opportunity, which has a flow through factor λ. In this case, the present value of that opportunity is given by the following:

$$PVGO = \left[\frac{-I_1(1 + \lambda i)}{(1 + r_R)(1 + i)} + \frac{(1 + \lambda i)\text{ROE}_R I_1(1 + \lambda i)}{(1 + r_R)^2(1 + i)^2} \right.$$

$$\left. + \frac{(1 + \lambda i)^2\text{ROE}_R I_1(1 + \lambda i)}{(1 + r_R)^3(1 + i)^3} + \cdots \right] \tag{4A.14}$$

$$= \frac{I_1(1 + \lambda i)}{(1 + r_R)(1 + i)} \left[\sum_{t=1}^{\infty} \frac{\text{ROE}_R(1 + \lambda i)^t}{(1 + r_R)^t(1 + i)^t} - 1 \right]$$

$$= \frac{I_1(1 + \lambda i)}{(1 + r_R)(1 + i)} \left\{ \text{ROE}_R \left[\frac{1 + \lambda i}{r_R(1 + i) + i(1 - \lambda)} \right] - 1 \right\}$$

5

Principles of Option Pricing

I. THE NATURE OF OPTIONS

The proliferation of option products has been one of the most important and exciting developments in world capital markets over the past two decades. An option is a prime example of a derivative security, since its value is derived from another underlying asset. More specifically, an option is the right to buy (or sell) a specified (or underlying) asset on (or perhaps before) a specified date at a price that is specified now. A right to buy is a call option, while a right to sell is a put option. The underlying asset can be any asset, financial or tangible. Among the most widely traded options are those on common stocks of individual companies, but there are also exchange-traded options on stock indexes, fixed income securities, currencies, and futures contracts. Many financial contracts, such as callable bonds or rental agreements, also contain implicit options. The date specified in the option contract is the expiration or maturity date, while the specified price is the exercise or strike price. The holder of the option exercises it by paying (or collecting in the case of a put) the exercise price and receiving (or giving up) the underlying asset. If the option can be exercised only at maturity, it is called a European option, while if it can be exercised any time up to and including the maturity date, it is an American option.

An option is also the classic example of a security with a state-contingent payoff, since its value at maturity depends on the state of the world prevailing at that time. We can think of a state of the world as an economic scenario, or contingency, in which the complete set of states of the world is defined in such a way that any possible occurrence at a given future date falls into one of these states or another. There are different ways to define these states, depending on what future indicator is most relevant to the value of the option. If we take an option on a stock, for example, a natural way to define the states of the world is in terms of all the possible values that the stock's price might take on as of a particular future date, such as the option's maturity date. If we use this approach, there is then a very explicit boundary between the set of states in which the option has a positive payoff and those in which its payoff is zero. Consider, for example, a European call option on a common stock with exercise price X and maturity date T. Our state-contingent variable is S_T, the price of the underlying stock at time T.[1] When we reach T, we will exercise the option if $S_T > X$, giving us a gross payoff of $S_T - X$ (that is, we can buy the stock for X from the writer of the option and immediately resell it in the market for S_T). If $S_T < X$, on the other hand, we throw the option away unexercised, and our gross payoff (not counting the cost of purchasing the option in the first place) is zero. This approach is illustrated in Figure 5.1, where the states in which the option has a positive payoff (in which the option is in the money) fall to the right of X, while those in which the option payoff is zero (that is, the option is out of the money) fall to the left of X. In the state in which S_T is exactly X, the option is just at the money.

Given these features of the option contract, our ultimate problem is to find out how to value the option. That is, what price would someone be willing to pay for a contract that gives the holder the rights just described? Before tackling that task directly, however, it is useful to introduce the state preference model of security prices. The state preference

FIGURE 5.1   Gross payoff on European call option as a function of underlying asset's price at maturity date

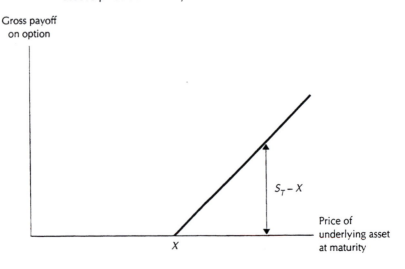

model affords us a way to determine the value of payoffs that occur in one or more future states of the world, but not in other states, which is exactly the payoff pattern provided by any option. While seemingly somewhat abstract, the state preference model has direct, practical application to the pricing of options.

In Section II, the basic elements of the state preference model are introduced, along with the crucial no-arbitrage principle of security pricing. These principles are then used to analyze boundaries on option prices in Section III and to develop the two-state or binomial option pricing model in Section IV. Finally, the Black-Scholes option pricing model is introduced in Section V. These option pricing tools are used subsequently in Chapters 6 and 7 to value a variety of types of options that are commonly embedded in fixed income and equity securities.

II. THE STATE PREFERENCE MODEL AND THE NO-ARBITRAGE PRINCIPLE

A. Essential Elements of the State Preference Model

The state preference theory is really a very direct extension of standard microeconomic theory. That theory, for example, can describe the supply of apples and oranges, and consumers' preferences for each, and it then offers an explanation of how a price is determined for apples relative to oranges that clears both markets. We can add a time dimension to this analysis by simply relabeling the axes on the graph. For example, instead of looking at two goods today, we can take as our two goods apples today and apples tomorrow. We can then determine a relative price, or terms of trade, that will govern how many apples are sold and consumed today and how many are stored for future sale. An interest rate is an example of this kind of price that links present and future periods.

In much the same way, we can apply standard microeconomic analysis to uncertain situations if we simply relabel the axes again so that they refer to apples in the future if one state of the world occurs versus apples in the future if a different state of the world prevails. Suppose I store apples today. Next year, two states of the world might occur: there might be good weather, in which case there will be a bumper crop of apples; or there might be a drought, in which case next year's apple crop will fail. The return on my asset (stored apples) is thus highly state-contingent. If the good-weather state occurs, apples will be plentiful next year, their prices will be low, and my stored apples will have a low value. On the other hand, if the drought state occurs, apples will be scarce and their price high, so my stored apples will be very valuable.

The state preference theory envisions that the market is really determining prices for dollars to be delivered in the future if and only if a particular state of the world occurs. The set of available securities and their payoff patterns determine the number of future dollars available in any particular state. Individual preferences determine the demand for those dollars. A farmer, for example, may have a high demand for dollars to be delivered in the drought state, since he knows that his income will be low in that state. If drought insurance were available, it would simply represent a contract with a state-contingent payoff (for example, a positive payoff if the drought state occurs, nothing if good weather occurs), and the farmer might be willing to pay a considerable amount for it. These supplies and demands will then determine market-clearing prices for dollars to be delivered in any of the possible states of nature.

What is important about these state prices is not so much how they are determined or the form that they take on, but rather that, once known, these state prices can be used to value any asset. Take the case of our stored apples. Suppose we know that a carload of apples will be worth $100 if the good-weather state occurs and $500 if the drought state occurs. Suppose further that we know the state prices, π_{gw} and π_d, corresponding to the two states. Specifically, π_{gw} represents the *present* value of $1 to be delivered next year if and only if the good-weather state occurs, while π_d represents the *present* value of $1 to be delivered next year if and only if the drought state occurs. Assume, for example, that $\pi_{gw} = .3$, while $\pi_d = .5$. These prices imply that the value today of a carload of apples to be stored until next year must be $(100)\pi_{gw} + (500)\pi_d = \$280$.

What if the actual price of a carload of apples today were $250? In that case, I would have an arbitrage opportunity. I would buy as many carloads of apples as I could for $250 each. If markets existed for state-contingent securities, I would simultaneously sell $100 to be delivered next year if and only if the good-weather state occurs and $500 to be delivered next year if and only if the drought state occurs for every carload of apples that I bought. These security sales would give me $(100)\pi_{gw} + (500)\pi_d = \$280$ per carload of apples purchased. I would thus pocket $30 per carload immediately. Note further that this transaction is riskless. As soon as I buy the apples, I can put them in storage. Regardless of which state of the world occurs next year, I can sell my stored apples for an amount sufficient to meet the obligation from my securities sales.

B. The No-Arbitrage Principle

There are organized markets for some types of state-contingent claims (for example, insurance, options, sports betting), but most of us probably do not think of ourselves as trading dollars for future delivery if and only if a particular future state occurs. It is natural to ask, then, whether it is necessary to the apple example that established markets in state-contingent securities actually exist. The answer is no, as long as we can combine other securities in a way that will produce the same pattern of payoffs across the two states of the world as the stored apples would. In that case, we simply sell that combination of securities. Therefore, even if there are no explicit markets in state-contingent securities for individual states of the world, we can still infer the state prices that are implicit in the traded securities as long as there is a sufficient number of securities with varying payoff patterns across the states. If existing securities were not priced in a manner consistent with these implicit state prices, arbitrage opportunities would be available.

In fact, it turns out that this identity between all arbitrage opportunities being fully exploited and the ability to determine state prices is a fundamental result of state preference theory as well as a crucial element in modern theories of asset pricing. In order to state this result in somewhat more general terms, let us consider a world in which there are N different assets and S possible future states of the world. Given these terms, we can define a giant payoff matrix, $\mathbf{R}$, specifying the payoff on each of the assets in each of the possible states of the world. We can represent $\mathbf{R}$ as follows:

$$\mathbf{R} = \begin{pmatrix} R_{11} & R_{12} & \cdots & R_{1N} \\ R_{21} & \cdot & \cdots & \cdot \\ \cdot & \cdot & \cdots & \cdot \\ \cdot & \cdot & \cdots & \cdot \\ \cdot & \cdot & \cdots & \cdot \\ R_{S1} & \cdot & \cdots & R_{SN} \end{pmatrix} \qquad (5.1)$$

If we then define an $N \times 1$ column vector of portfolio weights, $\mathbf{a}$, whose entries sum to one,

$$\mathbf{a} = \begin{pmatrix} a_1 \\ a_2 \\ \cdot \\ \cdot \\ \cdot \\ a_N \end{pmatrix} \qquad (5.2)$$

an investor's wealth in any future state of the world with portfolio $\mathbf{a}$ is simply given by $\mathbf{Ra}$. Moreover, if we define a row vector $\mathbf{P} = (P_1, P_2, \ldots, P_N)$, which specifies the price of each of the N assets, the current value of an investor's portfolio is given by $\mathbf{Pa}$.

With these definitions, we can then write the condition that there be no arbitrage opportunities available in the capital markets (the no-arbitrage condition) as follows:

$$\text{If } \mathbf{Ra} \geq 0, \text{ we must have } \mathbf{Pa} \geq 0 \qquad (5.3)$$

This expression says, "There is no free lunch." That is, if a portfolio generates nonnegative wealth, it must have a nonnegative cost, or value. Any portfolio that generates a positive payoff in some future states of the world, even if it is only one state, and no negative payoffs in other states, must have a positive value today.

For example, a profitable coupon-stripping opportunity, such as discussed in Chapter 1, would violate this condition. If an investor could buy whole bonds and sell strips profitably, the simultaneous purchase and sale would create a portfolio with future net cash flows of zero, because the inflows from the whole bonds would be just canceled by the obligation to pay off on the strips. If this portfolio generates a profit now, however, it means that the net cost of constructing it is negative, in violation of (5.3).

It then turns out that if the no-arbitrage condition (5.3), holds, there must exist a set of state prices, $(\pi_1, \pi_2, \ldots, \pi_n)$, where π_s represents the present value of a dollar to be delivered in the future if and only if state s occurs. These state prices can be used to value any asset. That is, if the price of asset n, with state-contingent payoffs $(R_{1n}, R_{2n}, \ldots, R_{Sn})$ is P_n, it must be the case that

$$P_n = \sum_{s=1}^{S} \pi_s R_{sn} \qquad (5.4)$$

This principle works in the other direction as well: If a set of state prices exists such that (5.4) holds for all assets, there can be no arbitrage opportunities in the capital markets. Thus, we can state our fundamental result as follows:

Theorem: A set of state prices exists that can be used to value any asset if and only if assets are priced so as to eliminate all arbitrage opportunities.[2]

As we will see in this and subsequent chapters, this result has many applications. In some cases, we will be able to use no-arbitrage relationships among the prices of traded assets to find the underlying state prices. In others, we will be able to use the state prices to discover relationships among asset prices that must hold if arbitrage opportunities have been eliminated. This application can be illustrated through two examples.

First, suppose there is a risk-free, one-year zero-coupon bond, which has a yield (using annual compounding) r_f, a face value of \$1 and a price $1/(1 + r_f)$. Suppose also that there is a full set of pure state-contingent securities available. That is, I can buy or sell today a dollar to be delivered in one year, if and only if state s occurs a year from now, at a price π_s. If I bought exactly \$1 to be delivered in each of the S states, I would have the equivalent of the risk-free bond. The fact that it pays \$1 a year from now with no risk means exactly that it pays \$1 in each and every possible state of the world. However two assets or portfolios that have exactly the same payoff pattern across all states of nature cannot sell at different prices today without creating an arbitrage opportunity. Thus, in equilibrium,

$$\sum_{s=1}^{S} \pi_s = \frac{1}{1 + r_f} \tag{5.5}$$

The second illustration concerns the principle of value additivity, which says that if the payoff on one asset is always some linear combination of the payoffs on two other assets, the price of the first asset must always be the same linear combination of the prices of the other two assets. Otherwise, an arbitrage opportunity would exist. To see why, we can first restate the premise as follows: In any state s, the payoff on asset c, R_{sc}, is equal to $AR_{sa} + BR_{sb}$, where R_{sa} and R_{sb} are the payoffs on assets a and b, respectively, and A and B are constants. The absence of arbitrage opportunities implies that we can write the price of asset c as

$$P_c = \sum_{s=1}^{S} \pi_s R_{sc} \tag{5.6}$$

The relationship among the asset payoffs, however, implies that

$$P_c = \sum_{s=1}^{S} \pi_s (AR_{sa} + BR_{sb}) = A \sum_{s=1}^{S} \pi_s R_{sa} + B \sum_{s=1}^{S} \pi_s R_{sb} = AP_a + BP_b \tag{5.7}$$

which proves our result. While the proof is quite simple, it should be noted that the result is not trivial, and it has many applications. For example, the validity of the net present value rule for corporate investment rests on the value additivity principle. As a result, we can value a new project separately from the firm's other assets, knowing that the new project's contribution to firm value can be accounted for by simply adding its net present value to the firm's existing value.

III. USING THE NO-ARBITRAGE PRINCIPLE TO PLACE BOUNDARIES ON OPTION PRICES

Consider a European call option, with exercise price X, on a share of common stock. The current price of that option is C_0, while the current price of the underlying stock is S_0. We will assume that this stock pays no dividends. We will also assume that riskless borrowing and lending is available at the rate r_f per period for maturities up to T periods.[3] Given these conditions, we can derive three properties of options. The first of these is as follows:

> *Property 1.* The current price of the European call option on the non-dividend-paying stock must be greater than or equal to the maximum of either zero or $S_0 - \dfrac{X}{(1 + r_f)^T}$.

That is, the option must be worth at least as much as the current stock price minus the present value of the exercise price. To understand this principle, consider a portfolio consisting of one share of the underlying stock plus an amount of borrowing that obligates us to pay a total of X at time T. The cost of this portfolio today is thus $S_0 - X/(1 + r_f)^T$. At time T, the stock will be worth S_T and the bonds will be worth X, so the portfolio's value at T will be $S_T - X$. Also, at time T the value of the European option will be the maximum of either zero or $S_T - X$ (we will write this condition as $\max[0, S_T - X]$). Thus, at expiration, the option must be worth at least as much as the portfolio. That being the case, however, the option must be worth at least as much as the portfolio today. For example, if the interest rate is 5%, a call option with a 5-period maturity and an exercise price of 50 on a stock whose current price is 45 must be worth at least $45 - 50/(1.05)^5 = 5.82$, because the option's payoff at time T is always at least as good as the payoff from borrowing $50/(1.05)^5$ today and buying the stock for a net outlay of 5.82.

If this property were not true, an arbitrageur could profit by selling portfolios and buying options, since the option payoffs would always be at least sufficient to pay off on the portfolios at T. The fact that the option's price must also be at least zero (it has some positive payoffs and no negative payoffs) proves Property 1. The next two properties concern the relationship between European and American options. Property 2 is as follows:

> *Property 2.* An American call option on a non-dividend-paying stock will never be exercised prior to expiration.

To understand this property, first recognize the fact that the American option confers the same right (that is, the right to exercise at T) on its holder as the European option, but some additional rights as well (for example, the right to exercise at any earlier date). The additional rights could always go unexercised, so they can never have negative value. Thus the American option's price, C_0^A, must be worth at least as much as the European option. The American option must therefore satisfy Property 1. But if that is true, $C_0^A > \max[0, S_0 - X]$, because $1/(1 + r_f)^T$ must be less than one. Since $S_0 - X$ is the amount an investor could get by exercising the American option now, early exercise cannot be optimal. The

investor would always do better to sell the option in the market for C_0^A.
Finally,

> *Property 3.* An American call option on a non-dividend-paying stock
> must have the same value as an otherwise-equivalent European call
> option.

Property 2 tells us that the additional choices conferred on us by
an American option aren't worth anything, because we would never find
it worthwhile to exercise those choices. Thus, the American and European options must sell for the same price.[4]
The discussion of the three properties thus far has all been based,
at least implicitly, on the no-arbitrage condition. The argument is that,
if the properties did not hold, there would be an opportunity to make a
profit. To reinforce the identity between no-arbitrage and the existence
of state prices, consider the same arguments in a state price setting.
Suppose that there are M possible values for the stock at time T. We can
think of these values as our states of the world, and if there is no arbitrage, there must be state prices, $\pi_1, \ldots, \pi_M$, which represent the
present value of \$1 to be delivered at time T if and only if a particular
stock price prevails. Denoting the stock price at time T if state s occurs
as S_{sT}, we can then write the current price of the European option as

$$C_0 = \sum_{s=1}^{M} \pi_s \max[0, S_{sT} - X] \qquad (5.8)$$

Then, by the definition of a maximum,

$$C_0 \geq \sum_{s=1}^{M} \pi_s (S_{sT} - X) = \sum_{s=1}^{M} \pi_s S_{sT} - X \sum_{s=1}^{M} \pi_s \qquad (5.9)$$

But the first term on the right side of the equality in (5.9) is just the current price of the stock, while the second term is the current price of an
\$X face value in zero-coupon bonds that mature at time T and have no
default risk. Since the price today of each bond is B_0, therefore

$$C_0 \geq S_0 - XB_0 \quad \text{(Property 1)} \qquad (5.10)$$

Furthermore, since $B_0 < 1$,

$$C_0 > S_0 - X \quad \text{(Property 2)} \qquad (5.11)$$

from which it follows that the American and European options must
have the same value (Property 3).
The importance of the assumption that the stock pays no dividend
should be noted, however. As we will see in the next section, there may
be cases when the stock pays a dividend in which early exercise of an
American call option may be optimal. In that event, the American option

must be worth strictly more than the otherwise-equivalent European option because we can collect the dividend by exercising early, whereas it is forgone if we wait until maturity. Cases can arise, particularly as the option nears expiration, in which the value of capturing the dividend can exceed the value of waiting.

One other property of option prices that follows from the no-arbitrage condition concerns the relationship among the prices of call options, put options, the underlying asset, and zero-coupon bonds. We will confine ourselves in this case to European options on non-dividend-paying stocks.

Suppose we buy a stock now, at a price S_0, and simultaneously write (that is, sell) a call and buy a put on that same stock. Both the call and the put mature at time T and have exercise price X. What are the payoffs to this portfolio at time T? If $S_T > X$, the put will expire worthless, but the stock will be called away from us by the holder of the call, and we will receive X. If $S_T < X$, the call will expire worthless, but we will exercise our put and receive X. If S_T is exactly equal to X, the call and the put will be worth zero and the stock will be worth X, so we will wind up with X whether or not either of the options is exercised. We have thus created a portfolio that pays X at time T, regardless of the state of the world. However, a zero-coupon bond with face value X that matures at T also has the same payoff. If arbitrage opportunities are driven out, then, we must have the following:

> *Property 4 (put-call parity).* If S_0 is the current price of a non-dividend-paying stock, C_0 the price of a European call option on that stock with exercise price X and maturity T, P_0 the price of a European put option on the stock with the same exercise price and maturity, and $B_0 = 1/(1 + r_f)^T$, the price of a zero-coupon bond with no default risk, maturing at T, it must be the case in equilibrium that

$$S_0 + P_0 - C_0 = \frac{X}{(1 + r_f)^T} \qquad (5.12)$$

IV. THE TWO-STATE (BINOMIAL) OPTION-PRICING MODEL

A. Using No-Arbitrage to Determine State Prices in a One-Period, Two-State World

While the properties discussed in the previous section help us to narrow down option prices somewhat, it would be more desirable to determine the option's precise value. It is clear from our no-arbitrage theorem that, if we can find the state prices, we can use them to value an option, or for that matter, any asset whose payoffs are fully defined over the same set of states. In general, this task is a formidable one, but in some simplified cases, we can use no-arbitrage arguments to value assets.

Consider, for example, a world in which just one period will elapse. A stock's current price is S (we will drop the zero subscript), and next period it will either rise to uS (where $u > 1$ expresses some constant) or fall to dS (where $0 < d < 1$ expresses another constant). This scenario is sometimes referred to as a two-state model, since there are only two relevant future states of the world. In addition to the stock, we will assume that there is a riskless bond, which pays $1 next period in either state of the world. Thus, if r_f is the yield on this bond, its current price is $B = 1/(1 + r_f)$.

If we define π_u as the up-state price (that is, the present value of $1 to be received next period if and only if the stock price moves up to uS) and π_d as the down-state price (the present value of $1 next year if and only if the stock price falls to dS), we can rewrite the prices of the stock and bond, respectively, as follows:

$$S = \pi_u uS + \pi_d dS \tag{5.13}$$

$$B = \frac{1}{1 + r_f} = \pi_u + \pi_d \tag{5.14}$$

These asset price definitions form a system of two equations in two unknowns that we can use to solve for the state prices. Multiplying (5.14) by dS and subtracting from (5.13) we can find π_u as follows:

$$\pi_u = \frac{1 + r_f - d}{(1 + r_f)(u - d)} \tag{5.15}$$

Substituting (5.15) into (5.14), we then find π_d as follows:

$$\pi_d = \frac{u - (1 + r_f)}{(1 + r_f)(u - d)} \tag{5.16}$$

To illustrate, suppose $u = 1.25$, $d = .8$, $S = 40$, and $r_f = .10$. We wish to value a call option on the stock with an exercise price of 34. We can first use (5.15) and (5.16) to find the state prices: $\pi_u = .6061$, $\pi_d = .3030$. As a check on our calculation, we can add these prices to determine that $\pi_u + \pi_d = .9091 = 1/1.1 = 1/(1 + r_f)$. Next, we determine that, if the stock price rises to 50, the holder of the option will exercise, earning a gross payoff of 16. On the other hand, if the stock price falls to 32, the option will expire unexercised, and the gross payoff will be zero. Thus the price of the call option is $C = (.6061)(16) + (.3030)(0) = 9.697$. Similarly, we could value a put option with the same exercise price. If the stock price rises to 50, the put will expire unexercised with a zero gross payoff, but if the price falls to 32, the option holder will exercise for a gross payoff of $(34 - 32) = 2$. Thus, the value of the put option is $(.6061)(0) + (.3030)(2) = .606$.

As a further check on these prices, we can see if they obey the put-call parity relationship in (5.12). Adding the value of the stock and put and subtracting the value of the call, we obtain $40 + .606 - 9.697 = 30.909$. This result checks with the present value of the exercise price, $34/1.1 = 30.909$, so put-call parity holds.

A variation on this example shows why the American and European call options need no longer have the same value for a dividend-paying stock. Suppose that our stock pays a dividend in both future states equal to δ times the stock price prevailing in that state. In this case, we need to recalculate the state prices to reflect the different pattern of payments on the stock. Since shareholders now receive a dividend, the current stock price can now be represented as follows:

$$S = \pi_u(1 + \delta)uS + \pi_d(1 + \delta)dS \qquad (5.17)$$

Combining (5.17) with (5.14) and solving for the state prices then results in the following:

$$\pi_u = \frac{1 + r_f - (1 + \delta)d}{(1 + r_f)(1 + \delta)(u - d)} \qquad (5.18)$$

$$\pi_d = \frac{(1 + \delta)u - (1 + r_f)}{(1 + r_f)(1 + \delta)(u - d)} \qquad (5.19)$$

For example, if the dividend rate, δ, is equal to .15, with all other values remaining the same as in our example just given, we have $\pi_u = .3162$ and $\pi_d = .5929$. Assume further that a holder of the stock receives the future dividend, while the holder of a call option does not, which would be the case if the dividend were paid just before maturity, so that uS and dS can be interpreted as ex-dividend prices. It is still the case here that the holder of a European call will exercise only if the stock price rises to 50, and the gross payoff is still $(50 - 34) = 16$, since the option holder does not receive the dividend. Thus the value of the European option is $(.3162)(16) + (.5929)(0) = 5.059$.[5] If the holder of an American option waits until next period to exercise the option, the payoff will be the same as on the European option. However, the holder of the American option can also exercise now and receive a payoff of 6, so early exercise is superior to waiting until next period and making the optimal exercise decision then. This result has occurred here because of the high dividend rate.

The advantage of holding on to an option is that it allows us to wait until next period to see what happens to the stock price before deciding whether or not to buy the stock. In this case, however, that advantage is outweighed by the fact that we capture the dividend if we buy the stock immediately, whereas we do not if we wait. For similar reasons, put-call parity does not necessarily hold when the underlying stock pays a dividend. These points are further illustrated in Problems 4 and 5 at the end of the chapter.

B. Extending the Two-State Model to Two Periods

The model in the preceding section allows us to calculate option prices easily, once we find the state prices, but a single-period model will not have many useful applications to real-world problems. To show how its range of applicability could be improved, we will extend the two-state stock price model to longer time horizons in two steps, considering the two-period case in this section before moving on to many periods in the next.

For simplicity, we will return to the case of a non-dividend-paying stock. We can handle the two-period case if we assume that the process governing movements in the stock price (the stochastic process) is the same in both periods. This assumption implies that stock prices will unfold over the two periods as shown in Figure 5.2. After one period, the stock price will be either uS or dS, as in the preceding section. Regardless of whether the stock price has gone up or down in the first period, it can again either rise by a factor u or fall by a factor d in the second period. Thus, if the stock price at the end of the first period is uS, it can either rise to u^2S or fall to udS in the second. Similarly, if the stock price

FIGURE 5.2   Possible paths for stock prices over two periods

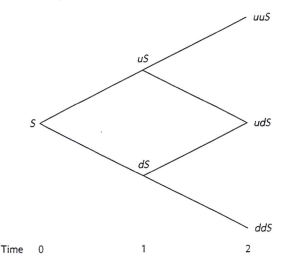

Time   0   1   2

is dS after the first period, it can either rise to udS or fall to d^2S in the second.

In the same manner, we will also assume that the yield curve is flat. That is, the per period yields on bonds of either one- or two-period maturities are the same, so the price today of a two-period zero-coupon bond with no default risk is $1/(1 + r_f)^2$, where r_f is the same as the yield on a one-period zero.

Now suppose that we want to determine state prices, π_u^1 and π_d^1, that give the values as of time 1 of \$1 to be paid at time 2, if and only if the up and down states, respectively, occur at time 2. We can represent the stock price at time 1 in terms of the possible state-contingent payoffs at time 2. Thus, if we start from uS,

$$uS = \pi_u^1 u^2 S + \pi_d^1 udS \tag{5.20}$$

Since the one-period zero-coupon bond yield in the second period is r_f, we can also write $1/(1 + r_f) = \pi_u^1 + \pi_d^1$ as our second pricing condition. Note, however, that this bond-pricing condition plus (5.20) is equivalent to (5.13) and (5.14), so the solution will be the same as given in (5.15) and (5.16). The same solution would also be obtained if we started from a price of dS at time 1.

This condition establishes that, as of time 1, a dollar to be delivered in time 2 if the up state occurs is π_u. What will its value be as of time 0? Figure 5.2 shows that we can receive that value, π_u, at time 1 if and only if the up state occurs in the first period. Since the value now of π_u to be received at time 1 if and only if the up state occurs is $\pi_u(\pi_u)$, we can say that the value today of \$1 to be received at time 2 if and only if two consecutive up moves occur is π_u^2. The same logic indicates that the value now of \$1 to be received at time 2 if and only if two consecutive down moves occur is π_d^2. However, the value today of \$1 to be received at time 2 if and only if an up and a down move occur must be $2\pi_u\pi_d$, since there are two ways in which this payoff could be obtained: An initial down move could be followed by an up move, or an up move could be followed by a down move.

Thus, the state prices corresponding to the three possible states that could occur at time 2, as indicated in Figure 5.2, are, reading down the diagram, π_u^2, $2\pi_u\pi_d$, and π_d^2. With these state prices, we are ready to value any asset whose time 2 payoffs are defined in terms of these three states. Take, for example, a two-period zero-coupon bond which pays \$1 in each of the three states. Its value today, B_0, must then be as follows:

$$B_0 = \pi_u^2 + 2\pi_u\pi_d + \pi_d^2 = (\pi_u + \pi_d)^2 = \left(\frac{1}{1 + r_f}\right)^2 \tag{5.21}$$

which is consistent with our assumption about the yield curve.

Let us now return to our numerical example. Assume once again that the underlying stock's price is currently \$40, that it can rise by 25% or fall by 20% in each of the next two periods, and that the risk-free rate is 10%. By the end of the second period, the stock can have three possible values, $u^2S = 62.5$, $udS = 40$, and $d^2S = 25.6$. The state prices corresponding to these three future states are $\pi_{uu} = \pi_u^2 = .3673$, $\pi_{ud} = 2\pi_u\pi_d = .3673$, and $\pi_{dd} = \pi_d^2 = .0918$. As a check on the state prices, they sum to $.8264 = 1/(1.1)^2$.

The value of a two-period, European call option with exercise price \$34, is then $(.3673)(62.5 - 34) + (.3673)(40 - 34) + (.0918)(0) = 12.672$. In contrasting this value with the analogous one-period call option value in Section IV.A, note the property that option values increase with maturity. The reason is that, given the underlying stochastic process, a longer maturity gives the option a greater chance to come into the money. Similarly, a two-period European put with exercise price \$34 is worth $(.3673)(0) + (.3673)(0) + (.0918)(34 - 25.6) = .7711$, which is consistent with put-call parity, since $40 + .7711 - 12.672 = 28.099 = 34/(1.1)^2$.

Another point that can be illustrated with this example is that Property 3 (European and American call options have the same value) from the previous section does not necessarily hold for put options, even on non-dividend-paying stocks. Given the current parameters, it would not be optimal to exercise an American put early. It would not be optimal to exercise immediately, since the put is not even in the money, given an initial stock price of \$40. Likewise, at time 1, it would not be optimal to exercise if the stock price were \$50. If the stock price had fallen to \$32 at time 1, early exercise would be profitable, but it would still not be optimal, because we could earn a gross profit of \$2 from early exercise. However, if we wait one more period, the stock price could either rise to \$40, in which case we get nothing, or it could fall to \$25.6, in which case we could exercise for a gross profit of \$8.4. Given a stock price of \$32 at time 1, then, the value of waiting one more period would be equal to the up-state price times zero plus the down-state price times 8.4, or $(.303)(8.4) = 2.55 > 2$. Thus the value of waiting exceeds the value of exercising early. For these particular parameter values, then, a two-period American put would have the same value as a two-period European put.

Suppose, however, that we change the exercise price to \$40, leaving all other parameters unchanged. In this case, it is not optimal to exercise immediately, nor would we want to exercise at time 1 if the stock price had risen to \$50. If the stock price had moved to \$32 at time 1, on the other hand, the holder of the put could earn \$8 by exercising. If the put holder waits until period 2, the payoff will be either zero or 14.4, so the value of waiting is $(.303)(14.4) = 4.36 < 8$. In this case, then, it is optimal to exercise early if the stock price falls during the first period.

The essential difference between puts and calls in this respect is that the payoff on the put is bounded. The stock price cannot possibly fall below zero, which limits the value of waiting. By contrast, there is no limit on the amount by which the stock price could rise, given enough time to wait, so a call option holder has more of a bias toward waiting. In the particular case at hand, the stock's price can rise by a greater percentage than it can fall in any given period. The stochastic process here is such that, once the price has fallen in the first period, it cannot possibly fall enough farther in the second to justify waiting another period.

C. The Binomial Model: Two-State Option Pricing with Many Periods

The extension of the two-state model to many periods is straightforward from this point. If we have T periods, and we wish to calculate the current state price for $1 to be delivered T periods from now if and only if the underlying asset's price has made n up moves and $(T - n)$ down moves at that time, we simply take π_u to the power of n times π_d to the power of $(T - n)$ and then count up the number of possible paths by which we could reach that point. It turns out that the number of such paths is the same as the coefficients in the binomial probability distribution. For this reason, the many-period, two-state model of asset prices is often referred to as the binomial model. Specifically, the current state price for the state in which n up moves and $(T - n)$ down moves have been made is given by the following:

$$\pi_{u^n d^{T-n}} = \binom{T}{n} \pi_u^n \pi_d^{T-n} \tag{5.22}$$

where

$$\binom{T}{n} = \frac{T!}{n!(T - n)!}$$

$$= \frac{T \cdot (T - 1) \cdot (T - 2) \cdots 1}{n \cdot (n - 1) \cdot (n - 2) \cdots 1 \cdot (T - n) \cdot (T - n - 1) \cdots 1} \tag{5.23}$$

It is relatively easy to enter (5.22) in a spreadsheet program to solve option pricing problems with quite a few periods. In particular, if m is the minimum number of up moves needed for a European call option with exercise price X to be in the money, the binomial model gives the value of the option as follows:

$$\sum_{n=m}^{T} [S(u^n d^{T-n}) - X](\pi_{u^n d^{T-n}}) \qquad (5.24)$$

There is another equivalent approach to valuing multiperiod options and other securities using state prices that is useful in spreadsheet computation. This approach is the method of rolling back the tree. The key to this approach is to note that, at any given point, regardless of which state we are in, we will make either an up move or a down move in the next period. Furthermore, because of the nature of the binomial model, the value now of a $1 payoff a year from now if an up move occurs is π_u, while the value of a $1 payoff a year from now if a down move occurs is π_d, regardless of the period or the state in which we currently stand.

Rather than calculating a large set of state prices using (5.22), then, it is often computationally convenient simply to start at the end of a value tree (that is, the farthest future point) and work back to the present one period at a time. Consider, for instance, the example in the preceding section, in which we valued a two-period European call option on a stock. The option has an exercise price of $34, and two periods from now, there are three possible values the stock price could take on: $62.50, $40, and $25.60. As shown in Figure 5.3, then, the possible values for the option at maturity are $28.5, $6, and $0, depending on which stock price occurs. Now move back one period. If we are in the higher of the two possible states at the end of the first period, the option's value within the next period will either move up to $28.5 or down to $6. Since

FIGURE 5.3   Binomial tree of stock prices and 2-period call option values

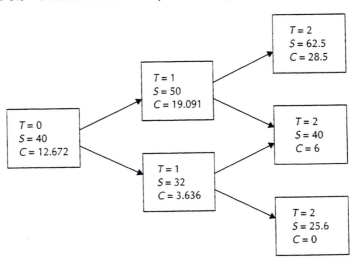

the one-period state prices are $\pi_u = .6061$ and $\pi_d = .3030$, the value of the option at this point (or this node in the tree) must be $(.6061)(28.5) + (.3030)(6) = 19.091$. Similarly, if we were instead in the lower of the two possible states at the end of the first period, the option's value next period could either move up to \$6 or down to zero, so it's value at this point must be $(.6061)(6) = 3.636$. Finally, if we move back to the present, the option's value could either move up to 19.091 or down to 3.636 over the next period, so its value now must be $(.6061)(19.091) + (.303)(3.636) = 12.672$, which is the same answer we obtained in the preceding section using the two-period state prices. The method described here may seem more roundabout in this simple example, but it is quite convenient in solving multiperiod problems with a spreadsheet, since the spreadsheet commands are simply repeated, period after period, as we move back through the tree.

Before moving on, it should also be noted that, in all of the examples used thus far in this chapter, the state variable, or the random variable whose possible future values distinguish among different future states of the world, has always been a stock price. However, the binomial model works in the same way with other state variables. In addition to stock prices, other economic factors such as interest rates or currency exchange rates may be used as state variables. Problems 2 and 3 at the end of this chapter provide examples of options in which the exchange rate is the underlying state variable, while Chapter 6 is largely devoted to option pricing models that take an interest rate as their state variable.

V. THE BLACK-SCHOLES OPTION-PRICING MODEL

If we divide the T periods in the binomial model into a very large number of small intervals, with smaller up and down moves taking place within each interval, we approach in the limit the continuous-time option-pricing model derived by Black and Scholes. This model gives the current value of a European call option, C, with maturity T, current price of the underlying, non-dividend-paying stock, S, exercise price, X, and instantaneous (that is, continuously compounded) risk-free rate, r_f, as follows:

$$C = SN(d_1) - Xe^{-r_fT}N(d_2) \tag{5.25}$$

where $N(d_1)$ and $N(d_2)$ are cumulative probabilities for a standard normal random variable. The values of d_1 and d_2 are in turn given by the following:

$$d_1 = \frac{\ln(S/X) + r_f T}{\sigma\sqrt{T}} + \frac{1}{2}\sigma\sqrt{T} \tag{5.26}$$

$$d_2 = d_1 - \sigma\sqrt{T} \tag{5.27}$$

where σ is the annualized instantaneous standard deviation of the underlying stock's price. This standard deviation is related to the up and down moves in a binomial model by $u = e^{\sigma\sqrt{T/n}}$ and $d = e^{-\sigma\sqrt{T/n}}$, where n is the number of moves (or binomial trials) that the stock makes in each of the T periods. An important point that is made clear by Equations (5.25) to (5.27) is that the call option's price depends on the variance of the stock's price but not on its expected rate of return. This point is significant for practical application, since a variance can be estimated from historical data with greater accuracy than can an expected return.

Instead of starting with the binomial model and approaching continuous time in the limit, we can also derive the Black-Scholes model directly using arbitrage arguments. That is, we can combine the underlying stock with call options and risk-free bonds in such a way as to form a riskless portfolio, whose return must then be r_f. This approach allows us to determine the value of the call option in terms of the known values of the stock and bond. The primary features of this derivation are sketched in the Appendix to this chapter.

This arbitrage derivation reinforces the idea that the Black-Scholes model, like the two-state model, is an arbitrage-based, rather than a utility-based, pricing model. That is, the Black-Scholes model does not tell us how option prices are related to the fundamental economic determinants of asset prices. It makes no assumptions about investor utility, so it cannot tell us, for example, how investors value the risk and return characteristics of options. Rather, the model is based on the observation that the risk and return characteristics of options are inextricably linked to those of stocks and bonds. However investors arrived at a valuation of those characteristics, that valuation is already embodied in stock and bond prices. The Black-Scholes model then tells us how call options must be priced relative to other securities, whose prices we already know, if arbitrage opportunities are to be eliminated.

A few comments are also in order here about the difference between the Black-Scholes and two-state option pricing models, on the one hand, and the option pricing properties that we derived in Section I.A on the other. In both cases, arbitrage arguments are used, but in the case of a proposition like Property 1, in Section III, we achieve only a boundary on the option's value. With the pricing models, by contrast, we achieve an exact numerical value. The difference lies in the fact that the properties derived in Section III made no assumption about the stochastic process governing movements in the underlying asset's price. Both the

TABLE 5.1   Cumulative standard normal distribution values

d	$N(d)$	d	$N(d)$	d	$N(d)$	d	$N(d)$
-3	0.0013	-1.78	0.0375	-1.16	0.123	-0.54	0.2946
-2.95	0.0016	-1.76	0.0392	-1.14	0.1271	-0.52	0.3015
-2.9	0.0019	-1.74	0.0409	-1.12	0.1314	-0.5	0.3085
-2.85	0.0022	-1.72	0.0427	-1.1	0.1357	-0.48	0.3156
-2.8	0.0026	-1.7	0.0446	-1.08	0.1401	-0.46	0.3228
-2.75	0.003	-1.68	0.0465	-1.06	0.1446	-0.44	0.33
-2.7	0.0035	-1.66	0.0485	-1.04	0.1492	-0.42	0.3372
-2.65	0.004	-1.64	0.0505	-1.02	0.1539	-0.4	0.3446
-2.6	0.0047	-1.62	0.0526	-1	0.1587	-0.38	0.352
-2.55	0.0054	-1.6	0.0548	-0.98	0.1635	-0.36	0.3594
-2.5	0.0062	-1.58	0.0571	-0.96	0.1685	-0.34	0.3669
-2.45	0.0071	-1.56	0.0594	-0.94	0.1736	-0.32	0.3745
-2.4	0.0082	-1.54	0.0618	-0.92	0.1788	-0.3	0.3821
-2.35	0.0094	-1.52	0.0643	-0.9	0.1841	-0.28	0.3897
-2.3	0.0107	-1.5	0.0668	-0.88	0.1894	-0.26	0.3974
-2.25	0.0122	-1.48	0.0694	-0.86	0.1949	-0.24	0.4052
-2.2	0.0139	-1.46	0.0721	-0.84	0.2005	-0.22	0.4129
-2.15	0.0158	-1.44	0.0749	-0.82	0.2061	-0.2	0.4207
-2.1	0.0179	-1.42	0.0778	-0.8	0.2119	-0.18	0.4286
-2.05	0.0202	-1.4	0.0808	-0.78	0.2177	-0.16	0.4364
-2	0.0228	-1.38	0.0838	-0.76	0.2236	-0.14	0.4443
-1.98	0.0239	-1.36	0.0869	-0.74	0.2296	-0.12	0.4522
-1.96	0.025	-1.34	0.0901	-0.72	0.2358	-0.1	0.4602
-1.94	0.0262	-1.32	0.0934	-0.7	0.242	-0.08	0.4681
-1.92	0.0274	-1.3	0.0968	-0.68	0.2483	-0.06	0.4761
-1.9	0.0287	-1.28	0.1003	-0.66	0.2546	-0.04	0.484
-1.88	0.0301	-1.26	0.1038	-0.64	0.2611	-0.02	0.492
-1.86	0.0314	-1.24	0.1075	-0.62	0.2676	0	0.5
-1.84	0.0329	-1.22	0.1112	-0.6	0.2743	0.02	0.508
-1.82	0.0344	-1.2	0.1151	-0.58	0.281	0.04	0.516
-1.8	0.0359	-1.18	0.119	-0.56	0.2877	0.06	0.5239

Black-Scholes and two-state models, on the other hand, make very specific assumptions about that process. In fact, this assumption is probably the key behind option-pricing models, and their predictions will be only as precise as the validity of that assumption. In particular, the stochastic processes assumed by most such models rule out the possibility of sudden, discontinuous jumps in stock prices, but as illustrated by the stock market crash of October, 1987, such jumps are not always absent in reality. The option properties of Section III, by contrast, are less precise but also more generally valid, since they are based on less stringent assumptions.

Let us now look at how the Black-Scholes model can be applied. Consider, for example, a European call option on a non-dividend-paying stock. The stock is currently selling for $30, the option's exercise price is

TABLE 5.1 cont. Cumulative standard normal distribution values

d	N(d)	d	N(d)	d	N(d)	d	N(d)
0.08	0.5319	0.68	0.7517	1.28	0.8997	1.88	0.9699
0.1	0.5398	0.7	0.758	1.3	0.9032	1.9	0.9713
0.12	0.5478	0.72	0.7642	1.32	0.9066	1.92	0.9726
0.14	0.5557	0.74	0.7704	1.34	0.9099	1.94	0.9738
0.16	0.5636	0.76	0.7764	1.36	0.9131	1.96	0.975
0.18	0.5714	0.78	0.7823	1.38	0.9162	1.98	0.9761
0.2	0.5793	0.8	0.7881	1.4	0.9192	2	0.9772
0.22	0.5871	0.82	0.7939	1.42	0.9222	2.05	0.9798
0.24	0.5948	0.84	0.7995	1.44	0.9251	2.1	0.9821
0.26	0.6026	0.86	0.8051	1.46	0.9279	2.15	0.9842
0.28	0.6103	0.88	0.8106	1.48	0.9306	2.2	0.9861
0.3	0.6179	0.9	0.8159	1.5	0.9332	2.25	0.9878
0.32	0.6255	0.92	0.8212	1.52	0.9357	2.3	0.9893
0.34	0.6331	0.94	0.8264	1.54	0.9382	2.35	0.9906
0.36	0.6406	0.96	0.8315	1.56	0.9406	2.4	0.9918
0.38	0.648	0.98	0.8365	1.58	0.9429	2.45	0.9929
0.4	0.6554	1	0.8413	1.6	0.9452	2.5	0.9938
0.42	0.6628	1.02	0.8461	1.62	0.9474	2.55	0.9946
0.44	0.67	1.04	0.8508	1.64	0.9495	2.6	0.9953
0.46	0.6772	1.06	0.8554	1.66	0.9515	2.65	0.996
0.48	0.6844	1.08	0.8599	1.68	0.9535	2.7	0.9965
0.5	0.6915	1.1	0.8643	1.7	0.9554	2.75	0.997
0.52	0.6985	1.12	0.8686	1.72	0.9573	2.8	0.9974
0.54	0.7054	1.14	0.8729	1.74	0.9591	2.85	0.9978
0.56	0.7123	1.16	0.877	1.76	0.9608	2.9	0.9981
0.58	0.719	1.18	0.881	1.78	0.9625	2.95	0.9984
0.6	0.7257	1.2	0.8849	1.8	0.9641	3	0.9987
0.62	0.7324	1.22	0.8888	1.82	0.9656		
0.64	0.7389	1.24	0.8925	1.84	0.9671		
0.66	0.7454	1.26	0.8962	1.86	0.9686		

$40, the instantaneous variance of the stock price is 0.64, the risk-free rate is 6%, and the option has six months remaining to maturity. What value does the Black-Scholes model predict for the option?

First, we can use (5.26) and (5.27) to calculate d_1 and d_2 as follows:

$$d_1 = \frac{\ln(30/40) + (.06)(.5)}{\sqrt{.64}\sqrt{.5}} + \frac{1}{2}\sqrt{.64}\sqrt{.5} = -.1727 \qquad (5.28)$$

$$d_2 = -.1727 - \sqrt{.64}\sqrt{.5} = -.7384 \qquad (5.29)$$

Note, in (5.28) and (5.29), that since both r_f and σ are quoted in annualized terms, T must also be quoted that way to be consistent. Thus a period of 6 months corresponds to $T = .5$.

Next, we need to consult Table 5.1 to determine the values of the

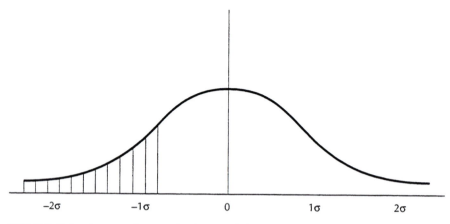

FIGURE 5.4   Area under standard normal density function

cumulative standard normal distribution function corresponding to d_1 and d_2. The standard normal distribution has a mean of zero and a standard deviation of one. Thus $d_2 = -.7384$ corresponds to a point that is 0.7384 standard deviations below the mean, and $N(d_2)$ corresponds to the area under the standard normal density function between minus infinity and $-.7384$, shown as the shaded area in Figure 5.4. Interpolating between values in Table 5.1, we can thus find $N(d_2)$ as .2302. In a similar fashion, we can find $N(d_1)$ from Table 5.1 as .4315. The Black-Scholes formula (5.25) then gives the value of the call option as

$$C = 40(.4315) - 30e^{-.06(.5)}(.2302) = 10.56 \qquad (5.30)$$

The Black-Scholes formula can also be used to value put options on non-dividend-paying stocks through the put-call parity relationship. Using the continuous-time version of (5.12), we can write the value of a put in terms of the stock price, the interest rate, and the call price as

$$P = Xe^{-r_f T} + C - S \qquad (5.31)$$

Then, substituting the Black-Scholes formula (5.25) for C, the formula for the value of the put is

$$P = Xe^{-r_f T}[1 - N(d_2)] - S[1 - N(d_1)] \qquad (5.32)$$

In our numerical example, the value of a put option on the same stock with 6 months until maturity and an exercise price of $40 is $40e^{-0.6(.5)} + 10.56 - 30 = 19.38$.

VI. SUMMARY

Options are rights to buy or sell specified assets at a specified price on or before a specified date. Whether or not this right will have value when the option matures depends on the future value of the underlying asset, so options are the classic example of a security with a state-contingent payoff.

It is not surprising, therefore, that the state-preference model of security pricing is useful in predicting the values of options. Even without making many assumptions besides the absence of arbitrage opportunities, we can establish certain properties of option prices. These properties include the ideas that a European call option on a non-dividend-paying stock will never be exercised early, that a European and American call option on a non-dividend-paying stock must have the same value and the put-call parity relationship (5.12).

If we are willing to go further and make assumptions about the stochastic process governing movements in the value of the underlying asset, we can sometimes solve for the relevant state prices and value options directly. The two primary models for doing so are the two-state (or binomial) model and the Black-Scholes model. The two-state model assumes that the underlying asset's value can move either up or down by constant factors in any given period, which in turn allows us to solve for the state prices in terms of the risk-free interest rate and the size of the up and down moves. The model can be extended to a large number of periods and can be used to value different types of options on stocks, bonds, and other securities.

The Black-Scholes model can be viewed as a continuous-time analogue of the two-state model, and it allows us to determine European call option values in terms of the underlying asset's current price and the variability of that price, the option's exercise price, the risk-free rate, the option's maturity, and the areas under a standard normal density function. In conjunction with the put-call parity relationship, we can also use the Black-Scholes formula to value put options.

SUGGESTIONS FOR FURTHER READING

Additional material on option valuation, hedging with options, and the no-arbitrage principle can be found in the following:

1. Benninga, Simon, *Numerical Techniques in Finance*. Cambridge, Mass.: MIT Press, 1989.

2. Brenner, Menachem, and Marti G. Subrahmanyam, "A Simple Approach to Option Valuation and Hedging in the Black-Scholes

Model," *Financial Analysts Journal,* 50 (March/April 1994), pp. 25–28.

3. Hull, John C., *Options, Futures and Other Derivative Securities* (2nd ed.). Englewood Cliffs, N.J.: Prentice Hall, 1993.

4. Kritzman, Mark, "What Practitioners Need to Know about Option Replication," *Financial Analysts Journal,* 48 (January/February 1992), pp. 21–23.

5. Rubinstein, Mark, "Derivative Assets Analysis," *Journal of Economic Perspectives,* 1 (Fall 1987), pp. 79–93.

6. Varian, Hal R., "The Arbitrage Principle in Financial Economics," *Journal of Economic Perspectives,* 1 (Fall 1987), pp. 55–72.

PROBLEMS AND QUESTIONS

1. Suppose that today's price quotations for the Eurodollar option contract (traded on the Chicago Mercantile Exchange) are as follows (the quotations were taken from a January newspaper):

Eurodollar (CME) $million; pts. of 100%

STRIKE PRICE	CALLS-SETTLE			PUTS-SETTLE		
	MAR-C	JUN-C	SEP-C	MAR-P	JUN-P	SEP-P
9175	0.63	0.69	0.60	0.16	0.43	0.68
9200	0.46	0.54	0.57	0.23	0.52	0.80
9225	0.31	0.43	0.46	0.33	0.65	. . .
9250	0.20	0.32	0.36	0.47	0.79	. . .
9275	0.12	0.24	0.28	0.64	0.94	. . .
9300	0.07	0.18	0.23	0.83	1.12	1.41

Each option allows the holder to buy or sell (in effect) a $1 million Eurodollar certificate of deposit. This CD begins on the option's expiration date and runs for three months at the prevailing 3-month LIBOR* rate. Strike prices are quoted in terms of basis points. That is, a strike price of 9250 corresponds to an interest rate of (10,000 − 9250) = 750 basis points, or 7.50%. If an investor buys a call option with a strike price of 9250, and if the actual 3-month LIBOR rate

---

* London interbank offered rate.

on the expiration day is 5.00% (that is, 500 basis points), then the option holder can, in effect, buy for 9250 a security that is worth 9500 (10,000 − 500). In actual fact, the option holder simply receives $25 for each basis point gain (that is, 1 basis point corresponds to .0001; for a $1 million 3-month CD, an annualized basis point corresponds to .0001 × $1 million × $\frac{1}{4}$ year = $25). Thus in the example above, the call holder simply receives $25 × 250 = $6250. Similarly, an investor owning a put with a 9250 strike price would receive 150 × $25 = $3750 if the actual LIBOR rate is 9.00% on the expiration day. Prices of the options themselves are also quoted in basis points (although note that the decimal point is moved over. Thus it costs 60 basis points, or $25 × 60 = $1500 to buy one September call option with a strike price of 9175. With this information as background, give brief answers to the following:

a) Why do the prices of the calls decrease with the strike price, while the prices of the puts increase with the strike price? Why do the prices of both puts and calls increase with the expiration date for the most part, but not exclusively (see the Sept. call with a strike price of 9175)? Why do you think a March call with a strike price of 9175 costs nearly 4 times as much as a March put with the same strike price? Why do you think a September call with a strike price of 9175 costs slightly less than a September put with the same strike price?

b) You are the Treasurer of a company that has issued $10 million of floating rate debt. Every quarter the interest rate on the debt is reset to the prevailing 3-month LIBOR rate plus 1%. It is January 8. The next three reset dates for your debt are March 14, June 13, and September 19 (these are also the expiration dates for the March, June, and September Eurodollar options). How can you use put options to ensure that the gross interest cost of your floating rate debt will be no more than 9% for the three-month periods starting March 14, June 13, and September 19? How much will it cost you to purchase this interest rate insurance?

2. The current exchange rate between German marks (DM) and U.S. dollars is 1.60 DM/$. One year from now, the exchange rate will be either 1.28 DM/$ or 2.00 DM/$. The current interest rate on a one-year DM-denominated risk-free bond is 5%. The current interest rate on a one-year dollar-denominated risk-free bond is 8%.

a) What are the state prices (measured in $) corresponding to the two possible values that the exchange rate could take on next year?

b) What is the value today (in $) of a European call option, expiring in one year, which allows the holder to buy $105 in exchange for

DM 168? What is the value today (in $) of a European put option, expiring in one year, which allows the holder to sell $105 in exchange for DM 168?

c) Suppose you convert $100 to DM today and invest the proceeds for one year at the DM interest rate. At the same time, you buy the call and sell the put described in (b). What is your total dollar rate of return over one year from this transaction? Briefly explain how this transaction illustrates the no-arbitrage principle.

3. The current yen/dollar exchange rate is 120 yen per dollar. One year from now, the exchange rate will be either 144 yen per dollar or 96 yen per dollar. Two years from now, the exchange rate will take on one of three values: 172.8 yen per dollar, 115.2 yen per dollar, or 76.8 yen per dollar. The current interest rate on a one-year dollar-denominated bond is 8%, while the current interest rate on a one-year yen-denominated bond is 5%.

a) Suppose you exchange $1 for yen today and invest it in a one-year yen bond. Your dollar payoff one year from now will depend on the exchange rate prevailing at that time. Calculate state prices, representing (1) the present value (in $) of $1 to be delivered in one year if and only if the exchange rate goes to 144 yen per dollar and (2) the present value (in $) of $1 to be delivered in one year if and only if the exchange rate goes to 96 yen per dollar.

b) A number of securities firms market range forward contracts. For example, the securities firm might agree to sell you ¥14 million in exchange for dollars two years from now. If the yen/dollar exchange rate at that time is above 140 yen/dollar, you must buy the yen from the securities firm at the rate of 140 yen per dollar. If the yen/dollar exchange rate at that time is below 100 yen per dollar, the securities firm agrees to sell you the yen at the rate of 100 yen/dollar. If the exchange rate at that time is between 100 and 140 yen/dollar, the securities firm will sell you the yen at the prevailing market rate. Describe this contract as a combination of options (be as precise as possible in describing the terms of the options).

c) How much should you be willing to pay the securities firm to enter into this range forward contract?

4. A stock's current price is $150. Each period the stock's price can go up by a factor (1.2) or down by a factor (1/1.2) = .8333. Next period, for example, the stock's ex-dividend price will be either 180 or 125. The current risk-free rate is 5%, and the stock pays a dividend at the rate, δ, of 3% per period. You own a call option on this stock that matures three periods from now. If you exercise this option at the end of any period, you are *not* entitled to receive that period's dividend on

the stock, but you will receive all future dividends as long as you own stock.

a) Suppose the exercise price on the call option is $150. If the option is European (that is, you can exercise the option only at the end of the third period) what is its value today? If the option were American (that is, you can exercise the option immediately, at the end of the first period, at the end of the second period, or at the end of the third period) what would its current value be? Given the values of the parameters, are there any circumstances under which you would exercise the option early? Briefly explain.

b) Now suppose that the exercise price on the call option is $50 rather than $150 (all other facts remain unchanged). If the option is European, what is its value today? If the option were American, what would its current value be? Briefly explain any differences between your answers to this part and your answers to (a).

5. **Spreadsheet Exercise.** A stock's current price is $20. Each period the stock's price can go up by a factor (1.3) or down by a factor (1/1.3). The current risk-free rate is 5% per period, and the stock currently pays no dividend. Call and put options on this stock, each with an exercise price of $10, mature five periods from now.

a) What are the current prices of 5-year European (that is, exercisable only at the end of five periods) put and call options (with exercise price = $10) on this stock? Show whether or not the put-call parity relationship holds for these options.

b) What are the current prices of 5-year American (that is, exercisable at the end of any of the next five periods) put and call options (with exercise price = $10) on this stock? Show whether or not the put-call parity relationship holds for these options, and briefly explain why it does or does not hold.

c) Suppose instead that the same stock now pays a dividend at the rate of 3% per period. All other facts remain the same as before (that is, $S_0 = \$20$, $u = 1.3$, $d = 1/1.3$, $r_f = .05$, $X = \$10$, $T = 5$ periods). By the end of the first period, for example, the stock either moves up to an ex-dividend price of $(1.3)S_0$ or down to an ex-dividend price of $S_0/1.3$. If you exercise a call option on this stock at the end of any period, you are *not* entitled to receive that period's dividend on the stock (thus, you buy at the ex-dividend price), but you will receive all future dividends as long as you own the stock. What are the current prices of 5-year European (that is, exercisable only at the end of five periods) put and call options (with exercise price = $10) on this stock? Show whether or not the put-call parity relationship holds for these options, and briefly explain why it does or does not hold.

d) Continuing to assume a 3% dividend rate, what are the current prices of 5-year American (that is, exercisable at the end of any of the next five periods) put and call options (with exercise price = $10) on this stock? Would the call option ever be exercised early? Explain why or why not.

6. Consider a stock that pays no dividend and whose current price per share is $40. The instantaneous variance of the stock price is .4 and the risk-free interest rate, quoted on a continuously compounded basis, is 4%.

   a) Use the Black-Scholes formula to calculate the values of European call and put options on this stock, where each option has a one-year maturity and an exercise price of $50.

   b) Using your answers to (a) as your base case, show how the values of the European call and put options change as each of the following events occurs (measure each of the changes, one by one, relative to the base case):

   (1) The option maturity goes from one year to ten years;
   (2) The instantaneous variance increases from .4 to .8;
   (3) The risk-free rate increases from 4% to 5%.

   c) Explain the option price changes you have calculated in (b).

7. **Spreadsheet Exercise.** Construct your own Table 5.1. As explained in Simon Benninga, *Numerical Techniques in Finance* (Cambridge, MA: MIT Press, 1989), the cumulative standard normal distribution function, $N(d)$, can be approximated, for $d \geq 0$, as follows:

$$N(d) = 1 - h(d)t(b_0 + b_1 t + b_2 t^2 + b_3 t^3 + b_4 t^4)$$

where $h(d) = (1/\sqrt{2\pi})e^{-x^2/2}$,
$t = 1/(1 + pd)$,
$p = 0.2316419$,
$b_0 = 0.319381530$,
$b_1 = -0.356563782$,
$b_2 = 1.781477937$,
$b_3 = -1.821255978$,
$b_4 = 1.330274429$.

You can calculate $N(d)$ for negative values of d by calculating $N(-d)$ using the approximation above and then setting $N(d) = 1 - N(-d)$.

8. **Spreadsheet Exercise.** Using the approximation for $N(d)$ from Problem 7, set up a spreadsheet to calculate option values using the Black-Scholes model. You can check your spreadsheet by using it to redo the examples in Problem 6.

9. (Note: This problem deals with setting up hedge portfolios, as described in the Appendix to this chapter.) The share price of Hedge Clippers, Inc., which pays no dividends, is $45. European call options written on the company's stock have an exercise price of $40 and mature in 90 days. The risk-free is 6% and the instantaneous variance of the stock's price movements is 9%. If you wish to hedge yourself against these price movements, what should you do in the following situations?
   a) If you own 200 shares of Hedge Clippers stock, how many call options should you buy or sell?
   b) If you own 10 put options (with the same exercise price and maturity as the calls), how many shares of stock should you buy or sell?
   c) If you own one call option, how many puts should you buy or sell?

Footnotes

[1] It should be noted, with apologies to the reader, that the notation in the options chapters is slightly different from that in earlier chapters. In Chapters 1 to 4, the notation P was used to denote the price of a bond or a stock. That notation is consistent with most other discussions of this material in the finance literature. In the case of options, however, the prices of stocks, bonds, call options, and put options must be addressed simultaneously. Rather than adopt subscripts to index the prices of different types of securities (for example, P_S, P_B), most other finance literature uses the notation S, B, C, and P to denote the prices of stocks, bonds, calls, and puts, respectively. Because many readers of this book may be using it in conjunction with other treatments, it was felt that it would be less confusing to maintain as much consistency with other literature as possible, rather than maintaining strict notational consistency within the book at the cost of being inconsistent with other discussions in the literature.

[2] A proof of this result can be found in Hal R. Varian, "The Arbitrage Principle in Financial Economics," *Journal of Economic Perspectives*, 1, (Fall 1987), 55–72.

[3] This assumption implies that, if B_0 is the current price of a riskless, T-period zero coupon bond, $B_0 = 1/(1 + r_f)^T$.

[4] It is worth noting at this point that Property 3 does not hold for put options, even on non-dividend-paying stocks. An example of this situation is provided in Problem 5 at the end of the chapter.

[5] It may seem strange that the call option should be worth less when the stock pays a dividend. This condition is really an artifact of using the same stock prices in both the non-dividend-paying and dividend-paying examples. In the non-dividend-paying case, a stock that is worth 40 today could be worth either 50 or 32 in the future. The state prices have been determined to translate into a certain risk-adjusted expected return for the shareholder that will be competitive with the 10% return

available on the riskless bond. In the dividend-paying case, on the other hand, the stock price could not only either rise to 50 or fall to 32, but it pays a 15% dividend yield as well. Using the same state prices as in the non-dividend-paying example would translate into an expected return that is more than commensurate with the 10% riskless return available on the bond, in which case the current stock price would have to rise above 40. If the stock is to sell at 40 today, the state prices must adjust. As can be seen from the calculations, the up-state price becomes smaller in the dividend-paying case, so the same dollar payoff is the up state becomes less valuable. The dividend-paying case, therefore, really corresponds to a whole different set of economic conditions, and under those conditions, call options are less valuable than under the set of conditions prevailing in the non-dividend-paying case.

Appendix to Chapter 5

I. DERIVATION OF THE BLACK-SCHOLES FORMULA

One way to derive the Black-Scholes formula for the value of a European call option on a non-dividend-paying stock is to combine shares of the stock and call options so as to form a hedge portfolio, or a portfolio whose value is insulated against changes in the value of the stock. If we let V_H be the value of the hedge portfolio, S the price of the stock, and C the price of the call option, we wish to find the number of shares, n_S, and the number of call options, n_C, such that the change in the value of the portfolio, dV_H, over a small time interval is equal to zero. Thus the portfolio must satisfy the following two conditions:

$$V_H = n_S S + n_C C \tag{5A.1}$$

$$dV_H = n_S ds + n_C dC = 0 \tag{5A.2}$$

These conditions are in turn satisfied if, for every one share of stock we hold, (that is, $n_S = 1$) we hold $n_C = \dfrac{-1}{\partial C/\partial S}$ call options.

Next, we will assume that changes in the price of the stock are governed by a particular stochastic process known as a geometric Brownian motion with drift, which implies that percentage changes in the stock price follow

$$\frac{dS}{S} = \mu dt + \sigma dz \tag{5A.3}$$

where μ is the instantaneous expected return, or drift term, dt is a small increment of time, σ is the instantaneous standard deviation of the rate of return, and dz represents the change in a stochastic variable

z, which follows a Wiener process. This latter process has the properties that changes in z are independent of one another, no matter how small the time interval, and that the variance of these changes grows linearly with the time interval. Our assumptions about the stochastic process further imply that percentage changes in the stock price are normally distributed over any finite time interval.

Given these assumptions, we can invoke Ito's lemma, a fundamental result of stochastic calculus, which implies that we can express changes in the value of the call option as

$$dC = \frac{\partial C}{\partial S} dS + \frac{\partial C}{\partial t} dt + \frac{1}{2} \frac{\partial^2 C}{\partial S^2} \sigma^2 S^2 dt \qquad (5A.4)$$

Turning back to (5A.2), if the hedge portfolio is free of risk, its percentage rate of return over any time interval should be the instantaneous risk-free rate, r_f, times the length of the interval, as follows:

$$\frac{dV_H}{V_H} = r_f dt \qquad (5A.5)$$

Then, combining (5A.2) with (5A.4) and (5A.5), and letting $n_S = 1$ and $n_C = \dfrac{-1}{\partial C/\partial S}$, we can write the change in the value of the hedge portfolio as

$$dV_H = r_f dt V_H = dS - \frac{1}{\partial C/\partial S}\left(\frac{\partial C}{\partial S} dS + \frac{\partial C}{\partial t} dt + \frac{1}{2} \frac{\partial^2 C}{\partial S^2} \sigma^2 S^2 dt \right) \qquad (5A.6)$$

which in turn implies

$$\frac{\partial C}{\partial t} = r_f V_H \left(-\frac{\partial C}{\partial S} \right) - \frac{\partial^2}{\partial S^2} \sigma^2 S^2 \qquad (5A.7)$$

The importance of (5A.7) is that setting up the riskless hedge portfolio has enabled us to eliminate the stochastic term, dS. This approach in turn allows us to find a solution using conventional differential equation solution techniques. Specifically, we can substitute (5A.1) for V_H in (5A.7), with $n_S = 1$ and $n_C = \dfrac{-1}{\partial C/\partial S}$, and solve subject to the boundary conditions that, (1) if the stock price is zero the option value must be zero, and (2) at maturity the value of the option must be equal to max[0, $S - X$]. Black and Scholes showed that the solution to this problem is given by text equations (5.25), (5.26) and (5.27).

It is worth noting in the solution that $\dfrac{-1}{\partial C/\partial S} = \dfrac{-1}{N(d_1)}$. Since $\dfrac{-1}{\partial C/\partial S}$ is the number of calls that should be held to hedge one share of stock, $\dfrac{-1}{N(d_1)}$ is sometimes referred to as the hedge ratio. It represents the ratio of calls to shares that should be held to create a hedge portfolio.

6

Fixed Income Securities with Call and Prepayment Options

Unlike the option-free bonds we examined in Chapters 1 to 3, many bonds have attached options of various types. One of the most common of these is a call provision, which gives the issuer the right to buy back the bonds at a prespecified price prior to maturity. An essentially equivalent option is the prepayment provision on a mortgage. For example, if the mortgage contract calls for no prepayment penalty, the mortgage allows the homeowner to prepay, or buy back, the outstanding mortgage balance at par prior to the mortgage's stated maturity.

In this chapter, we will focus primarily on bonds and mortgages with call and prepayment provisions, and we will analyze how these options affect the values and interest sensitivities of the securities to which they are attached. The same analysis is also applicable to other types of options that alter the schedule of principal payments on a bond. These include options that give bond issuers the right to increase a scheduled sinking fund payment (the double-up option) or to issue additional bonds in lieu of cash interest payments (pay-in-kind bonds), as well as options that give bondholders the right to extend the bond's maturity (extendible bonds) or to call for early repayment of principal (puttable bonds). We will save other types of option elements in stocks and bonds for Chapter 7, including bondholders' options to convert a bond into common stock (convertible bonds), issuers' options to default on a bond issue, and firms' options to undertake future investment opportunities or abandon existing ones.

I. DURATION AND CONVEXITY FOR CALLABLE BONDS

We will begin by analyzing how the addition of a call provision affects the bond's interest sensitivity. An option has positive value to the party who can decide whether or not to exercise it and negative value (that is, it is a contingent liability) to the writer. Since the bond issuer has the right to exercise a call provision, the bondholder has effectively written the option, and thus the bond has lower value to the holder than an otherwise equivalent option-free bond. If we let B_c be the price of a callable bond, B_{nc} the price of an otherwise equivalent noncallable bond, and C the market value of the issuer's call option, we can express the value of the callable as follows:

$$B_c = B_{nc} - C \qquad (6.1)$$

Then, as shown in the Appendix to this chapter, the relationship between the modified duration of the callable bond, D_c, and that of the noncallable, D_{nc}, is given by

$$D_c = D_{nc} \frac{B_{nc}}{B_c} (1 - \delta) \qquad (6.2)$$

where δ is the call option's delta, or the change in the value of the call option given a change in the value of the underlying noncallable bond.[1] The expression on the right-hand side of (6.2) is also referred to as the bond's call-adjusted duration.

Equation (6.2) tells us that the callable bond will have a duration that approaches that of the noncallable when the option's delta is near zero. This condition will occur when interest rates are so high (bond prices so low) that exercise of the call provision is extremely unlikely. Under those circumstances, the call provision is of virtually no value to the issuer, and the callable bond's price behaves very much like that of the noncallable. On the other hand, when interest rates are low (bond prices high), the call provision becomes very valuable. As exercise of the call becomes very likely, owning the call option is virtually akin to owning the bond itself, so changes in the value of the call option as interest rates change further are very close to changes in the value of the noncallable bond. In this case, the option's delta is close to one, and thus the duration of the callable bond approaches zero.

For at least some interest rate levels, therefore, a callable bond's duration grows shorter as interest rates fall and lengthens as interest rates rise, which is exactly opposite to the behavior of an option-free bond's duration. It is sometimes said that the callable bond exhibits negative convexity, to distinguish it from the option-free bond, which is said to have positive convexity. When a bond exhibits negative convexity, its duration moves in directions that are detrimental to the investor as yields change. For example, when yields are falling, the duration of the bond with negative convexity grows shorter, so the tendency of the bond's price to rise is dampened. In the case of a callable bond, this result occurs because falling yields make the bond more likely to be called, and the bond's call price acts as a ceiling on upward price movements. Conversely, when yields are rising, the duration of the bond with negative convexity grows longer, so the tendency of the bond's price to fall is accentuated. For the case of the callable bond, rising yields make a call less likely, so the bond's effective maturity lengthens.

More specifically, we can calculate whether a bond exhibits positive or negative convexity over a given range of yields if we derive an expression for call-adjusted convexity. As shown in the Appendix to this chapter, we can express the convexity, CON_c, of a callable bond in terms of the modified duration and convexity of the underlying noncallable bond and the call provision's delta and gamma (the change in the option's delta, given a change in the price of the noncallable bond) as follows:

$$CON_c = \frac{B_{nc}}{B_c} [CON_{nc} (1 - \delta) - B_{nc} \gamma (D_{nc})^2] \qquad (6.3)$$

As Equation (6.3) makes clear, one of the primary factors leading to negative convexity is a high value for the call option's delta, which would indicate that the call provision is well in the money and the likelihood of a call is high. These effects of options on bonds' duration and convexity are further illustrated in problems 1 to 5 at the end of the chapter.

II. MODELS FOR EXPLICITLY VALUING INTEREST RATE OPTIONS

A. A Simple Two-State Model

Calculation of call-adjusted duration and convexity, as described in the preceding section, requires estimates of the call option's delta and gamma. One way to obtain such estimates is to construct a model that captures the uncertainty in market interest rates and thus allows us to explicitly value the call provision for different interest rate levels.

A simple approach to this problem is simply to modify the basic two-state model, as developed in Chapter 5, using the interest rate rather than a stock price as our uncertain, or state, variable. Consider, for example, a world in which there are two future dates, 1 and 2. As of now, there are one- and two-period coupon-bearing bonds. These bonds have no default risk. Currently, the one-period yield is 10%. At the same time, a two-period bond with a 10% coupon currently sells for $990.[2] Suppose further that, at time 1, the one-period yield could either rise to 12% or fall to 8.5%. Since there is no default risk, all uncertainty will thus be resolved by time 1 here. That is, once we reach time 1, what was a two-period bond at time 0 becomes effectively a one-period bond. Since we know the one-period interest rate and the bond's payoff at time 2, we can determine its value at time 1. Although there are two periods here, uncertainty affects only the first period, and we can view this situation as essentially similar to a one-period setting.

There are two future states of the world here: the one-period interest rate will either rise to 12% or fall to 8.5%. We can value any security in this setting, then, if we can determine state prices for the two states. One way to determine the up-state price is to construct a portfolio of one- and two-period bonds with 10% coupons that will pay off $1 if the one-period interest rate rises to 12% and zero otherwise.[3]

If we assume a $1000 face value for all bonds, then at time 1, a two-period bond pays $100 in interest, and, since it has one period left to run, it is worth $1100/1.12 = $982.14 if the up state occurs. Thus the total up-state payoff on the two-period bond is $1082.14 if the one-period rate moves to 12%. If the down state occurs, on the other hand, the two-period bond is worth $1100/1.085 = $1013.82, so the total down-state payoff on the two-period bond is $1113.82. The one-period bond, by contrast, pays off $1100 regardless of which state occurs.

We thus wish to put together a portfolio of n_1^u one-period bonds and n_2^u two-period bonds such that the portfolio's total up-state payoff is $1, while its down-state payoff is 0. This scenario implies the following two conditions:

$$1100n_1^u + 1082.14n_2^u = 1 \qquad (6.4)$$

$$1100n_1^u + 1113.82n_2^u = 0 \qquad (6.5)$$

Using these two equations in the two unknowns, n_1^u and n_2^u, we can solve to find $n_1^u = .03196$ and $n_2^u = -.03157$. A one-period 10% coupon bond currently sells at par $1000), while a two-period bond currently sells for $990. Thus the cost of creating this portfolio is $(1000)(.03196) + (990)(-.03157) = .7122$.[4] This value in turn must represent the up-state price (that is, the value today of $1 to be delivered next period if and only if the interest rate goes to 12%), since it is the cost of creating the pure up-state-contingent security's payoff.

Similarly, we can find the down-state price by forming a portfolio of n_1^d one-period bonds and n_2^d two-period bonds that will pay $1 if the down state occurs (that is, the one-period rate falls to 8.5%) and zero otherwise. In this case, n_1^d and n_2^d must satisfy the following:

$$1100n_1^d + 1082.14n_2^d = 0 \qquad (6.6)$$

$$1100n_1^d + 1113.82n_2^d = 1 \qquad (6.7)$$

which in turn implies $n_1^d = -.03105$ and $n_2^d = .03157$. The cost of creating this portfolio is $(1000)(-.03105) + (990)(.03157) = .1969$, which represents the down-state price. As a check on our state prices, we can sum them to get $\pi_u + \pi_d = .7122 + .1969 = .9091$. This value is consistent with the current one-period rate of 10%, since the sum of the state prices is equivalent to a one-period zero-coupon bond.

With the state prices in hand, we can now value a wide range of securities. Suppose, for example, that we wish to value a two-period, 10% coupon bond that is callable at par at the end of the first period. One way to do this is directly to value an investor's payoffs from holding this two-period bond. In this particular case, the firm will find it worthwhile to call the bonds in the down state (that is, if the one-period rate falls to 8.5%, the firm can buy back for $1000 a security that would be worth $1013.82 if it were not callable). If the up state occurs, the bond is not called, and the investor receives $100 in interest plus a claim on a second-period payoff that is worth $982.14 as of time 1. If the down state occurs, the investor receives the $100 coupon payment, but the bond is called, so the investor also receives the $1000 call price. Thus the callable bond is worth $(1082.14)(.7122) + (1100)(.1969) = \$987.29$.

The same answer could also be obtained if we split up the callable bond into its component pieces. Recall from Section I that the value of a callable bond should be equal to the value of an otherwise equivalent noncallable minus the value of the call option. In this case, the firm exercises its call in the down state but not the up state so the value of the call must be equal to the firm's payoff in the down state $(1113.82 - 1000 = 13.82)$ times the down state price $(.1969)$, or 2.72. If the noncallable two-period bond sells for $990, a callable bond would sell for $990 - \$2.72 = \$987.28$, which is identical, within a small rounding error in the state prices, to our answer in the previous paragraph.

Several problems at the end of this chapter afford additional practice in this type of valuation analysis. This analysis is the basis for what is referred to as financial engineering, or rearranging simpler building block securities to form complex securities with special features. In the example at hand, we have decomposed the callable bond into its two building blocks, a noncallable bond and a call option. This approach in turn allows for a financial engineering transaction known as monetizing the call. Suppose a firm has a callable bond outstanding and wishes to realize the value of its call option without actually calling the bond (say, because the call is not yet in the money, or because the firm does not want to incur the transaction costs of calling the bond, or because the firm believes that the market is overvaluing the call option). The firm can then sell a call option to some other investor, allowing the investor to buy a one-period $1000 face value bond with a 10% coupon one period from now at an exercise price of par. The firm will receive $2.72 from this sale, and in thus monetizing its call, it has effectively converted its callable bond into a noncallable. Its own bonds are still callable, of course, but any profit the firm gains from calling will be immediately offset by its loss on the call it has written. Additional illustrations of the effect of embedded options on bond values using the same type of simple, two-state model employed in this section are provided in problems 6 to 8 at the end of the chapter.

B. A Binomial Model that Incorporates the Term Structure

One problem with the simple model just described is that it does not incorporate all the information that is currently available about expected future interest rate movements. As we saw in Chapter 3, the term structure of interest rates reflects investors' expectations about future interest rate levels and perhaps also, depending on which theory of the term structure one adheres to, their assessments of the uncertainty surrounding those expectations. Any model that we use to value interest rate options, then, will be more consistent with current market prices if it reflects these same investor expectations.

Suppose, for example, that the current spot rates for one-, two-, and three-period zero-coupon instruments are as shown in Table 6.1. Suppose further that we believe future one-period interest rates will follow a binomial process that is a discrete representation of a lognormal distribution with a volatility parameter, σ. Of course, as with any option pricing model, this assumption about the underlying stochastic process is crucial, and there has been even less agreement about the appropriate process for interest rates than there has for stock prices or other state variables. Nevertheless, if we accept the lognormal process as reasonable, we may infer that, beginning from the current one-period yield of 4%, the one-period rate one period from now will fall into one of two possible states of the world. We will refer to these as the up and down

TABLE 6.1   Spot rates for zero-coupon instruments of different maturity

MATURITY (# PERIODS)	YIELD (% PER PERIOD)
1	4%
2	4.5%
3	5%

states, but in this context the terminology is loose, because the down state need not refer to an actual decline in the one-period rate relative to its current level. Rather, the down state refers simply to the lower of the two possible interest rate levels. Furthermore, the lognormality assumption implies that, if r_u and r_d are the rates prevailing in the up and down states, respectively, these rates are related to each other as follows:[5]

$$r_u = r_d(e^{2\sigma})$$ (6.8)

To illustrate the working of this process, suppose we assume $\sigma = .10$ and that the up and down states are equally likely. Given the current one-period rate of 4%, let us guess that the rate in next period's down state will also be 4%, which implies that the rate in the up state must be $4e^{.2} = 4.8856\%$. However, these two rates imply that our guess about the down-state rate was not consistent with the existing term structure of interest rates.

To understand this concept, let us try to value a two-period zero-coupon bond using our up- and down-state rates, as illustrated in the tree of rates and values shown in Figure 6.1. At the end of two periods, a default-free zero-coupon bond with a $1 face value is worth $1, regardless of the level of interest rates. We can then work backward and find the value of the zero at the end of one period. There are two possible values, depending on whether we are in the up or down state, and these values are simply the value of the payoff at $t = 2$, discounted back at the

FIGURE 6.1   Binomial tree of interest rates and 2-period zero-coupon bond prices

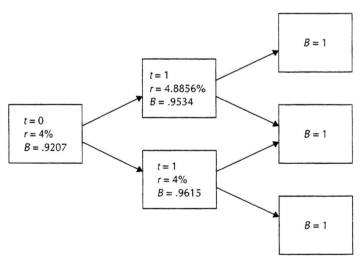

interest rate prevailing in that state. If we let B_{1u} and B_{1d} represent the time 1 values in the up and down states, respectively, then

$$B_{1u} = \frac{1}{1.048856} = .9534 \tag{6.9}$$

$$B_{1d} = \frac{1}{1.04} = .9615 \tag{6.10}$$

Recalling that the two states are assumed to be equally likely, we can then calculate the implied current value of the two-period zero by discounting the average of the up- and down-state values from (6.9) and (6.10) back to the present at the current one-period interest rate, as follows:

$$B_0 = \frac{\frac{B_{1u} + B_{1d}}{2}}{1.04} = \frac{\frac{.9534 + .9615}{2}}{1.04} = .9207 \tag{6.11}$$

We know, however, from the current term structure of interest rates in Table 6.1 that the current value of a two-period zero-coupon bond must be given by $B_0 = 1/(1.045)^2 = .9157$. Thus, our guess of a down-state rate of 4% one period from now turns out in retrospect to have been inconsistent with the expectations about future interest rates embodied in the current term structure. If the two had been consistent, both should have led us to the same value for the two-period zero.

At the same time, this inconsistency suggests a solution: What we need to do is choose the down-state rate, r_d, such that, when we let $r_u = r_d(e^{2\sigma})$, the current two-period zero-coupon bond value obtained from Equation (6.11) is the same as the value calculated using the two-period spot rate from the yield curve. Solving for this value, we find that $r_d = 4.5060\%$, which implies that $r_u = 5.5036\%$.[6] Performing the same calculations as in (6.9) and (6.10) gives $B_{1u} = .9478$ and $B_{1d} = .9569$. Using these values in (6.11) then gives us $B_0 = .9157$, which is consistent with the value obtained using the two-period spot rate. Thus, we can say that $r_d = 4.5060\%$ is the one possible choice for our binomial interest rate tree that is consistent with (a) the assumed lognormal interest rate process, (b) the assumed volatility of $\sigma = .10$, and (c) the current yield curve.

We can proceed in similar fashion, building up our interest rate tree for as many periods as we have spot rates. In the current example, we still have not used the three-period spot rate, so we could find the one-period rate, r_{dd}, that would prevail two periods from now if interest rates moved to the down state two periods in a row. If we had such a rate, we could find the one-period rate that would prevail two periods from now if rates made one down-state move and one up-state move, using the relationship

$$r_{ud} = r_{dd}(e^{2\sigma}) \qquad (6.12)$$

and in similar fashion, the one-period rate that would prevail in two periods after two successive up-state moves is given by

$$r_{uu} = r_{dd}(e^{4\sigma}) \qquad (6.13)$$

We then need to solve for the value of r_{dd} that, in conjunction with (6.12) and (6.13) plus the values of r_d and r_u that we found previously, gives the same value for a three-period zero-coupon bond when we roll back the binomial value tree that we obtain by using the three-period spot rate. It can be verified that the solution $r_{dd} = 4.8773\%$ results in a three-period zero value of .8638, which is the same as $1/(1.05).^3$ The complete binomial interest rate tree is thus as shown in Table 6.2.

The rates in this tree are essentially equivalent to state prices, because we can use them to discount back any set of cash flows that is defined over this set of interest rate states. Consider, for example, a three-period bond with a 6% coupon rate and a face value of 100. Assume initially that the bond is noncallable, so that it makes coupon payments of 6 each at the end of periods one and two plus a final payment of 106 at the end of period 3. Given these cash flows, we can value the bond using the interest rates in Table 6.2 by rolling back a tree of bond values, as shown in Figure 6.2. If we start at the end of period three, the bond is worth 106, regardless of the level of interest rates. Working back to the present, the bond's value at any node prior to period three is equal to the coupon payment at that node, plus the average of the bond's two possible future values, discounted back at the one-period interest rate prevailing at that node. Moving back successively to period 0, we find that the bond's value is 102.83.

TABLE 6.2 Binomial tree of one-period interest rate that is consistent with (a) a lognormal interest rate process, (b) a volatility $\sigma = .10$, and (c) the current spot rates in Table 6.1

	PERIOD	
0	1	2
$r = 4\%$	$r_u = 5.5036\%$ $r_d = 4.5060\%$	$r_{uu} = 7.2760\%$ $r_{ud} = 5.9571\%$ $r_{dd} = 4.8773\%$

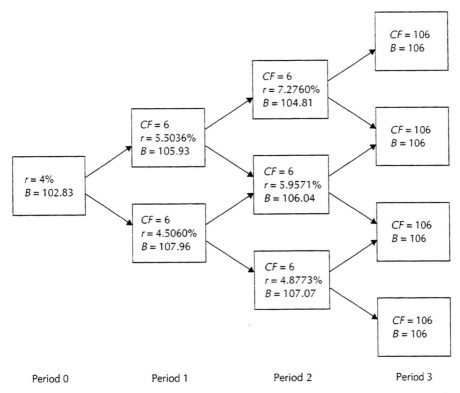

FIGURE 6.2   Value of noncallable bond at each node given cash flow, *CF*, and interest rate, *r*, at that node

We can again verify that this value is consistent with the current term structure of interest rates, because we know that this noncallable bond's value, given the spot rates in Table 6.1, is as follows:

$$B = \frac{6}{1.04} + \frac{6}{(1.045)^2} + \frac{106}{(1.05)^3} = 102.83 \qquad (6.14)$$

which checks with the value found from Figure 6.2.

We can use the interest rate tree to compare the value of this non-callable bond with that of an otherwise equivalent callable bond. Assume that the callable bond has one period worth of call protection (that is, the issuer may not exercise the call provision prior to one period from now), but it can be called at par at the end of either periods one or two. The issuer will want to exercise this call option whenever this reduces the value that the bondholders' claim would otherwise have. In doing so, the issuer thereby increases the value of shareholders' claim on the firm.

Looking back at Figure 6.2, we can identify the nodes at which the bond would be called as those at which the bond's value would exceed the current coupon plus the call price if the bonds were noncallable. That is, whenever the noncallable bonds' value exceeds 106, the issuer could benefit by calling them and buying them back for a total outlay of 106 per bond. Since bondholders will be aware of the issuer's optimal call strategy, however, they would never pay more than 106 for the bond at a node at which call is imminent. To value the callable bond, then, we simply have to go back through the tree in Figure 6.2, identify the nodes at which the bonds will be called, and set the bond's value equal to 106 at those nodes,[7] which has been done in Figure 6.3. Note that the bonds will be called at the bottom two nodes in period two (assuming we have reached either of those points without the bonds already having been called) and at the bottom node in period one. Using the same set of interest rates we derived previously, we can then roll back the tree of values and find that the current value of the callable bonds is 101.88.

FIGURE 6.3   Value of callable bond at each node given cash flow, *CF*, and interest rate, *r*, at that node

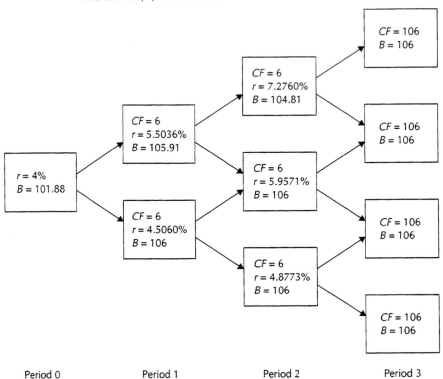

Period 0   Period 1   Period 2   Period 3

Therefore, comparing this value with the value of the noncallable, the value of the issuer's call provision is $102.83 - 101.88 = 0.95$.

In a similar fashion, once we have our interest rate tree in hand, we can use it to value any type of complex bond, as long as all of the uncertainty is confined to future movements in the one-year interest rate. These bonds include puttable bonds (bonds that can be sold back to the issuer), sinking fund bonds, and floating rate bonds with caps and floors (that is, limitations on the extent to which the coupon rate may be adjusted up or down).

III. OPTION-ADJUSTED SPREAD ANALYSIS

A. Standard Yield Spread Analysis

Many bond market participants prefer to think in terms of yields rather than dollar values. Thus, they might consider it more natural to measure the impact of a call provision on a bond in terms of the difference in yield to maturity between a callable and a noncallable bond.

Consider, for example, the three-year 6% coupon noncallable and callable bonds in our example in the preceding section. We found earlier that the prices of these bonds were 102.83 and 101.88, and the scheduled coupon and principal payments imply yields to maturity of 4.961% for the noncallable bond and 5.306% for the callable. Traditional yield spread analysis would simply subtract one yield from the other, and the analyst might infer that the inclusion of the call provision results in a 34.5 basis point yield spread between the two bonds.

B. The Static Spread

However, there are at least two potential problems with this type of analysis. First, a simple comparison of yields to maturity does not consider possible differences in the scheduled cash flow patterns of different bonds. Unless the term structure is completely flat, differences in the cash flow schedule could give rise to differences in yield, even apart from any effect of the call provision.

In an attempt to remedy this difficulty, an alternative yield spread measure called the static spread has come into use. In calculating the static spread, a bond's cash flows are discounted using spot rates from the yield curve rather than a single yield to maturity. Consider, for example, our same three-year callable bond. The scheduled cash flows are 6, 6, and 106 for years 1, 2, and 3, respectively. To find the static spread, we wish to find a constant spread, s, such that, when we add s to each of the spot rates in Table 6.1 and discount the corresponding cash flows, we get back to the market price of the bond. Specifically, the static spread in this case is the value of s such that

$$\frac{6}{(1.04 + s)} + \frac{6}{(1.045 + s)^2} + \frac{106}{(1.05 + s)^3} = 101.88 \qquad (6.15)$$

Solving for s, we find that the static spread is 34.5 basis points.[8]

Since Equation (6.14) implies that the static spread for the non-callable bond is zero, both the traditional analysis and the static spread analysis give us the same measure for the yield difference between the two bonds in this particular case because both bonds have identical patterns of scheduled cash flows. Suppose, on the other hand, that we use the same callable bond, but take as our point of comparison a three-year 6% noncallable bond with scheduled sinking fund payments of 30 in both years 1 and 2. The cash flows on this latter bond, including interest at 6% on the beginning-of-period outstanding balance are 36, 34.2, and 42.4 in periods 1, 2, and 3, respectively. Discounting these cash flows using the spot rates from Table 6.1, we find a value of 102.56 for this bond, which implies a yield to maturity of 4.682%. A traditional yield spread analysis would then say that there is a 62.4 basis point yield spread between this bond and the callable bond. However, part of this difference in yield arises because the yield curve is not flat and the two bonds, despite their identical maturity and coupon rate, have different cash flow patterns. We can filter out this portion of the difference in yields if we compare them with the static spread. The static spread for the sinking fund bond is zero, while for the callable bond it is 34.5 basis points. In this case, the difference in the bonds' static spreads gives us a better measure of the impact of the call provision than does the traditional yield spread.

C. Option-Adjusted Spread

The second problem with traditional yield spread analysis is that it does not take into account the fact that future interest rate changes will affect the cash flows on a callable bond. Under some interest rate scenarios, the bonds will be called and principal will be repaid sooner than scheduled. Under other scenarios, the bonds will be called at a different date or they may not be called at all. To account for this, variation option-adjusted spread analysis attempts to distinguish among different possible paths that future interest rates might take and explicitly to consider differences in cash flow patterns occurring along these different paths.

As its name suggests, the static spread analysis is static in the sense that a given set of spot rates implies just one set of forward, short-term interest rates for different future dates. If we rely on the pure expectations theory, we could interpret these forward rates as an expected path of future short rates. The static spread analysis is incapable, however, of including possible deviations around this expected interest rate path. By contrast, the option-adjusted spread analysis attempts to incorporate a dynamic element by simulating the different possible paths that the short rate might follow.

We can illustrate this concept for the same 6% three-year callable bond that we have been examining. Together, the possible future one-period rates that we derived for Table 6.2 imply that there are four possible interest rate paths over the next three periods. These paths are shown in A of Table 6.3. From Figure 6.3, we also know whether and when the bond will be called on any interest rate path. For example, the bond will be called at the end of period one for paths 3 and 4, at the end of the second period for path 2, and not at all for path 1. Thus, we can infer the cash flow patterns for the callable bond corresponding to the different interest rate paths, as shown in B of Table 6.3

Next, the option-adjusted spread analysis calls for us to discount each set of possible bond cash flows back to the present, using the one-period interest rates along the corresponding paths plus a constant interest rate spread (for example, 10 basis points), and average the four resulting present values. If this average present value exceeds the

TABLE 6.3   Option-adjusted spread analysis callable bond cash flows corresponding to different interest rate paths

A. Possible future paths for the 1-period interest rate

INTEREST RATE PATH #

		1	2	3	4
One-period rate	1	4.0%	4.0%	4.0%	4.0%
prevailing in	2	5.5036	5.5036	4.5060	4.5060
period:	3	7.276	5.9571	5.9571	4.8773

B. Callable bond cash flows for different one-period interest rate paths

INTEREST RATE PATH #

		1	2	3	4
Cash flow from	1	6	6	106	106
callable bond in	2	6	106		
period:	3	106			

callable bond's actual market value, we increase the spread and try again. If the average present value is below the bond's market value, on the other hand, we decrease the spread. The option-adjusted spread is that spread value such that the average present value across all the possible interest rate paths is just equal to the bond's market value.

If we discount the callable bond's cash flows, as shown in B of Table 6.3, using just the one-period rates along the different paths, as shown in A, the average of the four resulting values is 101.88. This value is, in fact, the current market value of the bond, which implies that the option-adjusted spread for this bond is zero.

This result makes sense if we consider that the bond has no default risk. The interest rates that we used to value the bond, when we rolled back the tree in Figure 6.3, were thus one-period risk-free rates. As long as we have considered all of the possible interest rate paths plus the cash flow consequences of being along any path, there is no difference between the set of rates used to set the bond's value and the set of possible one-period risk-free rates. That is, once we have properly adjusted the spread to take the option into account, the spread should disappear.[9] Otherwise, the bond would be mispriced, and in fact, option-adjusted spread analysis is often used in an attempt to identify mispriced bonds. More generally, for bonds subject to default risk, the option-adjusted spread, once we have removed the effect of the option, should just reflect the premium over risk-free interest rates that is being charged for default risk. Thus the analyst could try to identify mispriced bonds by comparing option-adjusted spreads with some independent estimate of what the bond's credit spread should be.

However, it should be noted that option-adjusted spread analysis is subject to a number of pitfalls and care should be taken in using it this way. Among the biggest of these pitfalls is the fact that the analyst must come up with a model of the process driving interest rates. The model completely determines the possible future interest rate paths, and in conjunction with assumptions we make about the issuer's policy for calling the bonds, determines the bond's value along any particular path. Inevitably, then, our measure of option-adjusted spread is highly sensitive both to the nature of the interest rate process and the assumed level of volatility. If we analyze a bond that is free of default risk, then, and come up with a nonzero option-adjusted spread, we can never be sure if the bond is really mispriced or if we are simply using the wrong interest rate model—that is, a model inconsistent with the investor expectations that are embodied in current market prices. It is important, then, that the analyst be explicit about the underlying model, so that decision-makers are at least aware of the basis on which their decisions are being made. It is also important to have some consistency checks between the model and other market prices, similar to the way in which we checked our interest rate model in Section II.B of this chapter for consistency with the observed yield curve.

IV. MORTGAGES AND MORTGAGE-BACKED SECURITIES

A. Investment Characteristics of Standard Mortgages

While numerous exceptions and variations can be found, the "standard" home mortgage contract in the U.S. calls for equal monthly payments over 30 years, where the monthly payment is calculated using a fixed interest rate and is such that the mortgage will be fully amortized (that is, the outstanding principal reduced to zero) by the maturity date. If these were the only features, the mortgage would be no different from any other annuity and would present no unusual problems for valuation and analysis. However, most home mortgages can be prepaid without penalty at any time during the life of the mortgage.

Effectively, the homeowner has a call provision that allows the mortgage to be repurchased at par. Because this option has a positive value that generally increases as interest rates fall (that is, the prepayment option has a positive delta), Equation (6.2) implies that the mortgage will have a shorter duration than an otherwise equivalent instrument that does not allow prepayment. In addition, as interest rates go lower, it becomes more likely that homeowners will refinance their mortgages at lower rates, so duration becomes even shorter as rates fall. Like callable bonds, then, mortgages can exhibit negative convexity over at least some range of interest rates. To make matters worse, mortgages are prepaid for reasons other than refinancing. Many homeowners prepay simply because they move to a new location, so demographic and other factors also play an important role in prepayments. Mortgage prepayments are thus extremely difficult to forecast accurately, and as a result, a mortgage's true duration can be quite uncertain.

In addition to unpredictable durations, mortgages on individual homes are traditionally plagued by a lack of liquidity, and default rates are often difficult to assess, particularly for investors with no knowledge of the locality in which the mortgages were originated. Because of these features, home mortgages were for some time relatively unattractive to investors who wanted securities with long and readily predictable durations for immunization purposes, and at the same time relatively safe and liquid securities.

A step in the right direction was the development in the 1970s of mortgage-backed pass-through securities. These securities represent claims to a diversified pool of home mortgages, and all payments of principal and interest on the underlying mortgages are passed through on a pro rata basis to the holders of the pass-through securities. The securities often include a guarantee, by a financial institution or government-backed agency, of timely payment of scheduled interest and principal as well. These securities offer enhanced credit quality and liquidity relative to the underlying mortgages, but they are still subject to an uncertain pattern of principal payments. Thus, mortgage pass-throughs still do not offer much help for investors looking for longer and relatively predictable durations.

B. CMOs

A later generation of mortgage-backed securities, known as collateralized mortgage obligations (CMOs), has provided a better answer to the problem of uncertain duration. These securities are based on the insight that, while the issuer of claims on a given pool of underlying mortgages has no control over the pool's total cash flow pattern, there is no reason why all investors must receive identical cash flow patterns. Rather, the overall cash flows can be divided and parceled out in different ways to different investor groups. For example, some groups might receive a pattern of cash flows with a shorter duration than the cash flows to the overall pool, while others might receive longer-duration cash flow patterns, as long as the average duration for the different groups is equal to the duration of the overall cash flow pattern.

The first CMOs simply divided the overall issue into classes, or tranches, which were distinguished by the order in which principal payments would be received. The first tranche, for example, might receive not only interest on its outstanding principal but also all initial principal payments, whether scheduled or not, for the pool as a whole. The other tranches would receive only interest payments on their outstanding principal, and this process would continue until the outstanding principal on the first tranche had been entirely paid down. At that point, the second tranche would start receiving all of the principal payments, and so on. Since it is clear under this design that the first tranches will be paid off earlier, these will presumably be more appealing to investors with shorter investment horizons, while investors with a desire for longer durations will prefer the later tranches.

Since this original, or "plain vanilla," CMO design still leaves some uncertainty about the actual duration experienced by any given class, some subsequent designs have focused on trying to reduce this uncertainty for one or more tranches. Since the uncertainty surrounding the pool as a whole is given, of course, reducing uncertainty for one tranche entails increasing it for some other tranche. One such design stipulates a planned amortization class (PAC), which is scheduled to receive a specific pattern of principal payments, much like a sinking fund bond. These payments will occur as long as the pattern of prepayments falls within some specified range. If prepayments occur at a rate toward the upper end of this range, the PAC bonds will be paid according to schedule, while other companion or support class bonds will simply be paid down faster than they otherwise would. If prepayments occur at a slower rate, but still inside the designated range, the companion bonds will be paid down at a slower rate. If prepayment rates fall outside the range, however, the companion bonds may have insufficient principal outstanding to absorb all of the excess prepayments, or conversely, the prepayments may be insufficient to meet the scheduled sinking fund, even if the companion bonds are receiving no principal payments. In such cases, the schedule of payments for the PAC bonds will have to be altered. Nevertheless, within the designated range of prepayment rates, the companion bonds insulate the PAC bonds from uncertainty about the pattern of cash flows. As with the plain vanilla bonds, the different classes in this structure will appeal to different groups of investors, who differ in what they are willing to pay to achieve relative cash flow certainty.

Still other CMO designs emphasize splitting the overall issue into classes with very different durations. For example, even though the underlying mortgages are fixed rate, the CMO could still designate a floating rate class of bonds, with interest indexed to some current market rate (for example, the London interbank offered rate, or LIBOR), as long as there is also an inverse floater class, which stipulates an interest rate that moves in the opposite direction from the index rate. The bonds in the inverse floater class would have quite long durations. As interest rates move up, for example, not only does the value of future payments on the inverse floater decline, but the current cash flow declines as well. Thus the inverse floater class is highly sensitive to short-term interest rate movements. In fact, since a perfect floater (one whose interest rate were continuously reset to market rates) would have a duration of zero, the duration of the inverse floater bonds will need to be approximately twice as long as that of the underlying mortgage pool if the durations of the two classes are to average out to the duration of the pool.

Another design that has been prevalent in recent years specifies interest only (IO) and principal only (PO) classes. As their names suggest, IO bonds receive all interest payments but no principal, while PO bonds receive all principal payments but no interest. In the case of IO bonds, an increase in interest rates will cause the remaining stream of payments to be discounted more heavily, but at the same time the length of the stream could be increased considerably, as prepayments become less likely and mortgages are paid off more slowly. If the second effect predominates, IOs will increase in value as interest rates rise. Conversely, a decline in rates will increase prepayments for refinancing purposes, interest rate streams will dry up faster, and the IO will decline in value. IO bonds, then, can exhibit negative durations.

A PO, on the other hand, works the opposite way. There is a set total of principal payments to be made on the underlying mortgages, so fluctuations in the PO's value will be determined largely by the length of the time period over which this total is paid. If rates decline, the total principal payment is accelerated through refinancings, and the POs appreciate in value. If rates increase, refinancing is less likely, principal payments are made over a longer period, and the PO declines in value.

Thus, the IO bonds exhibit a negative duration, the PO bonds a very long duration, and between them they average out to the duration of the underlying mortgage pool. As with other CMO structures, the intent is to find one class of investors to whom the IO bonds will appeal (perhaps for hedging purposes) and another class to whom the PO bonds will appeal.

While the basic purpose and working of the different CMO structures is relatively apparent, valuing these securities can be extremely complex. Not only does the analyst face difficulties in modeling future interest rate movements, as described in preceding sections of this chapter, but variations in prepayment patterns must be captured as well. This situation presents an extremely difficult forecasting problem, which we will not have room to delve into in this book, but it is crucial to the proper valuation of CMOs, since the sudden and sharp changes in value to which particular CMO tranches may be subject cannot be fully understood without a good understanding of how prepayments are likely to vary over different economic scenarios.

A great deal of analysis is currently available for CMOs, including option-adjusted spreads and other complex and sophisticated measures of potential investment performance. It should be kept in mind, however, that any such analysis is based on a particular model of interest rate movements and prepayments, and different models can yield widely differing results. It is important to be aware of the underlying models and their assumptions before basing decisions on this analysis.

V. SUMMARY

Many bonds are issued with attached options, exercisable by either the issuer or the bondholder. Such options can have considerable impact on a bond's value as well as its sensitivity to interest rate movements. In this chapter, we have analyzed bonds that give the issuer the right to buy the bond back and retire it prior to the scheduled maturity.

One way to analyze the effect of a call provision on a bond's interest sensitivity is to calculate call-adjusted duration and convexity measures. These measures can be expressed in terms of the duration and convexity of an ordinary noncallable bond plus certain characteristics of the option that reflect its sensitivity to changes in the underlying bond's price. These measures reveal that callable bonds, unlike option-free bonds, can exhibit negative convexity: As interest rates decline and call becomes more likely, the bond's duration can decrease, rather than increase.

Another approach to analyzing callable bonds is to try explicitly to value any attached option. This process entails constructing a model that allows us to value payments in different future states of the world, where the states are distinguished by different possible values for the short-term interest rate. The binomial option-pricing approach from the preceding chapter is amenable to this task. However, a desirable feature of any such model is to ensure that the possible future interest rate paths specified by our assumed interest rate process are consistent with the existing yield curve.

A third approach is option-adjusted spread analysis, in which we simulate possible future interest rate paths and then find the spread over the rates along these paths that sets the present value of cash flows, averaged over the different paths, equal to the bond's current market price. This approach attempts to adjust the bond's prospective rate of return for the presence of the call option.

Home mortgages present a particular case of callable bonds, but they have the added complication that prepayments also occur for reasons that may be unrelated to interest rate changes. A variety of mortgage-backed securities called collateralized mortgage obligations (CMOs) attempts to divide up the cash flows on a pool of underlying mortgages so that at least some classes of CMO securities will have longer and more predictable durations than the average mortgage in the pool. These securities pose complex valuation problems, and decision-makers must be careful to examine the assumptions underlying any prepared market analysis.

SUGGESTIONS FOR FURTHER READING

Additional material on interest rate option models, option-adjusted spread analysis, and mortgage-backed securities can be found in the following:

1. Babbel, David F., and Stavros A. Zenios, "Pitfalls in the Analysis of Option-Adjusted Spreads," *Financial Analysts Journal,* 48 (July/August 1992), pp. 65–69.

2. Black, Fischer, Emanuel Derman, and William Toy, "A One-Factor Model of Interest Rates and Its Application to Treasury Bond Options," *Financial Analysts Journal,* 46 (January/February 1990), pp. 33–39.

3. Bykhovsky, Michael, and Lakhbir Hayre, "Anatomy of PAC Bonds," *Journal of Fixed Income,* 2 (June 1992), pp. 44–50.

4. Carron, Andrew S., "Understanding CMOs, REMICs, and Other Mortgage Derivatives," *Journal of Fixed Income,* 2 (June 1992), pp. 25–43.

5. Cheyette, Oren, "OAS Analysis for CMOs," *Journal of Portfolio Management,* 20 (Summer 1994), pp. 53–66.

6. Fabozzi, Frank J., *Bond Markets, Analysis and Strategies* (2nd ed.). Englewood Cliffs, N.J.: Prentice Hall, 1993.

7. Finnerty, John D., and Michael Rose, "Arbitrage-Free Spread: A Consistent Measure of Relative Value," *Journal of Portfolio Management,* 17 (Spring 1991), pp. 65–77.

8. Hayre, Lakhbir S., "Understanding Option-Adjusted Spreads and Their Use," *Journal of Portfolio Management,* 16 (Summer 1990), pp. 68–69.

9. Kalotay, Andrew J., and George O. Williams, "The Valuation and Management of Bonds with Sinking Funds," *Financial Analysts Journal,* 48 (March/April 1992), pp. 59–67.

10. Kalotay, Andrew J., George O. Williams, and Frank J. Fabozzi, "A Model for Valuing Bonds and Embedded Options," *Financial Analysts Journal,* 49 (May/June 1993), pp. 35–46.

11. Kopprasch, Robert W., "Option-Adjusted Spread Analysis: Going Down the Wrong Path?" *Financial Analysts Journal,* 50 (May/June 1994), pp. 42–47.

12. Litterman, Robert, José Scheinkman, and Laurence Weiss, "Volatility and the Yield Curve," *Journal of Fixed Income,* 1 (June 1991), pp. 49–53.

PROBLEMS AND QUESTIONS

1. A 10-year bond has a coupon rate of 8%. Coupons are paid semiannually. The bond is callable, so it can be thought of as a package consisting of a 10-year noncallable bond with an attached call option, ex-

ercisable by the issuer. Shown below are prices for the call option and for the underlying noncallable bond at various market yields:

YIELD	PRICE OF CALL OPTION	PRICE OF NONCALLABLE BOND	
4%	14.80	132.70	(Prices quoted in decimals, not
6%	7.36	114.88	thirty-seconds)
8%	3.40	100.00	
10%	1.57	87.54	
12%	0.74	77.06	

a) What is the duration of the noncallable bond at each of the different yields?

b) Estimate the call-adjusted duration of the callable bond at each of the various yields (note that, for 6%, 8%, and 10%, call-adjusted duration will differ depending on whether the change in yields is upward or downward).

c) Explain why the duration of the noncallable and the call-adjusted duration move differently as yields change.

2. For various possible interest rates, the following are hypothetical prices for four securities: (1) a European put option, exercisable five years from now, which gives the holder the right to sell at par a five-year bond with an 8% coupon; (2) a European call option, exercisable five years from now, which gives the holder the right to buy at par a five-year bond with an 8% coupon; (3) a 10-year bond with an 8% coupon (payable semiannually) and with no options attached; (4) a five-year bond with an 8% coupon (payable semiannually) and with no options attached:

YIELD TO MATURITY	PRICE OF PUT	PRICE OF CALL	PRICE OF 10-YR BOND	PRICE OF 5-YR BOND
4%	$0.07	14.80	132.70	117.97
6%	1.01	7.36	114.88	108.53
8%	3.40	3.40	100.00	100.00
10%	6.31	1.57	87.54	92.28
12%	8.96	0.74	77.06	85.28

a) Use the prices above to determine the current value, at yields to maturity of 4, 6, 8, 10, and 12%, of a 10-year bond with an 8% coupon that is callable at par by the issuer after five years. Assume that the bond must either be called or not on only one date, which is exactly five years from now.

b) Show that the callable bond has the same price for each of the yields in (a) as a five-year 8% bond, which gives the issuer the right to sell holders at par another 5-year 8% bond five years from now (this bond will be referred to in (c) as a puttable bond). Why does this result represent an application of put-call parity?

c) Using the same technique described in the Appendix to this chapter for finding call-adjusted duration, find the put-adjusted duration of the puttable bond.

3. During the late 1980s, a number of U.S. corporations issued pay-in-kind (PIK) bonds. These bonds stipulated coupon payments every 6 months plus the repayment of principal at maturity. Their novel feature was that, at each coupon date for a specified period of time, the issuing firm could either make the coupon payment in cash or could give the bondholders additional bonds with a face value equal to the promised coupon payment and the same coupon rate and maturity date as the original bonds. For example, suppose the original bonds are issued today, carry a 15% coupon rate, and mature ten years from today. The pay-in-kind period covers the first five years of the bonds' life. Suppose that the bonds are also callable at par at any time during their life. In six months the first coupon date arrives, and the firm can either pay $75 in cash to the holder of each $1000 (face value) bond or can give the holder an additional pay-in-kind bond with a face value of $75, a coupon rate of 15%, and the same maturity date as the original bonds (that is, 10 years from today). The issuing firm can make this same choice on any coupon date during the next five years. After the first five years, however, it must make all scheduled payments in cash. This arrangement is subject to the qualification that the firm can call the bonds at any time by paying the holders (in cash) $1000 plus accrued interest for each $1000 face value bond outstanding.

a) Briefly describe this PIK bond as a combination of a plain, option-free bond plus options. If the firm exercises its option to pay in kind at each date during the five-year pay-in-kind period, what will be the face value of debt outstanding and the amount of the total semiannual coupon payments during the second five-year period in the life of the bonds?

b) Describe what happens to the PIK bond if the general level of market interest rates rises. In particular, as yields increase, what happens to the value of the firm's option to pay in kind? What happens to the value of the firm's call option? What happens to the value of the PIK bond relative to an otherwise equivalent option-free bond? What happens to the duration of the PIK bond relative to that of an otherwise equivalent option-free bond? (Be sure to indicate briefly the reasoning behind your answers.)

c) Describe what happens to the PIK bond if the general level of market interest rates falls. In particular, as yields decrease, what happens to the value of the firm's option to pay in kind? What happens to the value of the firm's call option? What happens to the value of the PIK bond relative to an otherwise equivalent option-free bond? What happens to the duration of the PIK bond relative to that of an otherwise equivalent option-free bond? (Be sure to indicate briefly the reasoning behind your answers.)

d) How would you describe the convexity of the PIK bond relative to an option-free bond?

4. A financial institution invests entirely in long-term loans on the asset side of its balance sheet. For simplicity, we will assume that all of the loans are identical in every respect, so we can treat the financial institution's portfolio as if it were one composite loan. These loans give the borrower an option to prepay at any time during the life of the loan. Right now, all of the loans have a market value of $100 per $100 face value (that is, they are selling at par). In the absence of the prepayment option, however, they would be selling for $111.11 per $100 face value. In the absence of the prepayment option, the loans would also have a duration of 8 years and a convexity of 95 at current yield levels. Because of the prepayment option, however, their actual duration and convexity are different from these values. The prepayment option's delta is 0.55 and its gamma is 0.03 at current yield levels. On the liability side, the financial institution finances itself partly with equity and partly with certificates of deposit, which all have five years to maturity (from today) and pay interest once per year at the rate of 5% per year. The certificates of deposit have no embedded options. For example, borrowers can withdraw the yearly interest payments, but they may not withdraw any of the principal prior to maturity. The certificates currently sell at par.

a) What are the duration and convexity of the financial institution's assets?

b) What are the duration and convexity of the financial institution's certificates of deposit?

c) If the financial institution wants the duration of its equity to be zero (refer back to Problem 5 in Chapter 2 for how to immunize the value of the financial institution's equity), what proportion of its assets should it finance with certificates of deposit?

d) Assuming the financial institution has adopted the capital structure you have found in (c), and assuming it starts with $100 million in assets, what will happen (give a number, not just a direction of movement) to the institution's market value of equity if all

market yield levels increase by 200 basis points? (Use your duration and convexity calculations from (a) to estimate the resulting
change in the market value of the institution's assets.)

e) Assuming the financial institution has adopted the capital structure you have found in (c), and assuming it starts with $100 mil-
lion in assets, what will happen (give a number, not just a direction of movement) to the institution's market value of equity if all
market yield levels decrease by 200 basis points? (Use your duration and convexity calculations from (a) to estimate the resulting
change in the market value of the institution's assets.)

f) Briefly explain why the value of the financial institution's equity
is not shielded from interest rate movements, despite the adoption
of a capital structure that sets the duration of its equity equal to
zero.

5. A bond with a 10% coupon rate, coupons payable semiannually, is
currently selling to yield 11%. The bond has exactly 25 years remaining to maturity, but it is callable at a price of 104. If the bond were
not callable, traders estimate that it would sell to yield 10%. At current prices and yields, the delta of the bond's call option is 0.3, while
its gamma is 0.02.

a) If the bond were noncallable, what would its modified duration
and convexity be?

b) Use your duration and convexity measures to estimate by how
much the price of the noncallable bond would change if bond
yields were to fall by 200 basis points. Compare this estimated
price change with the actual price change (computed by taking the
present value of the bond's cash flows at the lower yield).

c) Given that the bond is in fact callable, calculate its option-adjusted duration and convexity.

d) Use your duration and convexity estimates from (c) to estimate by
how much the price of the callable bond would change if yields
were to fall by 200 basis points. How can you interpret the difference between your answers to (b) and (d)?

6. The one-year interest rate is currently .10. One year from now, the
one-year interest rate will either be .15 or .05. A two-year pure discount bond is currently selling at a yield of .095.

a) How could you combine one-year and two-year pure discount
bonds so as to create a portfolio that pays $1 one year from now if
the one-year rate is .15 at that time and $0 if the one-year rate is
.05 at that time?

b) What should be the current price of a security that pays $1 one
year from now if the one-year interest rate is then .15 and $0 oth-
erwise?

c) What should be the current price of a security that pays $1 one year from now if the interest rate is then .05 and $0 otherwise?

d) What should be the current price of a two-year bond with a 10% coupon rate that can be called at face value one year from now? (This bond pays .10 per dollar of face value one year from now and is callable at that time for $1. If it isn't called, it pays $1.10 at the end of the second year.)

e) What should be the current price of a two-year floating rate note, whose coupon is reset annually? (This bond pays .10 one year from now. If the one year interest rate is .15 at that time, it pays 1.15 at the end of the second year; if the one-year interest rate is .05 at that time, it pays 1.05 at the end of the second year.)

f) What must be the current price of a two-year floating rate note whose interest rate is capped at 10%? That is, if the prevailing one-year rate one year from now is greater than 10%, the coupon rate on the floating rate note remains at 10%. Why must this note have the same current value as the two-year callable bond described in (d)?

7. Currently, the one-year zero-coupon interest rate is 6%. The one-year forward rate from the zero-coupon yield curve is 4%. After the fact, however, the one-year rate that prevails one year from now will be either 7% or 3%. All quoted rates are based on annual compounding.

a) Find the state prices corresponding to the two possible values the one-year rate could take on next year (that is, find the *present* value of $1 to be delivered next year if the one-year rate goes to 7% and the *present* value of $1 to be delivered next year if the one-year rate goes to 3%).

b) Consider a sinking fund bond with two years remaining to maturity, an 8% coupon rate, and coupons payable annually. Assume that the current coupon and sinking fund payments were just paid and that the entire bond issue now has $75 million in remaining principal outstanding. One year from now, the sinking fund schedule calls for an additional $25 million in principal to be retired at par. The bond issuer also has a double-up option, which allows a sinking fund payment of up to twice the scheduled amount. What is the current market value of the entire bond issue?

c) What is the value of the issuer's double-up option?

8. An ordinary sinking fund bond calls for periodic repayments of principal according to a set schedule over the life of the bond. For example, a two-year $100 million bond issue with a 6% coupon might call for a 40% sinking fund payment. At the end of the first year, the issuing firm would pay the $6 million coupon payment due at that time plus repay $40 million of principal. At the end of the second year, the

firm would then pay 60(1.06) = $63.6 million. An indexed sinking fund debenture (ISFD), in contrast, calls for a sinking fund payment that varies with the level of future interest rates. Consider, for example, a two-year ISFD, similar in all other features besides the indexation of the sinking fund payment to the ordinary sinking fund bond issue described above. A 40% sinking fund payment at the end of the first year would be considered the base case. If the prevailing interest rate one year from now were close to 6%, the firm would simply make a 40% sinking fund payment, and the bond would be identical to the ordinary sinking fund bond. If, however, interest rates one year from now had risen by 200 basis points or more above 6%, the required sinking fund payment would be reduced to zero. On the other hand, if interest rates one year from now had fallen by 200 basis points or more below 6%, the required sinking fund payment would be increased to 80%.

a) The one-year spot rate is currently 6%. The two-year spot rate is also currently 6%. One year from now, the one year rate will be either 2% or 10%. What are the state prices corresponding to the two possible values the one-year spot rate could take on next year (that is, what is the *present* value of $1 to be delivered next year if the one-year rate goes to 2% and the *present* value of $1 to be delivered next year if the one-year rate goes to 10%)?

b) What are the possible future cash flows on the ISFD as described, depending on what the prevailing interest rate is one year from now? Apply the state prices you determined in (a) to these cash flows to find the value of the ISFD.

c) Describe the ISFD as a combination of an ordinary sinking fund bond plus options. Show that you can express the value of the ISFD as a combination of the value of the ordinary sinking fund bond and the values of the options.

9. **Spreadsheet Exercise.** The current yield curve is as follows:

MATURITY (# PERIODS)	YIELD (% PER PERIOD)
1	8%
2	7.0%
3	6.5%
4	6.2%

You believe that, in the future, movements in the one-period interest rate will be governed by a discrete approximation to a lognormal distribution with a volatility parameter $\sigma = .15$.

a) What are the possible values for the one-period interest rate over the next three years that are consistent with the current yield curve?

b) What is the current value of a noncallable 8% coupon bond with a 4-year maturity?

c) What is the current value of an 8% coupon bond with a 4-year maturity that is callable at par at the end of periods 1, 2, or 3?

d) What is the callable bond's static spread?

e) What is the callable bond's option-adjusted spread? Briefly explain your answer.

Footnotes

[1] Note from the Appendix to Chapter 5 that a call option's delta is also equal to minus the reciprocal of the option's hedge ratio.

[2] From these prices we can also find one- and two-period zero coupon bond yields here. The one-period yield must be 10%, since a one-period coupon bond is indistinguishable from a one-period zero for purposes of calculating a yield. We can in turn express the value of the two-period coupon bond in terms of zero coupon yields as follows:

$$990 = 100 \, \frac{1}{(1 + y_1)} + 1100 \, \frac{1}{(1 + y_2)^2}$$

Since $y_1 = .10$, $y_2 = .1061$. Thus the yield curve is upward-sloping here.

[3] It is also possible to calculate prices that the two-period bond would take on one period from now under either of the two possible interest rate scenarios. Comparing these possible future prices with the current price, we could calculate up and down factors, u and d. Using the current one pe-riod rate as r_f, we could then calculate state prices from Equations (5.15) and (5.16). Some care must be taken under this approach to match state prices with the correct bond price. For example, up and down move-ments in bond prices correspond to decreases and increases in interest rates. Thus,we have to remember that the up state refers to the scenario in which interest rates decline. This approach can also become tricky with multiperiod problems. Depending on what is assumed about possi-ble future interest rate movements, the up and down factors may not necessarily repeat themselves throughout all future periods, as we as-sumed in our stock price examples in Chapter 5.

[4] The values of the state prices are susceptible to rounding error, so un-rounded values of n_1^u and n_2^u have been used in calculating π_u. The same applies to the calculation of π_d below.

[5] For further discussion of the implications of the assumed interest rate process, see Andrew J. Kalotay, George O. Williams, and Frank J. Fabozzi, "A Model for Valuing Bonds and Embedded Options," *Financial Analysts Journal*, 49, (May/June 1993), 35–46, on which this section is based.

[6] This solution can be found readily with a spreadsheet. For example, the value $r_d = 4.506\%$ was found using the Solver routine on Microsoft Excel.

[7] In performing these calculations on a spreadsheet, the computer can be instructed to set the callable bond's value at any node equal to the minimum of either (a) the coupon plus the call price or (b) the coupon plus the present value (at the one-period rate prevailing at that node) of the average of the values the bond could take on next period. If (a) represents the minimum value, the bond is called at that node, whereas if (b) is the minimum value, the bond is not called.

[8] Static spread values can be found readily on a spreadsheet. Such a value could be found, for example, using either the Solver or Goal Seek routines on Microsoft Excel.

[9] The difference between the static spread and the option-adjusted spread is sometimes referred to as the option cost, or the premium that the presence of the call option adds to the bond issuer's cost. In the example at hand, the option cost is thus 34.5 basis points.

Appendix to Chapter 6

I. CALL-ADJUSTED DURATION AND CONVEXITY

If we take Equation (6.1) in the text and differentiate with respect to y,

$$\frac{dB_c}{dy} = \frac{dB_{nc}}{dy} - \frac{dC}{dy} \tag{6A.1}$$

Multiplying by -1, dividing each term by B_c, and both multiplying and dividing the two right-hand side terms by B_{nc},

$$\frac{-1}{B_c}\left(\frac{dB_c}{dy}\right) = \left[\frac{-1}{B_{nc}}\left(\frac{dB_{nc}}{dy}\right)\frac{B_{nc}}{B_c}\right] - \left[\frac{-dC}{dy}\left(\frac{1}{B_{nc}}\right)\frac{B_{nc}}{B_c}\right] \tag{6A.2}$$

Writing the derivative of C with respect to y in terms of the underlying noncallable bond,

$$\frac{-1}{B_c}\left(\frac{dB_c}{dy}\right) = \left[\frac{-1}{B_{nc}}\left(\frac{dB_{nc}}{dy}\right)\frac{B_{nc}}{B_c}\right]$$
$$- \left\{\frac{dC}{dB_{nc}}\left[\frac{-1}{B_{nc}}\left(\frac{dB_{nc}}{dy}\right)\right]\frac{B_{nc}}{B_c}\right\} \tag{6A.3}$$

Finally, using the definition of modified duration (Equation [2.4] in Chapter 2), and defining the call option's delta as $\delta = dC/dB_{nc}$ results in Equation (6.2) in the text.

If we differentiate Equation (6A.1) again with respect to y and express the derivative of the bond's call provision in terms of the derivative of the underlying noncallable bond, as we did previously, the result is as follows:

$$\frac{d^2B_c}{dy^2} = \frac{d^2B_{nc}}{dy^2} - \left[\frac{d^2C}{dB_{nc}^2}\left(\frac{dB_{nc}}{dy}\right)^2 + \frac{dC}{dB_{nc}}\left(\frac{d^2B_{nc}}{dy^2}\right)\right] \tag{6A.4}$$

Multiplying the first term on the right-hand side of (6A.4) by B_{nc}/B_{nc}, the first term in brackets by $(B_{nc}/B_{nc})^2$, and the second term in brackets by B_{nc}/B_{nc} gives the following:

$$\frac{d^2 B_c}{dy^2} = \frac{d^2 B_{nc}}{dy^2} \left(\frac{B_{nc}}{B_{nc}} \right)$$
$$- \left[\frac{d^2 C}{dB_{nc}^2} \left(\frac{dB_{nc}}{dy} \right)^2 \frac{B_{nc}^2}{B_{nc}^2} + \frac{dC}{dB_{nc}} \left(\frac{B_{nc}}{B_{nc}} \right) \frac{d^2 B_{nc}}{dy^2} \right] \qquad (6A.5)$$

If we define an option's gamma as $\gamma = d^2 C / dB_{nc}^2$, then using this definition plus the definitions of the option's delta, the noncallable bond's modified duration (Equation 2.4), and its convexity (Equation 2.5), we can express (6A.5) as follows:

$$\frac{d^2 B_c}{dy^2} = CON_{nc} B_{nc} - [\gamma (D_{nc})^2 B_{nc}^2 + \delta CON_{nc} B_{nc}] \qquad (6A.6)$$

Finally, dividing both sides of (6A.6) by the price of the callable bond, B_c, and rearranging gives Equation (6.3) in the text.

7

Other Options Embedded in Bonds and Equities

I. OTHER BONDS WITH PRINCIPAL PAYMENT OPTIONS

In the preceding chapter, we saw examples of fixed income securities that give the issuer the option to accelerate the repayment of principal. There are a number of other option features that are often found in bonds and equities, and these options are the subject of this chapter. In Section I, we will analyze some bond structures that give either the issuer or the bondholder an option that determines the amount of the principal payment, depending on the level of a specified commodity or security price. In Section II, we will discuss convertible bonds and in Section III the default option on corporate debt. Finally, Section IV is devoted to option features of equity securities.

A. Currency- and Commodity-Linked Bonds

A simple example of a bond with an option affecting the principal payment is a dual currency bond that gives the issuer the option to pay, at maturity, either one specified amount in one currency or a different specified amount in a different currency. Suppose, for example, that we have a zero-coupon bond with one year remaining to maturity and a face value of US$ 100. The bond indenture stipulates that, one year from now, the issuer can choose to pay the bondholder either $100 or 13,000 yen. In effect, this bond is a combination of an ordinary zero-coupon bond plus a currency put option, exercisable by the issuer. The issuer will choose to pay the principal in yen if the ¥/$ exchange rate is greater than 130 ¥ per $ next year (that is, in that event ¥13,000 will be worth less than $100, so the issuer chooses to put ¥13,000 to the bondholders in exchange for $100) and will pay in dollars whenever the exchange rate is less than 130. If we can make an assumption about the process governing future movements in the ¥/$ exchange rate, which is the state variable in this case, and if we know the one-year interest rates in yen and dollars, we can value this bond using the standard option pricing techniques introduced in Chapter 5.

Suppose, for example, that the exchange rate currently stands at 130 ¥/$, that one year from now the exchange rate will move either to 140 ¥/$ or to 120 ¥/$, and that the current one-year interest rate is 6% for yen-denominated instruments and 8% for dollar-denominated instruments. We can determine state prices corresponding to the two possible future states of the world, using the same procedure we used in Chapter 5. If we want our state prices to be denominated in dollars, we can take the one-year dollar-denominated zero as our risk-free security, but we have to exercise some care about the "security" we use as our uncertain security. It might seem natural simply to use the exchange rate, but then we would be comparing our 8% risk-free security with the exchange rate, which bears no explicit return.

A better comparison is provided if we take $1 today, convert it to yen at the current exchange rate, invest this sum for one year at the 6% yen interest rate, and then convert the proceeds back to dollars at whatever exchange rate prevails next year. If the exchange rate moves to 120, the value of our initial $1 investment will be $130(1.06)/120 = 1.148333$, while if the exchange rate moves to 140, our initial $1 investment will be worth $130(1.06)/140 = .984286$. Using 1.148333 and .984286 as our up and down factors, respectively, we can then use Equations (5.15) and (5.16) to determine the state prices, as follows:

$$\pi_u = \frac{1.08 - .984286}{(1.08)(1.148333 - .984286)} = .5402 \qquad (7.1)$$

$$\pi_d = \frac{1.148333 - 1.08}{(1.08)(1.148333 - .984286)} = .3857 \qquad (7.2)$$

Given the state prices, we can value the bond by noting that it will pay $100 in the up state (the exchange rate goes to 120 ¥/$) and ¥13,000 = $13,000/140 = $92.857 in the down state. The value of the bond is then the sum of the values of its two state-contingent payoffs, or (100) (.5402) + (92.857)(.3857) = $89.84.

The same value could also be obtained by decomposing the dual currency bond into an ordinary zero minus a put option. The plain vanilla zero is worth $100/1.08 = \$92.59$. The put option costs the bondholder $(100 - 92.857) = \$7.143$ in the down state, so its value is $(7.143)(.3857) = \$2.755$. The combination of the bond and the option is then worth $\$92.59 - \$2.755 = \$89.84$.

In a similar vein, bonds have been issued where the principal payment is tied to the prevailing price of some other commodity as of the bond's maturity date. For example, Standard Oil issued four-year bonds in 1986 which promised holders a minimum principal payment plus any excess of the price of Oklahoma light sweet crude oil over $25 per barrel multiplied by 170 barrels. In this case, it is the bondholder who effectively has a call option that can be exercised against the issuer if the crude oil price four years from now exceeds $25 per barrel.[1] Other examples of securities whose principal payment contains an option element can be found in Problems 2 and 3 at the end of this chapter.[2]

II. CONVERTIBLE BONDS

A. Ordinary Convertibles

Convertible bonds give the bondholder the right to convert the bond into a specified number of shares of common stock of the issuing corporation. The bonds are also callable by the issuer at a prespecified price, but if the issuer exercises this call option, the bondholders may still convert the bonds to stock rather than accepting the call price. Valuing a convertible bond is somewhat more complex than the bonds with options that we have seen thus far because of the potential interaction between the choices that may be made by the issuer and the bondholders.

To illustrate, let's consider a convertible bond issue with three years remaining to maturity. The bonds have a 3% coupon rate, with coupons paid annually, and at the end of any year from now up to and including the bond's maturity date, bondholders may elect to convert each $1000 face value bond into 23 shares of the issuing company's common stock. That stock pays no dividend and is currently selling at a price of $40 per share. By the end of each future year the stock price will either move up by a factor 1.2 or down by a factor of .8 relative to its beginning-of-year level. The company can call the bonds at a price of 105 (that is, $1050 per $1000 face value bond) plus accrued interest either immediately or at the end of any year between now and the maturity date. The riskless one-year interest rate is 6.5%, and the yield curve is flat.

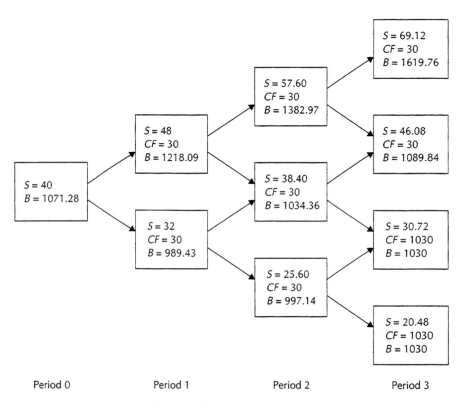

Period 0   Period 1   Period 2   Period 3

FIGURE 7.1   Value, *B*, of convertible bond at each node if it were noncallable, given cash flow, *CF*, and stock price, *S*, at that node.

To value the convertible bonds, we can first determine state prices, using Equations (5.15) and (5.16) with the issuing company's stock price as the state variable. The respective state prices are given by the following:

$$\pi_u = \frac{1.065 - .8}{(1.065)(1.2 - .8)} = .6221 \tag{7.3}$$

$$\pi_d = \frac{1.2 - 1.065}{(1.065)(1.2 - .8)} = .3169 \tag{7.4}$$

Next, we need to consider the optimal action by the bondholder at each node, which, for purposes of illustration, we will do in two steps. First, suppose the bonds were convertible but noncallable. The possible paths of future stock prices are shown in Figure 7.1, and if we move to the maturity date, the bondholders will choose to convert if the bonds' conversion value (that is, 23 shares times the prevailing share price) exceeds their face value.[3] At share prices above 1000/23 = $43.48, bond-holders will prefer to take the 23 shares, while at prices below that, they will prefer the face value principal payment on the bonds. In either case, bondholders also collect the final coupon payment. As shown in Figure 7.1, conversion will occur for the top two states (that is, $S = 69.12$, $S = 46.08$), but not in the other two states. Given the bondholders' optimal strategy, the value of the bonds is then shown for each of the possible nodes at the bonds' maturity date.

Next, we might notice that the bondholders' conversion option is really an American call option on a non-dividend-paying stock. As we saw in Chapter 5, such an option will never be exercised early, so we can value the convertible but noncallable bond by simply rolling back the tree from the maturity date using the state prices we calculated previously. At each node, the value of the bond will be the current coupon plus the value of waiting (that is, π_u times the bond's value if the stock price moves up plus π_d times the bond's value if the stock price moves down).[4] This calculation brings us back to a value of $1071.28 for the current period (it is assumed that the bond pays no coupon in the current period, either because the bond has just been issued or we are valuing it immediately after receipt of a coupon payment).

Unfortunately for bondholders, however, the issuer can now step in and spoil this scenario. Since the issuer can call the bonds at $1050 per bond, it will do so whenever the bond's value at a node prior to maturity exceeds $1050. By the maturity date, it is too late for the issuer. Notice, for example, in Figure 7.1 that the bond's value exceeds $1050 for each of the upper two nodes at maturity. If the issuer calls the bonds, bond-holders will simply convert and receive the same value shown in Figure 7.1 anyway. Prior to maturity, however, the issuer can take away value from the bondholders by forcing them to convert earlier than they would otherwise want to. Consider, for example, the uppermost node at the end of the second period. As shown in Figure 7.1, bondholders could achieve a value of $1383.02 by collecting their $30 coupon and waiting another period to see what happens to stock prices. If the firm called the bonds, however, it couldn't force the bondholder to receive $1050 plus accrued interest but it could force the bondholder to accept the conversion value plus accrued interest. In this case, the conversion value is 23 times $57.60, or $1324.80, so by calling the bonds the firm could keep bondholders' value to a total of $1354.80, in contrast to the $1383.02 they could achieve by waiting. Part of the value of any option stems from the right to wait and see what happens before making a decision, so the company's call provision effectively allows it to take away some of the bondholders' conversion option value. Because shareholders will benefit from bondholders' loss, the issuer will find it optimal to exercise this option at the uppermost node after two years, and as shown in Fig-

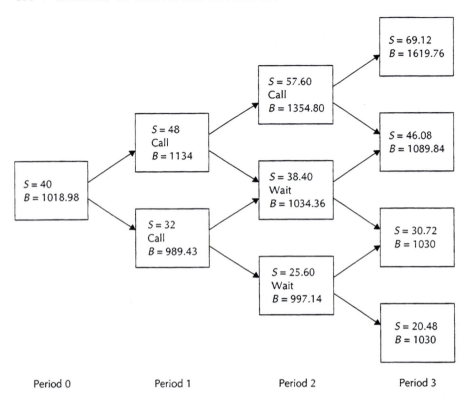

Period 0   Period 1   Period 2   Period 3

FIGURE 7.2   Value, B, of convertible bond at each node given that it is callable, with issuer's call strategy (call, wait) and stock price, S, shown at that node.

ure 7.2, the bond's value at this node will thus be $1354.80 rather than $1383.02.

Rolling back the tree in this fashion, as shown in Figure 7.2, allowing a bond call to occur whenever it is optimal for the issuer, we see that the current value of the bonds is $1018.98.[5] As in previous examples, we can also obtain the same value by decomposing the convertible bond into its component securities. First, the value the bond would have as straight debt is simply the following:

$$\frac{30}{1.065} + \frac{30}{(1.065)^2} + \frac{1030}{(1.065)^3} = 907.30 \qquad (7.5)$$

Second, the bondholders' conversion option can be valued by noting that, left on their own, bondholders would convert only in the two uppermost states at maturity. In the top state, in which the stock price is $69.12, bondholders gain $(23 \times 69.12 - 1000) = 589.76$ from converting. In the next state, in which the stock price is $46.08, bondholders gain (23 × 46.08 − 1000) = 59.84. By bringing these two amounts back to the present using the state prices, we see that the conversion option is worth $163.98. This same value could also be obtained by subtracting the straight bond value from the value the bonds would have if they were convertible but not callable. Finally, the issuer's call provision will be exercised if stock prices move up at the end of the first period.[6] From Figure 7.1, the value that the bonds would have at this node if they were not callable is $1218.09. By calling, the firm can force bondholders to convert early, giving them $1134. Thus the issuer gains (1218.09 − 1134) = $84.09 by calling, and multiplying this gain by π_u, the value of the call provision is $52.31. Adding these pieces together, the value of the convertible bond is 907.30 + 163.98 − 52.31 = $1018.97, which is accurate to within a rounding error.

B. LYONs

A new twist on ordinary convertibles is the liquid yield option note (LYON), introduced by Merrill Lynch in 1985. Other underwriters have also marketed securities with similar designs. A LYON is a zero-coupon bond that is convertible into the issuer's common stock. Like ordinary convertible bonds, a LYON is also callable. Since it is a zero-coupon bond, the LYON is sold initially at a deep discount and its value as straight debt increases over time as it approaches the maturity date. Because of this feature, the LYON stipulates an increasing schedule of call prices at which the issue can be called on various future dates. In addition, the LYON contains a put feature, exercisable by the bondholder, whereby the bond can be sold back to the issuer at an increasing schedule of prices over subsequent future dates.

If we are willing to ignore interest rate uncertainty and let the issuing company's stock price be our only state variable, the LYON affords no really new valuation issues that we have not previously seen with other securities. We need to specify the process governing stock price movements, solve for the appropriate state prices, and then use these to roll back a tree of bond values from maturity to the present. The addition of the put option does make the security more complex, however, and we need to account for the interaction between the issuer's and bondholders' options. At each node, for example, the issuer must decide whether to call the issue or let it remain outstanding. If the bond is called, the issuer must decide whether or not to convert, and if the bond is not called, the holder must decide whether to convert it early, continue holding it, or put it back to the issuer at the specified price. The value of these various actions the holder might take affects the issuer's optimal call strategy, and at the same time the issuer's right to call affects the value of the holders' options. Problem 5 at the end of this chapter gives an example in which you can value a LYON.

III. THE DEFAULT OPTION ON CORPORATE DEBT

Another application of option pricing that is useful in simplified settings is in valuing a company's equity. As Black and Scholes pointed out, the equity in a leveraged company can be viewed as a call option on the assets.[7] When the shareholders borrow against the firm's assets, it is as if they have sold the assets to the bondholders but retained a call option on those assets. If we assume, for simplicity, that all debt is zero-coupon debt, the promised payment at maturity (the face value) represents the exercise price of this option. If the option expires in the money (that is, the assets are worth more than the promised payment to the bondholders), the shareholders exercise their call by paying off the bondholders and taking back the assets. If the option expires out of the money, on the other hand, the shareholders default, and the bondholders retain title to the assets in lieu of receiving their promised payment. Thus, if we knew the asset value, A (which corresponds to S in the Black-Scholes formula), the promised payment on the debt and its maturity date, the risk-free rate, and the instantaneous standard deviation of the assets' value, we could use the Black-Scholes formula to value the company's equity.[8]

We can also invoke put-call parity to gain some further insight into the relationship between shareholders and bondholders. Writing put-call parity with the asset value A substituted for S, we can write the company's equity value, viewed as a call option as follows:

$$C = A - Xe^{-r_f T} + P \qquad (7.6)$$

where X is the promised payment on the debt and T is its maturity date. This expression suggests that we can also interpret the shareholders as owning the assets, A, as having made a promise to the bondholders that would have the value $Xe^{-r_f T}$ if it were risk-free, and as also having received a put option, or default option, from the bondholders. Under this interpretation, the shareholders retain title to the assets, but at the debt's maturity, they can choose to give control of those assets to the bondholders in exchange for having the bondholders' claim to the promised payment extinguished. We can also rearrange (7.6) to read as follows:

$$A = (Xe^{-r_f T} - P) + C \qquad (7.7)$$

Since C represents the value of the equity, and since the equity and debt must add up to the value of the assets, the first term (in parentheses) on the right hand side of (7.7) must represent the market value of the debt, which in turn is equal to the value the debt would have if it were risk-free, reduced by the value of the shareholders' put, or default, option.

Thus, standard option pricing techniques also allow us to value risky debt and the firm's associated default option. Two cautions are in order, however. First, as with the convertible bonds, we have accounted here only for movements in the firm's asset value, but have not considered interest rate uncertainty. Second, the assumption of zero-coupon debt greatly simplifies the analysis. Once we allow for coupon payments, we effectively have options on options, or what is known as compound options. For example, we have the option to default on the first coupon payment. If we do not, we thereby acquire the option to default on the second coupon payment, etc. For a lengthy series of coupon payments, this analysis can become quite complex.

IV. EQUITY WITH OPTION FEATURES

A. Innovative Equity Designs

Over the years, a number of innovative designs have appeared for equity securities with option features. In the 1980s, Americus Shareowners Service Corporation bought shares in a number of large, well-recognized U.S. corporations and put these shares into trusts with specified five-year lives. The trusts in turn sold two types of claims to investors. One type, the prime unit, entitled the holder to all dividends and voting rights over the life of the trust plus any stock price appreciation as of the trust's expiration date up to a specified maximum amount. The other type, the score unit, entitled the holder to any stock price appreciation as of the trust's expiration date in excess of that same specified amount. In effect, then, the score represents a European call option on the underlying stock, while the prime represents a long position in the stock plus a short position in the call option.

Primes and scores raise no new valuation issues that we have not seen earlier, but they are of interest because of the no-arbitrage relationship that links the prices of the primes, scores, and underlying stock. In fact, the trusts themselves afforded a mechanism for enforcing this relationship by offering to redeem a combination of a prime and a score at the trust's net asset value.[9] Because the trusts were ruled in 1986 to be taxable as corporations, no new trusts have been formed since that time.

Other equity securities have been issued with put features, affording investors some guarantee of a minimum return on their investment. Some initial public offerings of common stock, for example, have carried the issuing company's promise to buy back the stock from the holder at the offering price at the end of some specified period (for example, two years). These securities have some characteristics in common with convertible bonds, in that a convertible's value as straight debt provides a floor under the bond's value (subject to default risk) in much the same way that the put feature does on the puttable stock.[10]

B. Options Implicit in a Company's Future Cash Flows

Even for common equities of standard design, it is being increasingly recognized that option valuation techniques are useful for capturing the future choices firms can make that will in turn affect their cash flows. Consider, for example, a firm's growth opportunities. As discussed in Chapter 4, we represented those opportunities earlier as the present value of future net present values. However, ordinary discounted cash flow valuation techniques cannot capture the choice element in these future opportunities. Since the firm has not undertaken them yet, it can choose whether or not to adopt these projects when they arise. Similarly, a firm can choose to abandon projects that have already been undertaken.

If we model these opportunities as options, which can be exercised or not, a variety of new insights into common stock value are possible.[11] For example, options react differently to changes in interest rates or the uncertainty surrounding the underlying asset than do other types of assets. Thus, a firm whose stock value is disproportionately weighted toward growth options may react differently to interest rates and uncertainty than a firm whose value is more heavily weighted toward assets in place. In addition, certain types of investment outlays may be valuable to a firm not so much for the cash flow streams they create directly, but rather for the options they generate. Research and development expenditures, for instance, may create options for firms to market new products in the future, and these options may enhance a common stock's value now, even if they ultimately expire unexercised.

V. SUMMARY

In addition to the call and prepayment features analyzed in the preceding chapter, a number of other option elements may be present, either explicitly or implicitly, in debt and equity securities. For the most part, these elements introduce no real issues of option valuation that we have not previously encountered. They afford interesting illustrations, however, of the pervasiveness of options in the capital markets and of the working of the no-arbitrage principal.

A number of bond designs tie the amount or value of the principal payment to the level of some commodity or other price index at the bond's maturity. Bonds with currency options, for example, give the issuer a choice of paying the principal as either a specified amount in one currency or a specified amount in another currency. Since the ratio between the two specified amounts implicitly defines an exchange rate, the issuer will make this choice based on the market exchange rate prevailing at maturity. Other designs allow for adjustments in the principal payment, sometimes at the option of the issuer and sometimes the bondholder, depending on the level of commodity prices or equity prices.

Another common type of bond is the convertible bond. This design gives the bondholder the right to convert the bond into a specified number of common shares of the issuing company's stock, but it also gives the issuer the right to call the bonds. The issuer can then affect the value of the bondholders' conversion option, since by calling the bonds, it can force the bondholders to convert earlier than they would otherwise choose. A liquid yield option note (LYON) adds a new wrinkle to this design by giving bondholders a put option to sell the bonds back to the issuer.

Since the firm effectively sells its assets to bondholders if it doesn't meet the promised payments on its debt, the right to default can be viewed as a put option implicit in the bond contract. This option can be valued using available option pricing techniques.

Finally, equity securities can also contain option elements. These elements include explicit options, as in primes and scores or puttable equity, but also the options inherent in a company's future investment opportunities or in its ability to abandon existing projects.

SUGGESTIONS FOR FURTHER READING

Additional material on the design and valuation of securities with option elements, on the default option, and on the options inherent in firms' investment opportunities can be found in the following:

1. Black, Fischer, and Myron Scholes, "The Pricing of Options and Corporate Liabilities," *Journal of Political Economy,* 81 (May–June 1973), pp. 637–654.

2. Chen, Andrew H., and John W. Kensinger, "Uncommon Equity," *Continental Bank Journal of Applied Corporate Finance,* 5 (Spring 1992), pp. 36–43.

3. Damodaran, Aswath, *Damodaran on Valuation: Security Analysis for Investment and Corporate Finance.* New York: John Wiley & Sons, 1994.

4. Fabozzi, Frank J., *Bond Markets, Analysis and Strategies* (2nd ed.). Englewood Cliffs, N.J.: Prentice Hall, 1993.

5. Finnerty, John D., "An Overview of Corporate Securities Innovation," *Continental Bank Journal of Applied Corporate Finance,* 4 (Winter 1992), pp. 23–39.

6. Jarrow, Robert A., and Maureen O'Hara, "Primes and Scores: An Essay on Market Imperfections," *Journal of Finance,* 44 (December 1989), pp. 1263–1287.

7. Jones, E. Philip, and Scott P. Mason, "Equity-Linked Debt," *Midland Corporate Finance Journal,* 3 (Winter 1986), pp. 46–58.

8. Litterman, Robert, and Thomas Iben, "Corporate Bond Valuation and the Term Structure of Credit Spreads," *Journal of Portfolio Management,* 17 (Spring 1991), pp. 52–64.

9. McConnell, John J., and Eduardo S. Schwartz, "LYON Taming," *Journal of Finance,* 41 (July 1986), pp. 561–576.

10. McConnell, John J., and Eduardo S. Schwartz, "The Origin of LYONs: A Case Study in Financial Innovation," *Continental Bank Journal of Applied Corporate Finance,* 4 (Winter 1992), pp. 40–47.

11. Smith, Clifford W., Charles W. Smithson, and D. Sykes Wilford, "Managing Financial Risk," *Continental Bank Journal of Applied Corporate Finance,* 1 (Winter 1989), pp. 27–48.

12. Smithson, Charles W., and Donald H. Chew, "The Uses of Hybrid Debt in Managing Corporate Risk," *Continental Bank Journal of Applied Corporate Finance,* 4 (Winter 1992), pp. 79–89.

13. Trigeorgis, Lenos, and Scott P. Mason, "Valuing Managerial Flexibility," *Midland Corporate Finance Journal,* 5 (Spring 1987), pp. 14–21.

PROBLEMS AND QUESTIONS

1. **Spreadsheet Exercise.** A bond with four years remaining to maturity has a 4% coupon rate and a $100 face value. Coupons are paid once per year in US$. At maturity, the bondholder can elect to re-

ceive the principal payment as either $100 or the US$ equivalent, at exchange rates prevailing at that time, of £50. The current exchange rate between pounds and dollars is .60 £/$. Each year over the next four years, this exchange rate can either rise by a factor 1.2 or fall by a factor of .85. The current one-year interest rates are 5% on dollar-denominated instruments and 6% on pound-denominated instruments, and the yield curves are flat in both countries.

a) Describe this bond as a combination of other, more elementary securities.

b) What is the current value of this bond? Show that its total value is equal to the same combination of the elementary security values that you have described in (a).

2. Salomon Brothers has issued equity-linked securities, or ELKs. These are three-year notes, which pay interest at the rate of 6.75% per year (assume that interest is paid annually). Repayment of principal at the end of 3 years is tied to the stock price of Digital Equipment Corporation at that time. Specifically, for each $100 face value of notes held, the investor will be paid a principal amount equal to the value of three shares of Digital stock on the maturity date. However, this amount is subject to a maximum principal payment of $135 per $100 face value. Assume that Digital's stock is selling at $30 per share on the day the notes are issued and that the risk-free interest rate for instruments of one, two, or three years is 5%. Digital pays no dividend. Each year, Digital's stock price can either rise by a factor of 1.25 or fall by a factor of $\frac{1}{1.25}$ (= .8).

a) What should be the price of the ELKs per $100 face value on the date of issue?

b) How would you characterize the ELKs as a combination of other securities? Show that the price of the ELKs can be found by adding up the prices of the component securities.

c) What are the four possible yields to maturity that an investor could earn after the fact on the ELKs? (That is, given the possible Digital stock prices at maturity, what yields would these prices translate into for a holder of the ELKs?)

3. In 1986, the Kingdom of Denmark issued equity-linked notes, denominated in French francs and traded on the Paris Bourse. Each note had a face value of FF 10,000 and a coupon rate, payable annually, of 4.5%. Assume that, as of right now, the notes have exactly two years remaining to maturity. The notes were issued in two tranches, both of which have the same total face value. The principal payment on both tranches is contingent on the value at maturity of the French stock market index. In addition to paying annual coupons at the

4.5% rate (calculated as a percentage of the face value), the notes in the bull tranche make a principal payment equal to 25 times the value of the French stock market index at maturity, subject to a maximum principal payment of FF 20,000. In addition to paying annual coupons at the 4.5% rate, the notes in the bear tranche make a principal payment equal to FF 20,000 *minus* the principal payment on the bull notes. The stock market index currently stands at a level of 400. Each year, the index can either move up by a factor 1.5 (that is, $u = 1.5$) or down by a factor 0.5 (that is, $d = .5$). Assume for simplicity that none of the stocks in the index pays a dividend. The risk-free interest rate is 5% per year and the yield curve is flat.

a) Given the facts just stated, what should be the current market value of each FF 10,000 face value bull note?

b) Given the facts above, what should be the current market value of each FF 10,000 face value bear note?

c) Based on the entire note issue (that is, both bulls and bears combined), explain how much exposure the Kingdom of Denmark has to fluctuations in the French stock market index. Explain how the pricing of the bulls and bears combined represents an application of the put-call parity principal.

d) At the time of this issue, French securities regulation did not allow for the trading of either options or futures contracts on the French stock market index. Assume that that condition is still true today and that each pair of bull and bear notes is in fact selling for a combined sum of FF 20,000 (that is, together, each pair of notes is selling at par). Do you think this approach represents irrational pricing on the part of market participants, or can you give another plausible explanation? Does your answer give any insight into why the Kingdom of Denmark may have wanted to issue these notes in the first place?

4. **Spreadsheet Exercise.** A company has two types of securities outstanding: common stock and convertible bonds. The common stock is currently selling at a price of $30 per share. In every period the stock price will either move up by a factor 1.25 or down by a factor of .8. The riskless interest rate is 6%, and it is known that this rate will remain at the same level for the foreseeable future. The convertible bonds have a 4% coupon rate, they pay coupon payments annually (not semiannually), and they have five years remaining until maturity. At any date between now and maturity (including the maturity date) an investor can exchange his or her bonds for 30 shares of the company's common stock per $1000 (face value) bond (assume that

the act of converting does not itself have any effect on the stock price prevailing at that time—that is, that no dilution occurs when the company issues new shares to the converting bondholders). When an investor converts, the company must pay any interest accrued up to that time. The company can also call the bonds at 105 (that is, $1050 per $1000 face value bond) plus accrued interest at any date between now and maturity. If the bonds are called, however, the investor has the opportunity to convert to stock rather than accept the company's cash payment. The convertible bonds have no default risk.

a) Assuming, initially, that the underlying stock pays no dividend, what is the current market value of the convertible bonds? Show that this market value can be expressed as a combination of the values of (1) a nonconvertible, noncallable bond with a 4% coupon rate and five years remaining to maturity, (2) the bondholder's conversion option, and (3) the company's call option.

b) Assuming still that the underlying stock pays no dividend, will the firm ever wish to call the bonds before maturity? Explain why or why not. If the answer is yes, describe the circumstances under which the firm would want to call the bonds.

c) What would the value of the convertible bonds be if the call price changed from $1050 to $1040? If the call price changed from $1050 to $1060? Briefly explain your answers.

d) If all else remained the same as in (a), but the company now payed a dividend at an annual rate of 5%, what would happen to the value of the convertible bonds (note that, in the presence of the dividend, the up and down factors, 1.25 and .8 now refer to the stock's ex-dividend price)?

e) In the presence of the 5% dividend yield, what would investors' optimal conversion strategy be if the company could not call the bonds? How would this strategy be affected by the company's call provision?

5. **Spreadsheet Exercise.** A LYON issue has 10 years remaining to maturity. Each $1000 (face value) LYON may be converted into 9 shares of the issuing company's common stock at any time between now and maturity. The company's current stock price is $50 per share, it has a dividend yield of 2%, and each year the stock's ex-dividend price will either move up by a factor $u = 1.35$ or down by a factor $d = 1/u$. The risk-free rate is 8%, the term structure is flat, and there is no uncertainty about interest rates. At the end of each year, the LYONs may be either called by the issuer or put by the bondholder at the following prices.

YEAR	CALL PRICE	PUT PRICE
1	591.9	470.0
2	627.4	512.3
3	665.1	558.4
4	705.0	608.7
5	747.3	663.4
6	792.1	723.2
7	839.6	788.2
8	890.0	859.2
9	943.4	936.5
10	1000	1000

a) What is the value of the LYON?

b) How much value does the bondholders' put option add to the LYON?

6. Rollercoaster Inc., a wholly-owned subsidiary of Massive Corp., has assets with a current market value of $20 million. The standard deviation of the assets' value is 40 percent year. The company's capital structure consists of debt and equity. The debt is made up entirely of zero-coupon bonds that mature in five years. The bonds have a total face value of $15 million and are guaranteed against default by Massive, the parent company. Massive is considered sufficiently safe that no one expects it to be unable to honor this guarantee. The current risk-free interest rate prevailing in the market is 7%. Massive is considering selling its shareholdings in Rollercoaster, and is wondering what price it could hope to obtain.

a) If Massive sells its Rollercoaster shares but continues to serve as guarantor of Rollercoaster's debt, what is the maximum price it could hope to receive for the shares?

b) If Massive sells its Rollercoaster shares but does not guarantee Rollercoaster's debt, what is the maximum price Massive could hope to receive for the shares?

7. A firm has assets whose total market value is currently $10MM. The standard deviation of the assets' rate of return is 50% per year. It is financed with debt and equity, and the entire amount of debt consists of a zero-coupon bond issue that has ten years remaining until maturity. The debt has a face value (that is, the promised payment at maturity) of $8MM. The riskless interest rate, r_f, is 8%, and the term structure is flat, so this rate can be applied to riskless instruments of any maturity.

a) Using the Black-Scholes option pricing model, find the current market values of the firm's equity and debt.

b) Using the put-call parity relationship, find the value of the firm's option to default on its debt.
c) What would be the modified duration of the firm's debt if the debt were riskless? (Note: if $B_f = Xe^{-r_f T}$, where B_f is the value of the bonds if they are risk-free and r_f is the annualized instantaneous interest rate, the modified duration is the same as the Macaulay duration when discrete bond yields are used.) See if you can derive this equivalence by finding modified duration $= \dfrac{-\partial B_f / \partial r_f}{B_f}$, where $B_f = Xe^{-r_f T}$.
d) Let F be the face value of the firm's debt. Under certain assumptions, it can be shown that the value of a put option, P, on the firm's assets, with an exercise price of F, has the following sensitivity to changes in interest rates:

$$\frac{\partial P}{\partial r_f} = -T[1 - N(d_2)]Fe^{-r_f T}$$

where T and $N(d_2)$ have the same meaning as in the Black-Scholes option pricing model. Using this relationship, measure the sensitivity of the value, B, of the risky, zero-coupon issue to changes in the risk-free rate. You will find it useful to measure this sensitivity as $-\dfrac{\partial B / \partial r_f}{B}$ so that you can compare it with the duration of the equivalent riskless issue. This expression represents a kind of duration measure, but it is measured relative to the riskless interest rate rather than the bond's yield. (Suggestion: you might find the discussion of call-adjusted duration, Chapter 2, to be a useful framework for organizing your calculation).
e) Briefly explain why the sensitivity of the risky issue to the riskless rate, as measured in (d) is less than that of the equivalent riskless issue.

Footnotes

[1] See Clifford W. Smith, Charles W. Smithson, and D. Sykes Wilford, "Managing Financial Risk," *Continental Bank Journal of Applied Corporate Finance*, 1, (Winter 1989), 27–48.

[2] Bonds have also been issued in which the coupon payments contain option elements. In 1988, for example, Magma Copper Company issued 10-year notes which called for coupon payments indexed to prevailing copper prices, subject to maximum and minimum levels. The ceiling coupon payment effectively represents a put option held by the issuer, while the coupon floor level represents a call option held by the bondholder. See

Charles W. Smithson and Donald H. Chew, "The Uses of Hybrid Debt in Managing Corporate Risk," *Continental Bank Journal of Applied Corporate Finance*, 4, (Winter 1992), 79–89.

[3] An additional subtlety, which is ignored here for simplicity, is the fact that the company issues new shares when the bonds are converted. Anticipated dilution will be reflected in the company's share price, but there may still be some further adjustment in the stock price when this anticipation becomes a reality.

[4] The reader can also verify this principle by letting the bonds' value at each node be the maximum of the value of waiting another period and the value of converting at that node. It will be seen that the value of waiting exceeds the value of immediate conversion at every node prior to maturity.

[5] When performing these calculations with a spreadsheet, it is easier to consider the bondholders' and issuer's optimal strategies all at once. If the bond is called at any given node prior to maturity, bondholders can choose the maximum of either the call price or the conversion value. The bond issuer will then decide whether or not to call by choosing the minimum of the value bondholders will have if the bonds are called and the value they will have if we wait for another period.

[6] The bonds would also be called in the second period if stock prices moved up twice in succession (to a level of $57.60) and if the bonds had not already been called. However, since we can reach this node only by passing through a node where the bonds are called, the second-period node is irrelevant to the value of the call provision.

[7] See Fischer Black and Myron Scholes, "The Pricing of Options and Corporate Liabilities," *Journal of Political Economy*, 81, (May–June 1973), 637–654.

[8] A limitation of this analysis is that, strictly speaking, the formula can be used only when the company has zero-coupon debt. In that case, making the single payment at maturity or defaulting corresponds to the choice of whether or not to exercise a European call option at maturity. Coupon-paying debt is more complicated, since it represents a compound option, as discussed later in this section.

[9] See Robert A. Jarrow and Maureen O'Hara, "Primes and Scores: An Essay on Market Imperfections," *Journal of Finance*, 44, (December 1989), for empirical evidence that transaction costs and other factors kept this pricing relationship from being perfectly enforced.

[10] See Andrew H. Chen and John W. Kensinger, "Uncommon Equity," *Continental Bank Journal of Applied Corporate Finance*, 5, (Spring 1992), 36–43, for further discussion and description of equity securities with put option features.

[11] There are some special problems involved in valuing options on real assets, since if these assets are not traded it may be difficult to form the types of portfolios that underlie no-arbitrage option pricing arguments. This problem is discussed further in Robert S. Pindyck, "Irreversibility, Uncertainty and Investment," *Journal of Economic Literature*, 29, (September 1991), 1110–1148.

8

Forward and Futures Contracts

I. BASIC CHARACTERISTICS OF FORWARD AND FUTURES CONTRACTS

Forward and futures contracts represent firm commitments to buy or sell a specified asset on a specified future date at a price that is specified today. The fundamental difference, then, between option contracts and forward and futures contracts is that owning an option confers the *right* to buy or sell, whereas forward and futures contracts entail *obligations* to buy or sell.[1] An obligation to make a future sale is referred to as a short position, while an obligation to make a future purchase is a long position.

Forward and futures contracts can be used either to hedge against or speculate on changes in the price of the underlying asset. For example, a farmer who will soon harvest a wheat crop can hedge against changes in the price of wheat between now and the time the wheat is actually sold by selling wheat for future delivery (that is, taking a short position in wheat futures). Since the farmer can deliver the crop to satisfy his obligation to sell, he has effectively locked in a price at which the future sale will take place. Alternatively, an investor could speculate on wheat prices by taking a long or short position in the futures market without having either the wheat available to make a future sale or the cash available to make a future purchase. In a rough sense, the price that is determined in the futures market today represents market participants' best guess as to the wheat price that will actually prevail on the contract's delivery date. If an investor feels that this guess is too low, she could buy wheat for future delivery. On the delivery date, she could simultaneously take delivery of the wheat from the futures contract and

167

sell that wheat on the cash or spot market, using the proceeds from the spot sale to settle her purchase obligation from the futures contract. If she turns out to be right that the futures price is an underestimate of the future spot price, she will earn more from her spot sale than she has to pay to settle her futures purchase, and she can pocket the difference.

The difference between forward and futures contracts lies in the standardized features of futures contracts. A forward contract can be struck between any two parties, and its features can be custom-tailored to suit both parties' mutual needs or desires. Foreign currencies and the huge market for interest rate and currency swaps are two of the primary areas in which forward contracts are common. In both areas, commercial banks are among the predominant dealers, or market makers.

Futures contracts, on the other hand, are traded on organized securities exchanges (for example, the Chicago Board of Trade). Trading is confined to contracts on underlying assets of a few carefully specified deliverable grades, and these contracts expire on a single specified date in each of a list of delivery months. Exchange-traded contracts now cover not only physical commodities, such as copper and wheat, but also foreign currencies, fixed income securities, and stock market indices. The exchange typically specifies daily price limits for each contract. That is, futures prices can move up or down only within these limits in a given day. If one of the limits is reached, and no traders are willing to trade inside the limits, trading is halted. The exchange clearinghouse serves as a counterparty for each investor. For every investor who takes a short position, the exchange clearinghouse must find someone to take an offsetting long position if it is to remain hedged, but the long and short investors need not know each other's identity, because each transacts directly with the clearinghouse. This arrangement facilitates higher-volume, impersonal trading, because as long as each party trusts the exchange clearinghouse not to default, it need not worry about the creditworthiness of the investor with the offsetting position. The exchange, in turn, protects itself by asking each investor to post margin and by marking each account to market each day.

This process is perhaps best illustrated with an example: Suppose that on September 15, 1987, a company took down a $10 million floating rate loan. The interest rate on the loan was designated as the three-month LIBOR (London Interbank Offered Rate) plus 1%. Therefore, the rate for the first three months of the loan was 8.56% (the three-month LIBOR rate on that day was $7\frac{9}{16}\%$). However, the rate was to be reset quarterly, with the first reset date occurring on December 14.

The company could hedge itself against the interest rate risk inherent in the first reset date if it sold Eurodollar futures contracts for delivery December 14. This contract allows investors to make bets on the three-month LIBOR rate, since the underlying instrument is a three-month Eurodollar certificate of deposit (CD), and contracts are traded in Chicago, on the International Monetary Market, and in London. Each contract represents $1 million face value of Eurodollar CDs, so if the company wished to hedge the entire loan, it could sell 10 contracts. The initial margin is $2000 per contract, so the company must deposit $20,000 in cash or Treasury bills with the exchange. This is the company's initial equity in its position, and it represents a good-faith indication that the company intends to meet its obligation under the contract.[2]

Prices on this contract are quoted as percentages of 100. On September 15, for example, the prevailing futures price was quoted as 91.59, which corresponds to a LIBOR rate of 100 − 91.59 = 8.41%, or 841 basis points. Subsequently, each basis point's move in the futures price results in a credit or debit to the company's margin account of $25 per contract. Because the rate in question is an annualized quarterly rate, each extra annualized basis point on a $1 million CD corresponds to ($1MM) × (.0001/4) = $25 in quarterly interest.

On September 16, the futures price rose to 91.61. Because the company was a seller, this result means that the price had moved against it. If September 16 were the delivery date, the company would have to settle its contract by buying in the spot market for 91.61 and then selling on its futures contract for 91.59. Daily marking to market essentially means that the exchange acts as if each succeeding day is the delivery date, and thus it credits or debits each investor's margin account with that day's gains or losses. Since the price has moved against the company by 2 basis points on September 16, the company's account is debited by $500 ($25 per basis point times 10 contracts).

On subsequent days during the life of the contract, the futures price and the company's margin account moved as shown in Table 8.1.

TABLE 8.1   Daily marking to market on a Eurodollar futures contract, 1987

DATE	QUOTED PRICE	PRICE CHANGE FROM PREVIOUS DAY	(PRICE CHANGE) × 100 × 25 × 10	EQUITY
Sept. 15	91.59	—	—	$20,000
Sept. 16	91.61	+ .02	− 500	19,500
Sept. 17	91.62	+ .01	− 250	19,250
Sept. 18	91.73	+ .11	− 2750	16,500
Sept. 21	91.69	− .04	+ 1000	17,500
.	.	.	.	.
Oct. 9	90.85	.	.	38,500
.	.	.	.	.
Oct. 29	92.47	.	.	− 2,000
.	.	.	.	.
Dec. 15	91.64	.	.	18.750

During the first month, prices moved down, on balance, and the company gained. In fact, exchange rules would permit withdrawal from the margin account of amounts in excess of $20,000. In effect, it could be inferred that, during this period, market participants were revising upward their expectations of the three-month LIBOR rate that would prevail on December 15. Immediately after that, however, the stock market crash of 1987 occurred on October 19 and surrounding days, with a subsequent flight to liquidity by investors and a sharp decline in interest rates. As a result, the company's equity would have been completely wiped out by October 29. In fact, the exchange would never have voluntarily allowed the firm's equity to go negative. Once the margin account reaches a minimum level ($1500 per contract, or $15,000 total in this case), known as the maintenance margin, it would have received a margin call from its broker asking it to post sufficient additional funds immediately to bring the account back up to its initial level ($20,000 in this case). If the company could not meet the margin call, the broker would immediately liquidate the account, hoping to do so quickly before further price movements caused the company's equity to vanish altogether, thus exposing the exchange clearinghouse to a loss.

If the company were able to hang on through this period, however, and keep its margin up to required levels, the hedge would have ended on December 15 as nearly a break-even proposition. On that day, the company's position would have been liquidated, and it would have been free to take the balance of $18,750. The company's annualized interest rate on its loan for the three-month period beginning December 15 would have been the then prevailing LIBOR rate (which corresponds to the futures rate on the delivery date) of 8.36% + 1%. Thus, its total interest bill for the second three-month period would have been ($10MM) × (.0936/4) = $234,000. However, it lost $1250 on its futures position, so its effective interest cost would have been

$$\$235{,}250 = (\$10\text{MM}) \left(\frac{.0841 + .01}{4} \right)$$

The company has indeed succeeded in locking in an effective LIBOR rate of 8.41% for the second three-month period of the loan (although, with the benefit of hindsight, its interest cost would have been slightly lower in this case had it not hedged at all).

Although this example may be a bit extreme, because of the unusual economic conditions prevailing during this period, it does illustrate the importance of the mechanical details of futures contracts. The contract did allow the company to set up an effective hedge, which ultimately would have resulted in a small loss, but in the interim, the margin and marking-to-market features would have caused it to ride a roller coaster of daily price movements and to post additional margin on perhaps several occasions.

Despite the potential importance of these features, however, we will largely ignore them in the remainder of this chapter in order to keep the analysis as simple as possible. Much of our discussion of futures contract pricing will revolve around arbitrage arguments, and in keeping with our earlier arbitrage examples, we will largely ignore transaction costs. Thus, for purposes of the analysis in the remainder of this chapter, there will be no effective difference between futures and forward contracts.

II. ARBITRAGE PRICING OF FUTURES CONTRACTS ON INSTRUMENTS WITH NO PAYOUTS

A. The Basic Spot-Futures Pricing Relationship

If we let S_0 be the current spot price of a security that makes no cash payouts,[3] F_{0T} the current price of a futures contract, with a delivery date T periods from now, on the same amount of that underlying security, and r_f the per period risk-free rate of return, the relationship between the spot and futures prices must be given by the following:

$$F_{0T} = S_0(1 + r_f)^T \qquad (8.1)$$

To see why, consider the profit opportunities that would be available if (8.1) did not hold. If $F_{0T} > S_0(1 + r_f)^T$, an investor could borrow an amount S_0 now, invest the proceeds in the underlying security, and sell the underlying security for future delivery. Then, T periods from now, the investor could deliver that security in settlement of the futures contract obligation. He would also owe $S_0(1 + r_f)^T$ on his loan. He would receive F_{0T}, from delivering on the futures contract sale, however, which would be more than sufficient to pay off the loan and leave a profit. Thus, violation of (8.1) has afforded an opportunity to earn a riskless profit with no net investment.

Similarly, if $F_{0T} < S_0(1 + r_f)^T$, an investor could sell the underlying security short for S_0, invest the proceeds of the short sale in the riskless security, and buy the underlying security for future delivery. On the delivery date, the investor would have $S_0(1 + r_f)^T$ from her riskless investment. This amount would be more than sufficient to pay for delivery of the underlying security, and the delivered instrument could then be used to cover the short position. Again, we would have a violation of the no-arbitrage condition if (8.1) did not hold.

Let us now use (8.1) to check some going market prices for efficiency. Suppose we looked at the *Wall Street Journal* security price quotations on August 4, 1994, referring to trades that occurred August 3. A U.S. Treasury Bill futures contract was available on that day with a September 22 delivery date.[4] The delivery vehicle on that contract was in turn a Treasury bill with 13 weeks remaining to maturity as of September 22, which implies a bill maturing on December 22, 1994. In addition, Treasury bills were available in the spot market on August 3 that matured on September 22 and December 22, respectively. The market prices on these various instruments would have afforded an arbitrage opportunity if we could have used them to create two perfect substitutes with different prices.

Each T-bill futures contract covers $1 million (face value) of T-bills, which leads to two different ways that I could have had $1 million delivered to me on December 22, 1994: (1) I could have bought $1 million face value worth of spot T-bills maturing on December 22; (2) I could have bought one September 22 futures contract and simultaneously bought enough spot T-bills maturing on September 22 that I could use the proceeds to settle my futures purchase. Which was cheaper?

The quoted ask discount on the spot December 22 bills for trading on August 3 was 4.48. The bills then had 139 days to maturity, which implies a spot price (see Equation [1.5], Chapter 1) of

$$S_0 = (\$1 \text{ million}) \left[1 - (.0448) \frac{139}{360} \right] = \$982,702.22$$

Alternatively, the quoted price on the September futures contract for the same day was 95.38, which implies a discount of $100 - 95.38 = 4.62$. For $1 million in bills with 91 days to maturity, this result implies a price of

$$(\$1 \text{ million}) \left[1 - (.0462) \frac{91}{360} \right] = \$988,321.67$$

The quoted ask discount on the September 22 bill, which had 48 days to maturity, was 4.13, which implies a price per dollar delivered on September 22 of

$$\left[1 - (.0413) \frac{48}{360} \right] = .99449333$$

As of August 3, then, it cost $(.99449333)(988,321.67) = 982,879.31$ to provide $988,321.67 on September 22, which in turn, because of our futures purchase, would have guaranteed us the delivery of $1 million on December 22, 1994.

It thus appears that buying spot December 22 bills directly was a cheaper method (by about $179 per $1 million face value) of providing $1 million on December 22 than was the strategy of creating a synthetic

December 22 bill using the September 22 bill plus a futures contract. Following the maxim "Buy low, sell high" implies that we should have bought the spot December 22 bills and sold synthetics. However, if we sold synthetics, we would have had to do so at bid rather than asked prices. The bid discount on the September 22 bills was 4.17, which implies a price of

$$\left[1 - (.0417)\frac{48}{360} \right] = .99444$$

per dollar of face value. Thus the proceeds from selling $1 million face value in synthetic March 25 bills was $(.99444) \times (988,321.67) = \$982,826.60$. This change eliminates some, but not all, of our potential arbitrage profit. Several caveats are in order, though. First, the futures contract would also be subject to a bid-ask spread, but that value is not reported in the newspaper. Second, other components of transactions costs (such as brokerage fees) that are not contained in the bid-ask spread have not been captured here. Finally, as in the examples in Chapter 1, we cannot be sure that the reported prices from these two different markets, the spot T-bill market and the futures market, are actually contemporaneous. In order to execute an arbitrage transaction, we need price quotations that can be used to execute simultaneous trades.

One question that may arise here is where we have used condition (8.1). In our example, we multiplied the futures price, F_{0T}, by the spot price of the December bill (call it $S_{9/22}$) to see if that amount was equal to the spot price of the December 22 bill, $S_{12/22}$. The no-arbitrage condition could be written from this result as follows:

$$F_{0T} = \left(\frac{1}{S_{9/22}} \right) (S_{12/22}) \tag{8.2}$$

But then if we recognize that the price of a Treasury bill, like any zero coupon instrument, is equal to one over one plus the riskless rate raised to whatever power corresponds to the number of periods remaining until the bill's maturity, we can see that $1/(S_{9/22})$ in (8.2) plays the same role as $(1 + r_f)^T$ in (8.1). Thus our analysis in this illustration is equivalent to seeing whether or not (8.1) holds.

An alternative way to think about this arbitrage transaction is in terms of the forward rates that we discussed in Chapter 3. The December 22 bill contained an implicit forward rate for a 13-week bill that ran from September 22 to December 22. Similarly, the futures price defined a forward rate on a 13-week bill that ran from September 22 to December 22. Abstracting from any differences between forward and futures contracts, these two rates should be equal. An example of this way of looking at the arbitrage transaction is presented in Problem 3 at the end of the chapter.

B. Using Options to Create Synthetic Forward Contracts

It is also worth noting that there is an arbitrage pricing relationship between futures and option contracts on the same underlying asset. Suppose we buy a European call option and sell a European put option on the same asset with the same exercise price, X, and the same expiration date, T. At expiration, if the market price of the underlying asset exceeds X, we will exercise the call and the put will expire worthless. If the asset's price is less than X, on the other hand, the call will expire worthless but the put will be exercised against us. In either case, we wind up purchasing the asset for X at time T, so this combination asset position has the same effect as a forward contract.

To be exactly equivalent to a forward contract, however, the options position would have to have a net value of zero today, since neither party to a forward contract need pay any money today to enter it. This condition will be met if we set the exercise price on both options equal to the forward price, F_{0T}, because (8.1) then implies that the exercise price of the options is equal to $S_0(1 + r_f)^T$, and from the put-call parity relationship in Equation (5.12), $C_0 - P_0 = S_0 - S_0 = 0$. If the exercise price of the options is unequal to the forward price of the underlying asset, on the other hand, the prices of the call and put will not be equal to one another, so we will have positive or negative net proceeds from the options position. In this event, if we want to create the equivalent of a forward contract we can combine the options position with borrowing or lending in an amount just sufficient to give us a zero net cash flow today. An example of this type of synthetic forward creation is given in Problem 4 at the end of this chapter.

III. PRICING FUTURES CONTRACTS ON INSTRUMENTS WITH PAYOUTS

A. The Basic Arbitrage Pricing Relationship for Stock Index Futures

In addition to such instruments as Treasury bills, there are also traded futures contracts on stock indices, such as the S&P 500. One complication in pricing the stock index contracts is that the underlying stocks pay dividends. It will prove convenient in the analysis that follows to work with dividend yields, which can be compared directly with the risk-free interest rate. In addition, since we can better control for changes in the underlying stock index value if we work with very small time intervals, we will use continuously compounded interest rates and dividend yields here rather than the discretely compounded rates used in the preceding section.

Suppose that F_{0T} is the current price of a stock index futures contract with delivery date T. If we wished to invest a sum of money today at the continuously compounded risk-free rate, r_f, we would need to invest $F_{0T}e^{-r_fT}$ in order to ensure that we could meet a futures purchase obligation for one unit of the underlying portfolio of securities that make up the index at T.

On the other hand, we could own the index stocks directly. Suppose that the stocks pay a continuously compounded certain dividend yield, δ. If we purchased $e^{-\delta T}$ units of the stock today and reinvested all dividends received in the stock, our holding of the stock would grow at the continuously compounded rate δ. Thus, at time T, we will have $(e^{-\delta T})(e^{\delta T}) = 1$ unit of the stock index.[5]

Since these two transactions represent two ways of winding up in exactly the same position (that is, holding one unit of the index at time T), their present value must be the same. The present value of the first transaction, buying the index unit through a futures contract, is $F_{0T}e^{-r_fT}$. The present value of the second transaction, buying $e^{-\delta T}$ units of the stock now at a price S_0 is $S_0e^{-\delta T}$. Thus, if arbitrage opportunities are to be eliminated, the index futures price must be such that

$$F_{0T} = S_0 e^{(r_f - \delta)T} \qquad (8.3)$$

If we compare (8.3) with the continuous-time analogue of (8.1), $F_{0T} = S_0 e^{r_fT}$, we can see that the dividend yield acts as an opportunity cost. If we were to sell stock now and buy it back for future delivery, investing the sale proceeds in the interim at the risk-free rate, we would be sacrificing the dividend yield that we could be earning on the stock. Thus, selling the stock, investing at the risk-free rate and buying the stock for future delivery is not equivalent to owning the stock all along, unless we adjust for the forgone dividends from direct stockholding.

To illustrate how closely market prices adhere to condition (8.3) in practice, let us look at some market prices from August 5, 1994, for the S&P 500 index. The level of the index on that date was 457.09, while the December index futures price was 459.80. The S&P dividend yield for that date was quoted as 2.83%. The futures contract expired on the third Friday of the month, or December 16 in this case, and the Treasury bill maturing closest to that date, or December 15, had an asked discount on August 5 of 4.63%.

To find a continuously compounded risk-free interest rate, note first that the Treasury bill had 128 days to maturity on October 24. We will cheat slightly and call this 129 days, pretending that the T-bill's actual maturity is December 16, and thus equating it with the delivery date on the futures contract. Together, the asked discount of 4.63% and a 129-day maturity imply a T-bill price of .98340917 per dollar of face value. We can then translate this price into an equivalent continuously compounded interest rate by finding r_f such that $e^{-r_f(129/365)} = .98340917$. Solving gives $r_f = .047337$.

Since dividends are typically paid quarterly, let us assume that the 2.83% dividend yield is a quarterly compounded rate. To find the equivalent continuously compounded δ, we can set e^δ as follows:

$$e^\delta = \left(1 + \frac{.0283}{4}\right)^4$$

which implies $\delta = .0282$. Then, putting together the pieces, $S_0 e^{(r_f-\delta)T} = (457.09)e^{(.047337 - .0282)(129/365)} = 459.55$, which is within 0.05 of 1% of the futures price.

As in some of our bond pricing examples, we would not necessarily expect (8.3) to hold exactly for newspaper price quotations, since these do not include transaction costs, nor can we be absolutely sure that the futures, spot, and T-bill prices represent contemporaneous quotations. Nevertheless, we would expect (8.3) to come very close to holding if we had actual contemporaneous quotes, because it is not difficult to engage in index arbitrage transactions. In fact, as it has become easier and cheaper to trade "baskets" of securities, either on or off the exchanges, we would expect condition (8.3) to be enforced all the more stringently by securities traders.

B. Calendar Spreads

Condition (8.3) can also be used to look for arbitrage opportunities between two different futures contracts on the same index but with different delivery dates. Let us call these two dates T_f, the far delivery date, and T_n, the near maturity date, where $T_f > T_n$. Using (8.3) for both T_f and T_n, taking the ratio of the two futures prices and simplifying then implies the following:

$$\frac{F_{0T_f}}{F_{0T_n}} = e^{(r_f-\delta)(T_f-T_n)} \tag{8.4}$$

If the left-hand side of (8.4) is less than the right, the far futures price is too low relative to the near futures price. Thus we can profit by buying the far contract and selling the near, a transaction referred to as buying the spread. Conversely, if the ratio of the futures prices exceeds the right-hand side of (8.4), the far futures price is too high relative to the near, and we should sell the spread, or sell the far contract while simultaneously buying the near. Such transactions are referred to as calendar spreads or time spreads.

Suppose, for example, that we hold an index portfolio and that the left-hand side of (8.4) is less than the right-hand side. We first continue to hold the index and buy the spread. We also buy a T-bill futures contract that will deliver to us at T_n a Treasury bill that will mature at T_f. When we reach T_n, we deliver our index portfolio to satisfy our futures sale for T_n. We then use the proceeds from this sale to fulfill our obligation to purchase the T-bill under the T-bill futures contract. Then, at T_f we use the proceeds from the maturing T-bill to buy back the index portfolio under our far index futures contract. In effect, we have continued to hold the index portfolio, but we have also taken advantage of the relative mispricing of the near and far futures contract. Looked at another way, we can say that the ratio of the futures prices defines a value of $(r_f - \delta)$. If this implied value is less than the actual market value, we would do better to borrow at the implied value by selling stock at T_n and committing to repurchase it at T_f, and then investing the proceeds of our borrowing at the going market rate of interest in the meantime.

C. Covered Interest Arbitrage

A covered interest arbitrage transaction offers another illustration of the relationship between futures and spot prices for securities that make payouts. The key to this transaction is recognition of the fact that there are always a number of ways to provide a given number of U.S. dollars on some future date. Suppose, for example, that our investment horizon is three months. The most straightforward method for providing a given sum of U.S. dollars three months from now is simply to invest in a riskless, dollar-denominated debt instrument with a three-month maturity. However, we might also choose a roundabout method by first converting US$ into any of a number of foreign currencies, investing in a foreign currency-denominated debt instrument with a three-month maturity, and simultaneously entering a forward agreement to change the foreign currency back into US$ three months from now at an exchange rate that is determined today. If one of these transactions affords a cheaper method of providing a given number of US$ in three months (or equivalently, provides more US$ for the same initial outlay), we should go long in the cheap transaction and short in the more expensive.

TABLE 8.2   Interest rate and exchange rate quotations for US$ and £

		BID	ASKED
3-month interest rates	£ Sterling	$10\frac{9}{16}\%$	$10\frac{11}{16}\%$
	US$	$5\frac{1}{16}\%$	$5\frac{3}{16}\%$
Spot and 3-month	$/£ Spot	1.7535	1.7655
forward exchange rates	$/£ Forward	1.7292	1.7415

To be specific, suppose we face the interest rates and exchange rates for U.S. dollars and pounds sterling that are shown in Table 8.2. Since pound-denominated interest rates are so much higher, it might appear at first glance that we could profit by borrowing in US$ and lending in £. If we do so, we will have to borrow at $5\frac{3}{16}\%$ (you will be correct if you always assume that you will get whichever side of the bid-ask spread is least advantageous to you in any transaction), so at the end of three months we will owe

$$\left(1 + \frac{.051875}{4}\right) = 1.01296875$$

per US$ borrowed. We can immediately convert each US$ borrowed into $(1/1.7655) = £.566412$ (again, we use the least advantageous rate) in the spot exchange market, and if we lend this amount for three months, we will have

$$.566412\left(1 + \frac{.105625}{4}\right) = £0.581369$$

at the end of that period. Finally, at the same time that we lend pounds, we can contract in the three-month forward market to convert these pounds back into US$. Thus, we can convert £ back into US$ three months from now at the rate 1.7292 $/£, so we can assure ourselves of receiving $.581369(1.7292) = \$1.005303$ three months from now. Unfortunately, that is less than we owe on our US$ borrowing, so the arbitrage transaction has not netted us any profit.

If we make a loss going in one direction, perhaps we can earn a profit going back in the other direction. If we borrow a £ now, we will owe

$$\left(1 + \frac{.106875}{4}\right) = £1.026719$$

at the end of three months. We could convert the £ we borrow into US$ 1.7535 in the spot exchange market, and if we lend this amount for three months we will have

$$1.7535 \left(1 + \frac{.050625}{4} \right) = \text{US\$ } 1.775693$$

at the end of that period. Simultaneously with our lending transaction, we can contract to convert US\$ back to £ three months from now at the rate $1/1.7415 = .574218$ £/US\$. Thus, at the end of three months we will have $.574218(1.775693) = £1.019634$. Unfortunately, this amount is less than we owe on our £-denominated debt, and our attempt at arbitrage has failed once again. We are left to conclude that the condition known as interest rate parity holds and these price quotations afford no arbitrage opportunities.

One might ask in what way this transaction is similar to the stock index arbitrage transaction we examined previously. To understand this concept, note that equality in returns from lending in US\$ or converting to £, lending in £ and contracting in the forward market to convert back to US\$, gives rise to the following interest rate parity condition:

$$(1 + r_{US}) = \left(\frac{£}{\$} \right)_S (1 + r_{UK}) \left(\frac{\$}{£} \right)_F \tag{8.5}$$

which can be rearranged to read

$$\left(\frac{\$}{£} \right)_F = \left(\frac{£}{\$} \right)_S \frac{(1 + r_{UK})}{(1 + r_{US})} \tag{8.6}$$

Taking into account the fact that we are using discrete rather than continuous compounding here, Equation (8.6) is similar to (8.3) in that, when we sell \$ for £, simultaneously agree to buy back the dollars in the future, and lend in £ in the interim, we are forgoing the opportunity to lend in \$. Thus the US interest rate is an opportunity cost here, in the same way that the dividend yield is an opportunity cost if we sell stock now, agree to buy it back in the future, and lend the sale proceeds in the interim. Additional applications of the interest rate parity relationship are given in Problems 2, 5, and 7 at the end of this chapter.

IV. COMMODITY FUTURES

Commodity futures follow the same basic principles as stock index futures or other contracts on assets with payouts, but they require further adjustment for storage cost and convenience yield. Storage cost is simply the cost of storing physical commodities, such as gold or wheat, until they can be delivered at a future date. The convenience yield includes any benefits of actual ownership of the commodity that are not available from holding futures contracts. For King Midas, for example, the convenience yield of gold includes the utility he derives from admiring it in his coffers, a benefit that no mere slip of paper could duplicate. For a commodity like wheat, the convenience yield might include the benefit of being able to consume the wheat immediately should a shortage occur in the spot market.

The required adjustments can be performed most readily if we can express both the storage cost and the convenience yield as continuously compounded proportions of the commodity's value. Viewed in this way, the convenience yield is exactly analogous to the dividend yield on a stock index, while the storage cost is analogous to a negative dividend yield. Thus, if we let these proportions be w for the storage costs and c for the convenience yield, respectively, we can use arguments exactly like those in the preceding section to write the no-arbitrage condition for commodities, as follows:

$$F_{0T} = S_0 e^{(r_f + w - c)T} \tag{8.7}$$

where S_0 is the spot price of the commodity.

V. SUMMARY

Futures and forward contracts represent firm commitments (rather than rights, as options do) to buy or sell a specified asset at a specified price on a specified future date. Futures contracts are distinguished from the more flexible forward contracts by their standardized features, including designated contract months, deliverable grades, margin accounts, and daily marking to market. For purposes of this chapter, however, the important feature of both is the future obligation to buy or sell. Because of this, forward and futures contracts have a variety of potential uses as vehicles for both hedging and speculating.

Some of the most useful futures pricing relationships can be derived from the no-arbitrage condition, which implies the relationship (8.1) between futures and spot prices and the risk-free interest rate for securities with no cash payouts. One application of (8.1) is the determination of whether or not the implied forward rate in longer-term Treasury bills is equal to the rate implicit in futures prices.

This no-arbitrage relationship must be modified for dividend yields when we move to stock index futures, as in Equation (8.3). This equation is in turn the basis for determining whether or not index arbitrage transactions are profitable. When we compare Equation (8.3) for two index futures contracts with the same underlying index portfolio but different delivery dates, as in (8.4), we can determine whether or not a calendar spread is profitable.

In a similar manner, we can modify Equation (8.3) to incorporate another interest rate as the opportunity cost, as in the interest rate parity condition (8.6). We can also modify Equation (8.3) for storage costs and convenience yields, as in (8.7), to price futures contracts on physical commodities.

SUGGESTIONS FOR FURTHER READING

Additional discussion of the development, uses, and valuation of forwards, futures, and related financial instruments can be found in the following:

1. French, Kenneth R., "Pricing Financial Futures Contracts: An Introduction," *Continental Bank Journal of Applied Corporate Finance,* 1 (Winter 1989), pp. 59–66.

2. Hull, John C., *Options, Futures and Other Derivative Securities* (2nd ed.). Englewood Cliffs, N.J.: Prentice Hall, 1993.

3. Kritzman, Mark, "What Practitioners Need to Know About Commodity Futures Contracts," *Financial Analysts Journal,* 49 (March/April 1993), pp. 18–21.

4. Miller, Merton H., Burton Malkiel, Myron Scholes, and John D. Hawke, Jr., "Stock Index Futures and the Crash of '87," *Continental Bank Journal of Applied Corporate Finance,* 1 (Winter 1989), pp. 6–17.

5. Rawls III, S. Waite, and Charles W. Smithson, "The Evolution of Risk Management Products," *Continental Bank Journal of Applied Corporate Finance,* 1 (Winter 1989), pp. 18–26.

6. Remolona, Eli M., "The Recent Growth of Financial Derivative Markets," *Federal Reserve Bank of New York Quarterly Review,* 17 (Winter 1992–93), pp. 28–43.

7. Smith, Jr., Clifford W., Charles W. Smithson, and D. Sykes Wilford, "Managing Financial Risks," *Continental Bank Journal of Applied Corporate Finance,* 1 (Winter 1989), pp. 27–48.

PROBLEMS AND QUESTIONS

1. Return to Problem 6 in Chapter 6. Assume all of the same initial conditions (that is, the current one-year interest rate is .10; one year from now, the one-year rate will either rise to .15 or fall to .05; and the current two-year pure discount rate is .095). Now consider the following two problems:

a) Suppose there is a futures market. A long position of one futures contract obligates the buyer to purchase a one-year pure discount bond, with a face value of $1, one year from now. What must be the current futures price on such a contract?

b) How could you use one-year pure discount bonds plus the futures contracts described in (a) to create the equivalent of a two-year noncallable bond? (Think about how you could use the pure discount bond plus the futures contract to create the same pattern of cash flows as on the two-year noncallable.) What will be the current cost of creating a synthetic two-year noncallable bond with a 10% coupon and a $1000 face value? Why must this value be the same as that of the two-year callable bond, described in (d) of Problem 3, Chapter 7, plus the value of the call option?

2. Return to the example of the currency option bond in Section I of Chapter 7. Assume all of the same initial conditions (that is, the current yen/dollar exchange rate = 130, the exchange rate one year from now will either go up to 140 or down to 120, the current one-year US$ interest rate = 8%, and the current one-year ¥ interest rate is 6%). Now consider the following problem: Suppose you enter into a forward contract. Your counterparty agrees to deliver 130 yen to you one year from now. You will pay for these yen next year in dollars. However, even though you need not pay anything now, the number of dollars you will pay in the future (that is, the forward exchange rate) is determined today. If there are no arbitrage opportunities, what should this forward exchange rate be? Is the rate you have calculated consistent with interest rate parity?

3. Look at the example of the Treasury bill arbitrage transaction in Section II.A of this chapter. What is the implied forward rate on the December 22 bill? What T-bill interest rate (that is, yield) is implicit in the futures contract that expires on December 22? Are these two rates the same? How close are they to one another?

4. You can buy or sell European put and call options on the common stock of Forward-Looking Corporation (FLC). Both the puts and the calls expire six months from now and have an exercise price of $45. FLC stock has a current price of $40 per share, and it pays no dividends. The continuously compounded risk-free interest rate is 6% per year. You would like to create a synthetic forward contract that will allow you to take delivery of 100 shares of FLC stock six months from now at a price of $45.

a) How can you create such a synthetic forward contract using put and call options on FLC stock? Do you also need to engage in any borrowing or lending truly to duplicate a forward contract.

b) Suppose you expect the price of FLC stock six months from now to be $52 per share. What is your expected profit from the synthetic forward position?

5. The current exchange rate between U.S. dollars (US$) and German marks (DM) is 0.60 US$/DM. The current yields on one- and two-year risk-free zero-coupon bonds in each of the two currencies are as follows:

CURRENCY DENOMINATION OF BOND		
	US$	DM
One-year yield	.075	.050
Two-year yield	.1033	.060

a) Based on current one- and two-year yields, what are the forward interest rates for one-year loans, beginning one period from now, in each of the two currencies?

b) If there are no arbitrage opportunities, what must be the forward exchange rate for an exchange of US$ for DM to occur one year from now?

c) If there are no arbitrage opportunities, what must be the forward exchange rate for an exchange of US$ for DM to occur two years from now?

d) Can you point to any possible economic factors that might explain the relationship between current and forward interest rates and exchange rates in the two currencies? Does your explanation rely on any implicit theory of security pricing? Briefly explain.

e) A European call option on DM 10,000 expires in two years and has a strike price of US$ 6500 (that is, two years from now the holder of the option has the right to pay US$ 6500 and buy DM 10,000). The current price of this option is US$ 620. A European put option on DM 10,000, which expires in two years and has a strike price of US$ 6500, is currently selling for $670. Do these option prices afford any arbitrage opportunity? If so, explain what the opportunity is and how you would go about exploiting it.

6. The current (that is, spot) exchange rate between German deutsche marks (DM) and U.S. dollars (US$) is 1.72 DM/US$. The current market yields on zero-coupon instruments of selected maturity in the two currencies are as follows:

	ONE-YEAR	TWO-YEAR	THREE-YEAR
US$	4%	5%	6%
DM			4%

a) Given existing prices, what do you think should be the exchange rate on a forward contract in which the parties agree to exchange US$ for DM three years from now?

b) You are the treasurer of a company looking to find the best possible terms on which to raise debt funds in the international capital markets. Your investment banker suggests that you might consider issuing three-year principal exchange rate linked securities (PERLs). Each PERL would pay annual coupons in US$ at the rate of 5% per US$ 100 face value. At maturity, three years from now, principal would also be paid in US$. Instead of receiving a fixed principal payment of US$ 100, however, bondholders would receive the US$ equivalent, at exchange rates prevailing at that time, of DM 162.45. Use the forward rate you have calculated in (a) to calculate the present value (in US$) of the principal payment on this PERL. At what total price, per US$ 100 face value, do you think you could issue these PERLs today?

c) As a second possibility, the investment banker suggests an issue of three-year reverse PERLs. These securities would also pay annual coupons in US$ at the rate of 5%. However, the principal would be paid in DM, and bondholders would receive the DM equivalent, at exchange rates prevailing at that time, of US$ 100. At what total price, per US$ 100 face value, do you think these reverse PERLs could be issued today?

d) A third possibility suggested by the investment banker is that you could issue a three-year bond with annual coupon payments at the rate of 5%, payable in US$. At maturity, three years from now, the issuer could choose to make a principal payment equal to either the US$ equivalent of DM 162.45 or the DM equivalent of US$ 100, both measured at the exchange rate prevailing at that time. Explain what additional information you would need to value this third security. Would its value, per US$ 100 face value, be greater or less than that of the PERLs and reverse PERLs? Briefly explain.

7. The current exchange rate between US$ and UK£ is .7 £/$ (or 1.42857 $/£). The interest rate, r_{US}, on a two-year dollar-denominated riskless loan is currently 5%.

a) Suppose you simultaneously (1) lend $1/(1 + r_{UK})^2$ pounds for two years at the interest rate, r_{UK}, for a pound-denominated two-year riskless loan; (2) buy a European put option that allows you to sell one pound in exchange for $ two years from now at an exercise price $X = \$1.50$; and (3) borrow $\$X/(1 + r_{US})^2$ for two years, where $X = \$1.50$, at the riskless two-year $ rate. Describe the payoff from this strategy two years from now, depending on whether the

$/£ exchange rate prevailing at that time is greater or less than $1.50 per £. How does this payoff compare with the payoff on a European call option that allows you to buy one pound for $ two years from now at an exercise price $X = \$1.50$?

b) Explain why your answer to (a) implies that

$$C = \frac{\left(\frac{\$}{£}\right)_S}{(1 + r_{UK})^2} - \frac{X}{(1 + r_{US})^2} + P$$

where C and P are the current prices of the currency call and put options, respectively, and $(\$/£)_S$ is the current spot exchange rate between $ and £.

c) Explain why your answer to (b) further implies that

$$C - P = \frac{\left(\frac{\$}{£}\right)_{F2} - X}{(1 + r_{US})^2}$$

where $(\$/£)_{F2}$ is the currently prevailing forward exchange rate between $ and £ for an exchange that will take place two years from now.

d) If the current price of the currency call option is $\$.078326$, while that of the currency put option is $\$.258232$, find the forward exchange rate, $(\$/£)_{F2}$.

e) Find the current interest rate, r_{UK}, for a pound-denominated two-year riskless loan.

Footnotes

[1] The first part of this statement refers only to option owners, however. An option writer does have an obligation to sell the underlying asset to or buy it from the holder of a call or put option, respectively, if the option holder chooses to exercise.

[2] It should be emphasized that this margin deposit represents good-faith money rather than a down payment. It is sometimes asserted that futures contracts entail substantial leverage. However, it is incorrect to compare the $2000 initial margin with the $1 million contract size and conclude that the contract has a leverage ratio of 500 to 1. As can be seen in the example, the futures contract holder's position is adjusted daily on a dollar-for-dollar basis with changes in the futures price. With true leverage, on the other hand, gains or losses on the levered asset are magnified 500 to 1 in the borrower's equity.

[3] The reader is cautioned to note that S is used here to denote the spot price of the underlying asset, whereas S has been used to denote the

value of a common stock in preceding chapters. While the underlying asset could be common stock, as in the case of stock index futures, it could also be other securities or commodities. This notation is used in this chapter because it is most consistent with other discussions in the literature that the reader may also be consulting.

[4] The delivery date for the T-bill contract is the first Thursday after the third weekly T-bill auction in the delivery month. Weekly auctions are held each Monday, with the bills auctioned being available on Thursday of that week. Since the delivery vehicle on the futures contract is a bill with 13 weeks remaining to maturity, and since 13-week bills are sold at each auction, this procedure ensures that there will always be an adequate supply of the delivery vehicle available at each delivery date.

[5] To understand this concept, suppose that the initial stock index price, S_0, is 100 and that the dividend yield is 5%. If we start with one unit of the stock index and consider a very short time horizon, $T = .01$ years, the dividend over this period will be $100 \times .05 \times .01 = .05$. Assuming that the time interval is sufficiently short that the stock price has not had a chance to change, the dividend can be used to purchase $.05/100 = .0005$ units of the index. Thus our shareholding has grown by 0.05% over .01 years, which translates into an annualized growth rate of 5%. It can thus be seen that the assumption of continuous compounding is needed to ensure that over any infinitesimal time interval, new index units can be purchased at the beginning-of-period stock price. The stock price does change over longer intervals, of course, but as long as the dividend *yield* stays constant (that is, the actual dividend payment adjusts so that it is always a constant percentage of the beginning-of-period index price, whatever that beginning-of-period price may be), shareholdings will always grow at the continuously compounded rate δ.

II

Analysis of Portfolios
of Securities

9

Investor Preferences and Attitudes Toward Risk

I. THE THEORY OF INVESTOR PREFERENCES

As we saw in Part I of this book, we can go quite a way in finance without saying anything very specific about investor preferences. Except for our discussion of the term structure in Chapter 3, most of our discussion of security valuation throughout Part I relied on the no-arbitrage principle, and we had little need for explicit discussion or modeling of investor preferences, which is fortunate in many ways, since an investor's set of preferences, or utility function, is a very subjective concept. It is resistant to precise measurement, and thus few assertions about investor utility can be verified empirically.

Although the no-arbitrage principle is quite useful in valuing individual securities, its ability to help us in managing portfolios of securities is limited. In portfolio selection, we need to know not only the value of a security but also its risk-return profile. We need to know how one security's risk and return characteristics interact with those of other securities to determine the overall portfolio's risk-return profile. We will find some general principles of portfolio selection that are widely applicable, but ultimately the choice of a particular risk-return combination is a subjective one. We will thus begin our discussion of portfolio analysis by considering investor preferences and attitudes toward risk in this chapter.

A. Expected Wealth vs. Expected Utility: The Concept of Risk Aversion

As modern probability theory developed in the seventeenth century, investor attitudes toward risk were initially ignored. For some time, it was assumed that the attractiveness of a gamble could be characterized by the expected value of its payoff. However, in 1728, Nicolas Bernoulli posed the St. Petersburg Paradox: Suppose someone tosses a fair coin repeatedly. You receive $1 if heads comes up on the first toss, $2 if heads comes up for the first time on the second toss, $4 if heads comes up for the first time on the third toss, $8 if heads comes up for the first time on the fourth toss, and 2^{n-1} if heads comes up for the first time on the nth toss. With a probability of .5 that either a head or a tail will turn up on any given toss, the expected payoff, or expected wealth, $E(W)$, from playing this game is given by the following:

$$E(W) = 1\left(\frac{1}{2}\right) + 2\left(\frac{1}{4}\right) + 4\left(\frac{1}{8}\right) + 8\left(\frac{1}{16}\right) + \cdots + 2^{n-1}\left(\frac{1}{2}\right)^n$$

$$= \frac{1}{2} + \frac{1}{2} + \frac{1}{2} + \cdots = n\left(\frac{1}{2}\right)$$

(9.1)

This equation implies, however, that as n increases without limit someone will be willing to pay an unlimited amount for the right to play this game. Since that assumption runs counter to both intuition and observations of human behavior, it was eventually conceded that expected wealth is an insufficient measure of the value of a gamble.

A resolution to this paradox came in 1738 when Nicolas' cousin, Daniel Bernoulli, proposed that, instead of maximizing the expected value of their wealth, individuals act so as to maximize the expected utility of their wealth. At the same time, it was assumed that the relationship between the typical individual's utility of wealth, $U(W)$, and the level of wealth, W, has the concave shape depicted in Figure 9.1. This function exhibits the property known as diminishing marginal utility of wealth, because its slope becomes progressively flatter as wealth increases. This slope implies that an additional dollar of wealth adds less to the investor's utility when the initial wealth level is large than when it is small, which in turn implies that the investor is risk-averse.

To understand this concept, consider an investor who is offered a gamble that pays $1000 with probability .6 and $0 with probability .4. The expected wealth from this gamble is $E(W) = .6(1000) + .4(0) = \$600$. The utility function depicted in Figure 9.2 also indicates that, with a utility level of 100 (the units of measure for utility are subjective and are not comparable across investors) for $W = \$1000$, and a utility

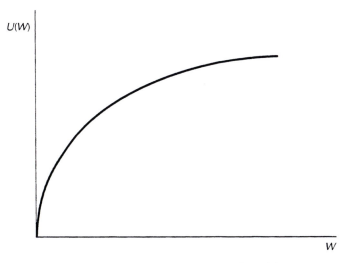

FIGURE 9.1   Investor utility as a concave function of wealth

level of 0 for $W = \$0$, the expected utility of this gamble is $E[U(W)] = .6(100) + .4(0) = 60$. At the same time, the utility function indicates that the expected utility of this gamble is less than the utility of $600 for sure, as is depicted in Figure 9.2, in which the utility of $600 for sure is approximately 90. The diagram also indicates that the level of certain wealth that would yield the same utility level as the expected utility of

FIGURE 9.2   Expected value of a gamble vs. certainty equivalent

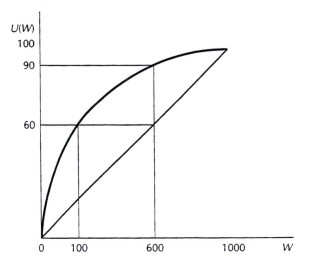

the gamble [that is, the level of W such that $U(W) = 60$] is approximately $100. Thus, the individual depicted here is quite risk-averse, since he or she would be just as willing to accept $100 for sure as a gamble with an expected payoff of $600. The amount of wealth for sure that would leave an individual just as well off as a gamble with a particular expected value, in this case $100, is known as the certainty equivalent of the gamble. The difference between the certainty equivalent and the expected payoff of the gamble, $600 − $100 = $500 in this case, is referred to as the investor's Markowitz risk premium. It indicates the additional payoff the investor would need to expect before he or she would be just willing to accept the gamble in lieu of $100 for sure.

The investor's degree of risk aversion here is embodied in the curvature of the utility function. Consider, in contrast, an individual with the linear utility function, $U(W) = .1(W)$, as depicted by the diagonal line in Figure 9.2. In this case, the utility of $600 for sure is 60, the same as the expected utility of a gamble with an expected payoff of $600. Thus, the investor's certainty equivalent for this gamble (or any other gamble) is equal to the gamble's expected payoff. This equivalence in turn implies that the investor needs no risk premium at all to accept the gamble, and thus the investor is referred to as risk-neutral.

II. MEASURING RISK AVERSION

A. The Markowitz Risk Premium

It is generally assumed that the average investor is risk-averse, at least toward significant portfolio management decisions, but at the same time, that any two given investors can differ markedly in terms of the degrees of risk aversion they exhibit. Thus, it is useful to have some measures of risk aversion that we can use to characterize differences in investor preferences. Since we saw in the previous section that the degree of risk aversion is related to the curvature in the utility function, it is natural to look for measures of the degree of curvature.

One such measure is the previously defined Markowitz risk premium. The difference between the expected value of a gamble and the investor's certainty equivalent tells us how much the utility function is bowed out relative to a diagonal line connecting the utilities of the two payoffs from the gamble, as shown in Figure 9.2. The greater is the risk premium, the greater is the curvature of the utility function, and thus the more risk-averse is the investor. The Markowitz risk premium can also be interpreted as the amount that an investor would pay to insure against a particular risk.

Suppose, for example, that the individual depicted in Figure 9.2 has $600. In the upcoming year, there is a 60% chance that he will inherit an additional $400, leaving him with $1000. However, there is also a 40% chance not only that there will be no inheritance but that a thief will steal the existing $600, leaving him with nothing. Thus the individual has an expected future wealth level of $600, but after the fact, the actual level will be either $1000 or nothing. Suppose in addition that a wealth insuror offers to guarantee the individual's wealth, which means that the insuror will fully reimburse any losses due to theft but also that the individual must relinquish to the insuror his claim on any inherited money. The individual will thus have gross wealth of $600, regardless of which outcome occurs. The insuror will also charge a fee for this service, though. What amount will the individual be willing to pay to enter this bargain? According to Figure 9.2, the answer is $500, the individual's Markowitz risk premium, because the individual will be just as well off with a certain wealth of $100 as he is with his current uncertain wealth, which has an expected value of $600. Thus, if he pays $500 for the insurance, he will have $100, regardless of which outcome occurs.

B. The Arrow-Pratt Measures

Kenneth Arrow and John Pratt defined two alternative measures of risk aversion, based on the insight that the degree of curvature in a function is related to its second derivative.[1] In this sense, the measures are similar to the convexity concept, which as we saw in Chapter 2, measures the curvature of the price-yield relationship for a bond. The first of these measures is the coefficient of absolute risk aversion, defined as follows:

$$ARA = -\frac{U''(W)}{U'(W)} \qquad (9.2)$$

where U' and U'' are the first and second derivatives, respectively, of the individual's utility function. For a utility function with positive but diminishing marginal utility, as depicted in Figures 9.1 and 9.2, the first derivative will be positive while the second is negative, so the negative sign in front makes the whole coefficient positive.

The second measure is the coefficient of relative risk aversion, defined as follows:

$$RRA = -W\frac{U''(W)}{U'(W)} \qquad (9.3)$$

Slightly rearranged, *RRA* can also be interpreted as an elasticity, as follows:

$$RRA = -W\frac{U''(W)}{U'(W)} = -W\left(\frac{\dfrac{d^2U}{dW^2}}{\dfrac{dU}{dW}}\right) = -\frac{d\left(\dfrac{dU}{dW}\right)\Big/\dfrac{dU}{dW}}{\left(\dfrac{dW}{W}\right)} \quad (9.4)$$

That is, *RRA* measures the percentage change in marginal utility given a percentage change in the individual's wealth. By contrast, *ARA*, which differs only by omitting the *W*, measures the percentage change in marginal utility, given an absolute change in wealth.

Intuitively, one would expect the coefficient of absolute risk aversion for a given individual to decrease with wealth, while the coefficient of relative risk aversion might be roughly constant across different wealth levels. That is, an individual starting with $100 would probably be more cautious about entering a bet in which she could win or lose $100 than she would be if she started with $1 million. At the same time, however, she might have similar feelings about a bet that could win or lose her 10% of her wealth whether she started with $100 or $1,000,000.

This intuition can then be used to check the reasonableness of various mathematical functions that might represent the utility function. Consider, for example, the following quadratic utility function:

$$U(W) = aW - bW^2 \quad (9.5)$$

where *a* and *b* are constants. This function has been used to justify making portfolio decisions based on the mean and variance of the probability distributions of security returns. However, as shown in the Appendix to this chapter, it has the undesirable properties that both *ARA* and *RRA* increase with wealth, so it implies that investors become more averse to risk, both absolutely and in relative terms, as they become wealthier.

Two alternative utility functions that exhibit decreasing absolute but constant relative risk aversion are the power function,

$$U(W) = -W^{-1} \quad (9.6)$$

and the logarithmic function,

$$U(W) = \ln W \quad (9.7)$$

The properties of these functions are demonstrated in the Appendix.

III. A MEAN-VARIANCE UTILITY FUNCTION

In the next chapter, we will find it convenient to have investors base their portfolio choices on the mean and variance of security return distributions. One way to justify this approach is to assume that investors have quadratic utilities, but as we saw in the previous section, that function has some undesirable properties. Alternatively, it can be shown that, if security returns are normally distributed and investors have constant relative risk aversion, their utility functions can be represented as follows:[2]

$$U(\tilde{R}_p) = E(\tilde{R}_p) - \frac{1}{2} A \sigma^2(\tilde{R}_p) \qquad (9.8)$$

where $\tilde{R}_p$ is the uncertain return on the investor's portfolio, $E(\tilde{R}_p)$ is the expectation, or mean, of that return distribution, and $\sigma^2(\tilde{R}_p)$ is the variance of the return distribution. For notational simplicity, we will hereafter drop the tildes, keeping in mind that the security returns are random variables, and we will denote the variance of the portfolio return distribution by σ_p^2.

The coefficient A represents the investor's degree of relative risk aversion, and, by assumption, it is constant for a given investor. The value of A can, of course, differ across investors. It is because of the assumption of constant RRA that the utility function is characterized in terms of security returns rather than wealth or security value. That is, we can use a constant risk aversion coefficient as long as we are talking about percentage changes in investor wealth rather than absolute investor wealth. We can also think of A as representing the personal trade-off between expected return and variance that an individual investor is willing to make. To understand this concept, think of the utility function as an implicit function of $E(R_p)$ and σ_p^2, in which case

$$\frac{dE(R_p)}{d\sigma_p^2} = - \frac{\dfrac{\partial U}{\partial \sigma_p^2}}{\dfrac{\partial U}{\partial E(R_p)}} = \frac{1}{2} A \qquad (9.9)$$

Equation (9.9) says that A determines the amount of additional expected return a given investor requires to be willing to take on an additional unit of risk, or variance.

Our mean-variance utility function is not without its drawbacks. It is not empirically true, for example, that security returns are normally distributed, although it is more nearly true when one is talking about portfolio returns rather than individual security returns. Nevertheless, this function is relatively easy to work with, and its assumption of constant relative risk aversion is reasonably consistent with intuition. Thus, we will use Equation (9.8) to characterize investor utility throughout Part II of this book.

IV. SUMMARY

Despite the inherent subjectivity of the topic, we need to be able to say something about investors' attitudes toward risk before we can analyze their optimal portfolios of risky securities. That is, we need to say something about their degree of risk aversion, or about the shape of their utility functions.

One measure of risk aversion is the Markowitz risk premium, or the difference between the expected payoff on a gamble and an investor's certainty equivalent, which can be interpreted as the amount the investor would be willing to pay to avoid the gamble. Two other measures are the Arrow-Pratt coefficients of constant and relative risk aversion, which are based on the second derivative, or degree of curvature in the utility function, given either an absolute or percentage change in the investor's wealth.

These measures can be used to evaluate whether a specific form for the utility function is reasonable. A case can be made, for example, that the typical investor might exhibit decreasing absolute but roughly constant relative risk aversion. In the analysis in Part 2 of this book, we will use a utility function that assumes constant relative risk aversion and that expresses utility in terms of a trade-off between the mean and variance of the investor's portfolio return distribution.

SUGGESTIONS FOR FURTHER READING

A review of basic principles and an assessment of the current state of the theory of investor preferences under uncertainty can be found in the following:

1. Harlow, W. V., and Keith C. Brown, "Understanding and Assessing Financial Risk Preferences: A Biological Perspective," *Financial Analysts Journal,* 46 (November/December 1990), pp. 50–62.

2. Kritzman, Mark, "What Practitioners Need to Know About Utility," *Financial Analysts Journal,* 48 (May/June 1992), pp. 17–20.

3. LeBaron, Dean, Gail Farrelly, and Susan Gula, "Facilitating a Dia-

logue on Risk: A Questionnaire Approach," *Financial Analysts Journal,* 45 (May/June 1989), pp. 19–24.

4. Machina, Mark J., "Choices Under Uncertainty: Problems Solved and Unsolved," *Economic Perspectives,* 1 (Summer 1987), pp. 121–54.

PROBLEMS AND QUESTIONS

1. Suppose your utility function can be characterized by $U(W) = \ln W$, and you are facing a gamble in which you stand either to win or to lose $2000. Each outcome has a probability of .5. How much would you be willing to pay to avoid this gamble if your initial wealth were $5000? How much would you be willing to pay if your initial wealth were $1,000,000? How would your answer differ if your utility function were characterized instead by $U(W) = -W^{-1}$?

2. A storeowner faces a probability of .02 that a hurricane will reduce the value of his store to $1 during the next year. There is also a probability of .03 that a hurricane will reduce the store's value to $500,000, and a probability of .95 that no hurricane will occur, in which case the store is worth $1,000,000. An insurance company is willing to insure the store at its current market value. That is, if a hurricane occurs, the insurance company will pay the difference between $1 million and the store's value after the storm. If the storeowner's utility function is $U(W) = \ln W$, what is the maximum amount he will be willing to pay to buy this insurance?

3. Many people purchase lottery tickets. This purchase represents an exchange of a sure amount of wealth (the cost of the ticket) for an uncertain amount (that is, a payoff of either zero or the lottery jackpot). Moreover, the expected payoff on the lottery ticket is less than the cost of the ticket. Many of the same people purchase property insurance. This purchase represents an exchange of an uncertain amount of wealth (the value of the property uninsured) for a certain amount (the insured value of the property). Does this purchase represent rational behavior? If so, how can it be explained?

Footnotes

[1] See Kenneth J. Arrow, *Essays in the Theory of Risk-Bearing* (Chicago: Markham Publishing Co., 1971); and John W. Pratt, "Risk Aversion in the Small and in the Large," *Econometrica,* 32 (January/April 1964), pp. 122–36.

[2] A nontechnical discussion of the justification for a mean-variance utility function can be found in Zvi Bodie, Alex Kane, and Alan J. Marcus, *Investments,* 2nd ed. (Homewood, Ill.: Richard D. Irwin, 1993). This discussion is based in part on a more formal treatment in Paul A. Samuelson, "The Fundamental Approximation Theorem of Portfolio Analysis in Terms of Means, Variances and Higher Moments," *Review of Economic Studies,* 37 (October 1970), pp. 537–42.

Appendix to Chapter 9

The risk aversion properties of some commonly used utility functions can be derived as follows.

I. QUADRATIC UTILITY

The equation $U(W) = aW - bW^2$ implies that $U'(W) = a - 2bW$ and $U''(W) = -2b$. Since marginal utility must be positive (that is, the individual always receives some amount of additional satisfaction from additional wealth), it must also be the case that $(a - 2bW) > 0$. Then, using the definition of ARA in text Equation (9.2),

$$ARA = \frac{2b}{a - 2bW} \tag{9A.1}$$

and

$$\frac{dARA}{dW} = \frac{(a - 2bW)(0) + 4b^2}{(a - 2bW)^2} > 0 \tag{9A.2}$$

Similarly, from text Equation (9.3),

$$RRA = \frac{2bW}{a - 2bW} \tag{9A.3}$$

and

$$\frac{dRRA}{dW} = \frac{(a - 2bW)(2b) + 4b^2W}{(a - 2bW)^2} > 0 \tag{9A.4}$$

Thus, both *ARA* and *RRA* increase with wealth for a quadratic utility function, contrary to what intuition might suggest is typical behavior.

II. POWER FUNCTION UTILITY

The equation $U(W) = -W^{-1}$ implies $U'(W) = 1/W^2$ and $U''(W) = -2/W^3$. It may seem odd, incidentally, that the utility level is negative with the power function. However, the actual value of utility is somewhat arbitrary. What is important is that marginal utility is always positive (that is, more wealth is preferred to less) and also diminishing. Using (9.2) and (9.3), $ARA = 2/W$, and $RRA = 2$. Thus, $dARA/dW = -2/W^2 < 0$, and $dRRA/dW = 0$.

III. LOGARITHMIC UTILITY

The equation $U(W) = \ln W$ implies $U'(W) = 1/W$ and $U''(W) = -1/W^2$. Using (9.2) and (9.3), $ARA = 1/W$, and $RRA = 1$. Thus, $dARA/dW = -1/W^2 < 0$, while $dRRA/dW = 0$. Both the power and logarithmic utility functions, then, exhibit decreasing absolute but constant relative risk aversion.

10

Fundamentals of Portfolio Analysis: The Generic Portfolio Problems

I. PROPERTIES OF MEAN AND VARIANCE

Now that we have some general principles in hand concerning investor choices in the face of risk, we are ready to begin the analysis of investor portfolio selection. In this chapter, we will examine some basic, or generic, portfolio problems. The principles and techniques emerging from these problems can be combined in various ways to design a wide range of portfolio strategies. In subsequent chapters, especially Chapter 12, we will then employ these basic tools to analyze more complex portfolio problems.

If we assume that all investors have utility functions of the form given in Equation (9.8), the mean and variance of security and portfolio return distributions will be the focus of investors' attention as they make their portfolio choices. In view of the importance of these two characteristics, it will be useful at the outset to review some basic properties of mean and variance as well as the covariance between two securities' returns.

A. Definitions

Suppose we have a security, x, whose random return, $\tilde{r}_x$, can take on any one of S possible values, depending on which state of the world or economic scenario, s, occurs. If $\tilde{r}_x$ takes on the value r_{xs} when state s occurs, and if the probability of state s occurring is p_s, the mean, or expected value, of security x's return distribution is defined as:

$$E(r_x) = \sum_{s=1}^{S} r_{xs} p_s \qquad (10.1)$$

Thus, the mean return is a probability-weighted average of the different possible returns on the security. The variance, which measures the degree of variation in the possible returns around this mean value, is defined as follows:

$$\sigma_x^2 = \sum_{s=1}^{S} [r_{xs} - E(r_x)]^2 p_s \qquad (10.2)$$

We will use the variance as our measure of risk. It should be noted, however, that by squaring the terms in the summation in Equation (10.2), the variance gives the same treatment to returns that are above the mean that it does to returns below the mean. One might well argue that a measure that places greater emphasis on deviations below the mean would give a better picture of the types of deviations that investors wish to avoid. Our justification for sticking with the variance is that portfolio return distributions tend to be more nearly symmetrical than those of individual securities, in which case a symmetrical measure of risk is perfectly acceptable. Nonetheless, it is worthwhile to keep in mind that the variance is a better risk measure for portfolios than it is for individual securities.

In the analysis that follows, we will also have occasion to use the standard deviation, σ_x, which is just the positive square root of the variance, as follows:

$$\sigma_x = \sqrt{\sigma_x^2} \qquad (10.3)$$

This expression is sometimes more convenient to work with, since it is measured in units (for example, percentage rates of return) that are comparable to those in which mean returns are measured.

Finally, when we are working with two securities, x and y, it will be useful to have a measure of the extent to which their returns vary in the same or opposite directions, given a particular economic scenario. Thus we define the covariance between their returns as follows:

$$\text{cov}(r_x, r_y) = \sum_{s=1}^{S} [r_{xs} - E(r_x)][r_{ys} - E(r_y)]p_s \qquad (10.4)$$

Note that if the returns on both x and y are either above or below their means in the same economic scenario, this difference contributes positively to the covariance. On the other hand, if the return on one of the securities exceeds its mean in the same scenario in which the return on the other security falls below its mean, this difference contributes negatively to the covariance. It is in this sense that the covariance is a measure of the degree to which the two securities' returns vary together.

It is also convenient, on occasions, to work with a measure of covariation that is standardized for the sizes of the two securities' return standard deviations. Thus we define the correlation coefficient, ρ_{xy}, by dividing the covariance by the product of the respective standard deviations of the two securities, as follows:

$$\rho_{xy} = \frac{\text{cov}(r_x, r_y)}{\sigma_x \sigma_y} \tag{10.5}$$

The correlation coefficient takes on values between $+1$ and -1.

It should also be noted that, while expressions like (10.1), (10.2), and (10.4) are similar in form to those found in statistics books for calculating sample means, variances, and covariances, their meaning here is rather different. In principle, the possible returns and probabilities of their occurrence are all forward-looking here, since we are dealing with future states of the world and their effect on different securities' returns. In practical applications, it is not uncommon to calculate sample means, variances, and covariances from past security returns and to use these as approximations to the inputs needed to solve portfolio problems. It should be emphasized, however, that these values are only approximations, predicated on the assumption that the future will be like the past, whereas expressions such as (10.1), (10.2), and (10.4) refer to the true characteristics of the probability distributions of security returns.

B. Securities Whose Returns Are Linearly Related to Those of Another Security

We will have occasion in the analysis that follows to calculate means, variances, and covariances for securities whose returns are a linear transformation of some other security's returns. This term simply means that the return in any given economic scenario on one security can be found by multiplying and/or adding a constant to the return on the other security. Thus the returns on securities x and y are linearly related if $r_{ys} = a + br_{xs}$ for all of the possible states of the world. If that is the case, it can be shown that the mean and variance of security y's return distribution and its covariance with some other security z's return distribution are calculated as follows:

$$E(r_y) = a + bE(r_x) \tag{10.6}$$

$$\sigma_y^2 = b^2\sigma_x^2 \tag{10.7}$$

$$\text{cov}(r_y, r_z) = b\text{cov}(r_x, r_z) \tag{10.8}$$

These three expressions can be derived by substituting the relationship $r_{ys} = a + br_{xs}$ into Equations (10.1), (10.2), and (10.4), respectively, and simplifying. They are useful in portfolio analysis, since we can think of portfolios as linear, weighted combinations of individual securities. They will also prove useful in the active-passive portfolio management application in Chapter 12, where we will assume that one component of each security's return bears a linear relationship to that of the overall market portfolio.

C. Portfolio Mean and Variance

We will also have occasion to calculate means and variances for portfolios of securities whose returns are not linearly related. For a two-security portfolio, consisting of securities x and y, with the fraction a_x of the portfolio invested in x and $(1 - a_x)$ invested in y, the mean and variance of the portfolio's returns can be expressed as follows:

$$E(r_p) = a_x E(r_x) + (1 - a_x)E(r_y) \tag{10.9}$$

$$\begin{aligned} \sigma_p^2 &= a_x^2\sigma_x^2 + (1 - a_x)^2\sigma_y^2 + 2a_x(1 - a_x)\text{cov}(r_x, r_y) \\ &= a_x^2\sigma_x^2 + (1 - a_x)^2\sigma_y^2 + 2a_x(1 - a_x)\rho_{xy}\sigma_x\sigma_y \end{aligned} \tag{10.10}$$

More generally, for a portfolio with n securities, $1, 2, \ldots, n$, and portfolio weights $a_1, a_2, \ldots, a_n$ such that $\Sigma_{i=1}^n a_i = 1$, the mean and variance of the portfolio return distribution are given by the following:

$$E(r_p) = \sum_{i=1}^n a_i E(r_i) \tag{10.11}$$

$$\sigma_p^2 = \sum_{i=1}^n a_i^2\sigma_i^2 + \sum\sum_{i \neq j} a_i a_j \text{cov}(r_i, r_j) \tag{10.12}$$

II. THE GENERIC PORTFOLIO PROBLEMS

Using the definitions and properties outlined above, plus the mean-variance utility function defined in Equation (9.8), we will now solve a series of generic portfolio problems. With the solutions to these problems in hand, we will be able to gain insight into a number of more complex portfolio management problems by identifying them as variations on or combinations of these generic problems.

A. Portfolio Problem 1: A Risk-Free Asset and One Risky Asset

The simplest of the generic portfolio problems concerns the optimal combination of a risk-free asset with one risky asset. The risk-free asset has a certain return, r_f (and therefore zero variance), while the risky asset, x, has an expected return, $E(r_x)$, and a variance of return, σ_x^2. We will first examine the set of investment opportunities presented by this choice and then apply the investor's utility function to find the optimal point. If these two assets are the only possible choices and the investor allocates the fraction a_x of the total portfolio to asset x, $(1 - a_x)$ is necessarily allocated to the risk-free asset. Thus, from (10.9) and (10.10), the mean and variance of the portfolio return are given by the following:

$$E(r_p) = a_x E(r_x) + (1 - a_x) r_f \tag{10.13}$$

$$\sigma_p^2 = a_x^2 \sigma_x^2 \tag{10.14}$$

To facilitate graphing both expected return and risk using the same scale, we will find it easier to work with standard deviation rather than variance, and (10.14) implies $\sigma_p = a_x \sigma_x$. We can analyze how the risk-return tradeoff varies with the portfolio proportions by differentiating both $E(r_p)$ and σ_p with respect to a_x and dividing one by the other as follows:

$$\frac{dE(r_p)}{d\sigma_p} = \frac{\dfrac{dE(r_p)}{da_x}}{\dfrac{d\sigma_p}{da_x}} = \frac{E(r_x) - r_f}{\sigma_x} \tag{10.15}$$

Thus, we find that this trade-off is a constant independent of a_x, which implies that the set of investment opportunities is linear, as shown in

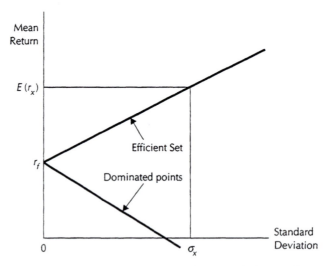

FIGURE 10.1 Investment opportunity set with one risk-free and one risky asset

Figure 10.1. The upper segment, pointing upward and to the right, corresponds to values of a_x greater than zero. Between the points $(0, r_f)$ and $[\sigma_x, E(r_x)]$, a_x takes on values between 0 and 1. Beyond and to right of the point $[\sigma_x, E(r_x)]$, a_x takes on values greater than one, which implies that $(1 - a_x)$ is negative. This scenario corresponds to taking a short position in the risk-free asset and using the proceeds to invest more than 100% of the portfolio's net value in the risky asset. Throughout this chapter, we will treat short positions as equivalent to issuing the security that is sold short. The issuer must then pay the return on this security to the buyer, so taking a short position in the risk-free asset is equivalent to borrowing at the risk-free rate of return.[1] Taking a short position in the risk-free asset in this case entails an increase in portfolio expected return (on each dollar of proceeds from a short sale, the investor expects to earn $E(r_x)$ but must pay only r_f. At the same time, however, the short position entails an increase in risk, since $\sigma_p = a_x\sigma_x$, where $a_x > 1$.

The investor could also take a short position in the risky asset $(a_x < 0)$, investing the proceeds in the risk-free security $(1 - a_x > 1)$. Such positions correspond to the downward-sloping line segment in Figure 10.1. Note, however, that these short positions entail a reduction in expected return (the investor earns only r_f on each additional dollar of short-sale proceeds, but expects to pay $E[r_x]$) and at the same time an increase in risk (since the standard deviation is the positive square root of the variance, $\sigma_p = |a_x|\sigma_x$, where $|a_x| > 1$). Since risk-averse investors will accept lower returns only if they can reduce their risk, this direction is not a desirable one in which to move. Note further that, for any point on the downward-sloping line segment in Figure 10.1, it is possible to find a point on the upward-sloping segment that gives a higher expected return for the same level of risk. In this sense, we say that the points on the downward-sloping segment are dominated. No risk-averse investor would consider one of these points, regardless of his or her specific degree of risk aversion, so we can eliminate these points from consideration and focus our attention on the remaining points, which we refer to as the efficient set.

We cannot say which point on the efficient set a given investor will choose, however, without more specific knowledge of his or her utility function. The investor's portfolio optimization problem then consists of choosing a_x to maximize utility. Using (10.13) and (10.14), this function can be represented as

$$\max_{a_x} U(r_p) = E(r_p) - \frac{1}{2} A\sigma_p^2 = a_x E(r_x) + (1 - a_x)r_f - \frac{1}{2} a_x^2 A\sigma_x^2 \quad (10.16)$$

Differentiating the utility function with respect to a_x, and setting the derivative equal to zero

$$\frac{dU}{da_x} = E(r_x) - r_f - Aa_x\sigma_x^2 = 0 \quad (10.17)$$

and solving for a_x gives an expression for the optimal portfolio proportion, a_x^*, as follows:

$$a_x^* = \frac{E(r_x) - r_f}{A\sigma_x^2} \quad (10.18)$$

Equation (10.18) completely characterizes the solution to Portfolio Problem 1. It says that the optimal proportion of the portfolio to invest in the risky asset increases with the asset's expected risk premium (the excess of its expected return over the risk-free rate) and decreases with its variance. In addition, more risk-averse investors (as indicated by higher values of A) will allocate smaller proportions to the risky asset.

B. Portfolio Problem 2: Two Risky Assets and No Risk-Free Asset

Our second generic problem, like the first, considers only two assets for the investor's portfolio, but in this case both of them are risky. Following the same steps as in Problem 1, we will first analyze the set of investment opportunities.

The investor's expected portfolio return and variance are given by Equations (10.9) and (10.10), and we can differentiate these with respect to a_x to see how the investor's risk-return trade-off varies with the portfolio proportions. The derivative of the expected return in (10.9) is just $dE(r_p)/da_x = E(r_x) - E(r_y)$. To facilitate graphical presentation, it will be more convenient to differentiate $\sigma_p = (\sigma_p^2)^{1/2}$, as follows, rather than differentiating (10.10) directly:

$$\frac{d\sigma_p}{da_x} = \frac{1}{2}\left(\frac{2a_x\sigma_x^2 - 2(1-a_x)\sigma_y^2 + 2\operatorname{cov}(r_x, r_y) - 4a_x\operatorname{cov}(r_x, r_y)}{\sigma_p}\right) \quad (10.19)$$

Then, simplifying (10.19), calculating the ratio of the two derivatives, and using the definition of correlation from (10.5) yields the risk-return trade-off along the investor's opportunity set, as follows:

$$\frac{dE(r_p)}{d\sigma_p} = \frac{\dfrac{dE(r_p)}{da_x}}{\dfrac{d\sigma_p}{da_x}} = \frac{[E(r_x) - E(r_y)]\sigma_p}{a_x\sigma_x^2 - (1-a_x)\sigma_y^2 + (1-2a_x)\rho_{xy}\sigma_x\sigma_y} \quad (10.20)$$

In contrast to the constant risk-return trade-off in Portfolio Problem 1, (10.20) is messy and depends on the portfolio composition, as summarized in the value of a_x. However, we can gain insight into this trade-off by examining it for special values of the correlation coefficient, ρ_{xy}. For example, if $\rho_{xy} = 1$ (that is, the returns on x and y are perfectly positively correlated), $\sigma_p^2 = [a_x\sigma_x + (1-a_x)\sigma_y]^2$, and

$$\frac{dE(r_p)}{d\sigma_p} = \frac{E(r_x) - E(r_y)}{\sigma_x - \sigma_y} \quad (10.21)$$

In this case, then, the slope of the investment opportunity set is constant and hence forms a straight line, as in the case of Portfolio Problem 1. If $\rho_{xy} = -1$ (that is, returns on x and y are perfectly negatively correlated), $\sigma_p^2 = [a_x\sigma_x - (1-a_x)\sigma_y]^2$, and either $\sigma_p = a_x\sigma_x - (1-a_x)\sigma_y$ or $\sigma_p = (1-a_x)\sigma_y - a_x\sigma_x$, depending on the value of a_x. Thus the slope of the risk-return trade-off is given by

$$\frac{dE(r_p)}{d\sigma_p} = \pm\frac{E(r_x) - E(r_y)}{\sigma_x + \sigma_y} \quad (10.22)$$

and the opportunity set can be represented as two straight-line segments, one with a positive slope and one with a negative slope. For values of the correlation coefficient between -1 and $+1$, the opportunity set is a curve that lies within the area bounded by the straight-line segments corresponding to $\rho_{xy} = +1$ and to $\rho_{xy} = -1$. This set is illustrated in Figure 10.2 for a numerical example in which $E(r_x) = .15$, $\sigma_x = .20$, $E(r_y) = .08$, and $\sigma_y = .09$ for values of ρ_{xy} ranging between $+1$ and -1.[2]

Except for the case in which the two risky securities' returns are perfectly correlated, Figure 10.2 shows that there is always some benefit

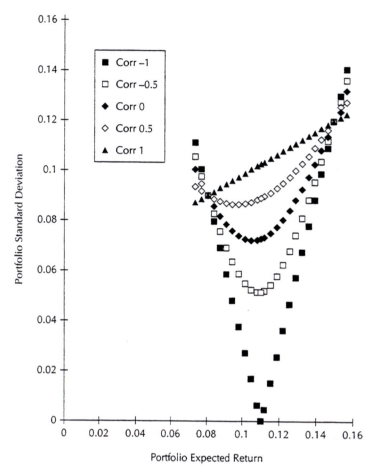

FIGURE 10.2   Investment opportunity set for different correlation levels

from diversifying, or from combining the two securities in the same port-folio. When $\rho_{xy} = +1$, the portfolio standard deviation is just the weighted average of the individual securities' standard deviations, so there is no benefit from combining the securities. As long as the securi-ties are less than perfectly correlated, however, it is possible to achieve portfolio standard deviations that are less than the weighted average of the separate standard deviations. Moreover, this risk-reduction benefit from combining securities increases as the correlation goes down, be-cause the lower the correlation, the greater is the tendency for fluctua-tions in one security's returns to offset those of the other security. For example, if $\rho_{xy} = 0$ or less, it is possible to achieve a portfolio standard deviation that is less than either of the individual security standard deviations, and if $\rho_{xy} = -1$, it is possible to eliminate risk altogether.

It is also useful to note in Figure 10.2 that, for any level of correlation, there is a combination of the two securities that minimizes risk. In cases in which this minimum-risk portfolio includes both securities, this point marks a boundary of the efficient set. That is, points above and to the left of the minimum-risk point are dominated, because there is some other point on the opportunity set that entails a higher expected return for the same risk. In fact, because of its importance as a boundary point, it will prove useful to derive the portfolio proportions that correspond to the minimum-risk portfolio, which we can do by setting the derivative of (10.10) with respect to a_x equal to zero and solving for a_x, as follows:

$$\frac{d\sigma_p^2}{da_x} = 2a_x\sigma_x^2 - 2(1 - a_x)\sigma_y^2 + 2\rho_{xy}\sigma_x\sigma_y - 4a_x\rho_{xy}\sigma_x\sigma_y = 0 \quad (10.23)$$

$$a_x = \frac{\sigma_y^2 - \rho_{xy}\sigma_x\sigma_y}{\sigma_x^2 + \sigma_y^2 - 2\rho_{xy}\sigma_x\sigma_y} \quad (10.24)$$

The proportion of the minimum-variance portfolio invested in y is $1 - a_x$, where a_x is given by (10.24). Additional properties of the minimum-variance portfolio are illustrated in Problems 1 and 2 at the end of the chapter.

We are now ready to solve Portfolio Problem 2. As in Portfolio Problem 1, we first write down the investor's utility maximization problem, as follows:

$$\max_{a_x} U(r_p) = E(r_p) - \frac{1}{2} A\sigma_p^2 = a_x E(r_x) + (1 - a_x)E(r_y)$$

$$- \frac{1}{2} A[a_x^2\sigma_x^2 + (1 - a_x)^2\sigma_y^2 + 2a_x(1 - a_x)\rho_{xy}\sigma_x\sigma_y] \quad (10.25)$$

Taking the derivative of (10.25) with respect to a_x, setting it equal to zero, and solving for a_x gives the optimal proportion a_x^* that should be invested in security x, as follows:

$$a_x^* = \frac{E(r_x) - E(r_y)}{A(\sigma_x^2 + \sigma_y^2 - 2\rho_{xy}\sigma_x\sigma_y)} + \frac{\sigma_y^2 - \rho_{xy}\sigma_x\sigma_y}{\sigma_x^2 + \sigma_y^2 - 2\rho_{xy}\sigma_x\sigma_y} \quad (10.26)$$

Notice that a_x^* has two components and that the second term on the right-hand side of (10.26) is just the minimum-variance portfolio proportion, as given in (10.24). This second term can be thought of as the investor's hedging demand for security x, since it represents the amount of x the investor would hold if her only interest were in minimizing risk. Note also that the second term does not depend on the investor's degree of risk aversion. The first term, on the other hand, does depend on A and can be thought of as the investor's speculative demand for security x. The numerator represents the additional return the investor could expect from substituting a dollar of security x for a dollar of y in her portfolio. Equivalently, the numerator could be thought of as the return on a portfolio with a 100% long position in security x and a 100% short position in security y. The denominator (ignoring A for the moment) is equal to $\sigma^2(r_x - r_y)$, the variance of this portfolio, which we can think of as a measure of the additional risk the investor would undertake by substituting a dollar of x for a dollar of y. Thus the speculative demand reflects the terms on which the investor can speculate or take a chance on extra expected return for extra risk by substituting x for y. Moreover, the investor's willingness to make this trade will depend on the level of risk aversion as embodied in A. The more risk-averse the investor (that is, the larger is A), the smaller the speculative demand becomes. In the extreme, an infinitely risk-averse investor would have no speculative demand at all and would hold only the risk-minimizing proportion of security x. Problem 3 at the end of the chapter further illustrates the implementation of the solution to Portfolio Problem 2.

C. Portfolio Problem 3: Many Risky Assets and No Risk-Free Asset

We can generalize Portfolio Problem 2 by considering n risky assets (with still no risk-free asset). The investment opportunity set can be characterized in much the same way as in Portfolio Problem 2. That is, the set of available opportunities depends not only on the characteristics of the n risky securities individually, but also on their correlations with one another. Most of the points on the opportunity set, as in Figure 10.2, will represent combinations, or portfolios of the risky assets. As before, some of these combinations will be dominated and can be eliminated from consideration, even without specific knowledge of the investor's utility function. The points that remain comprise the efficient set, and different investors may choose different points on this efficient set, depending on their degrees of risk aversion.

Using matrix notation, we can write the investor's portfolio optimization problem, or choice of a preferred point on the efficient set, as

$$\max_{\mathbf{a}} U(\mathbf{a}'\tilde{\mathbf{r}}) = \mathbf{a}'\mathbf{r} - \frac{1}{2} A \mathbf{a}' \Sigma \mathbf{a} \qquad (10.27)$$

where

$$\mathbf{a} = \begin{pmatrix} a_1 \\ a_2 \\ \cdot \\ \cdot \\ \cdot \\ a_n \end{pmatrix} \tag{10.28}$$

is the $n \times 1$ column vector of portfolio weights, or proportions invested in each of the n securities (which must add up to one), and $\mathbf{a}' = (a_1, \ldots, a_n)$ is its transpose;

$$\tilde{\mathbf{r}} = \begin{pmatrix} \tilde{r}_1 \\ \tilde{r}_2 \\ \cdot \\ \cdot \\ \cdot \\ \tilde{r}_n \end{pmatrix} \tag{10.29}$$

is the $n \times 1$ column vector of random returns on the n securities and $\mathbf{r}$ is the analogous column vector of expected returns;

$$\Sigma = \begin{bmatrix} \sigma_1^2 & \mathrm{cov}(r_1, r_2) & \cdots & \mathrm{cov}(r_1, r_n) \\ \mathrm{cov}(r_2, r_1) & \sigma_2^2 & \cdots & \mathrm{cov}(r_2, r_n) \\ \cdot & \cdot & \cdots & \cdot \\ \cdot & \cdot & \cdots & \cdot \\ \mathrm{cov}(r_n, r_1) & \mathrm{cov}(r_n, r_2) & \cdots & \sigma_n^2 \end{bmatrix} \tag{10.30}$$

is the variance-covariance matrix of security returns, and $\mathbf{a}' \Sigma \mathbf{a}$ is the portfolio variance. The solution to (10.27) is complex, as it involves a potentially large system of simultaneous equations. However, it can be obtained in rather straightforward fashion using matrix algebra and a computer. For example, the optimization routines available on spreadsheet software can be used to solve such problems rather readily. Examples of such spreadsheet solutions are given in Problems 9 and 10 at the end of the chapter. As shown in the Appendix to this chapter, the solution has the same form as that of Portfolio Problem 2 in that the optimal weight for any security can be separated into two components, one reflecting that security's weight in the minimum-variance portfolio (that is, the investor's hedging demand) and the other reflecting the investor's willingness to incur added risk to obtain a higher expected return (that is, the investor's speculative demand).

The setup of Portfolio Problem 3 can also be used to obtain an additional insight into the benefits from diversification. Consider, for example, n different risky securities, each of which has the same return variance, σ^2, and any pair of which has the same correlation coefficient, ρ, with any other security. Suppose further that we always assign an equal portfolio weight, $1/n$, to each security. To write the variance for this portfolio, note from (10.30) that there are n^2 total terms. Included in this total are n variance terms, the n diagonal terms in (10.30), and $n^2 - n$ covariance, or off-diagonal, terms. Moreover, the covariance terms always appear in pairs, since $\text{cov}(r_i, r_j) = \text{cov}(r_j, r_i)$, so there are $(n^2 - n)/2$ distinguishable covariance terms. Using the definition in (10.12), we can write the portfolio variance as follows:

$$\sigma_p^2 = n\left[\left(\frac{1}{n}\right)^2 \sigma^2\right] + \left(\frac{n^2 - n}{2}\right)\left[2\left(\frac{1}{n}\right)^2 \rho\sigma^2\right]$$

$$= \frac{\sigma^2}{n} + \left(\frac{n - 1}{n}\right)\rho\sigma^2$$

(10.31)

As the number of securities, n, becomes large, the first term in (10.31) becomes very small, and the portfolio variance approaches $\rho\sigma^2$, the average covariance between securities. We saw in the discussion of Portfolio Problem 2 that, with two securities, we can eliminate all risk if the securities are perfectly negatively correlated. In this case, however, we can eliminate all portfolio risk even if the average correlation between securities is zero, as long as we have a large number of them. More generally, we can reduce risk through diversification by (1) adding securities to the portfolio that have low or negative correlation with the securities already in the portfolio and (2) by combining a large number of securities, as long as they are not perfectly positively correlated with one another. This latter point is illustrated in Problem 4 at the end of the chapter.

D. Portfolio Problem 4: Two Risky Assets and a Risk-Free Asset

We are now ready to combine two risky assets with a risk-free asset. As in previous portfolio problems, we can first characterize the set of investment opportunities and then analyze the investor's choice of a particular point. In this case, we can construct the investment opportunity set in two parts: First, we can examine combinations of the two risky assets, in isolation from the risk-free asset, and construct an efficient set of these risky securities, exactly as we did in Portfolio Problem 2. This

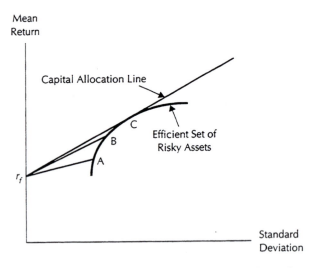

FIGURE 10.3   The capital allocation line and the optimal combination of risky assets

efficient set is depicted by the curved line in Figure 10.3. Second, we can analyze the risk-return combinations that can be achieved by combining long or short positions in the risk-free asset with these efficient combinations of risky assets. Consider, for example, combinations of the risk-free asset with the specific risky portfolio represented by point A in Figure 10.3. Since we can think of point A as if it were a single risky asset, we know from the discussion of Portfolio Problem 1 that the set of opportunities available from combining the risk-free asset with point A consists of the points along the straight line from r_f on the vertical axis through point A. Likewise, the opportunities available from combining the risk-free asset with any other point on the efficient set of risky assets lie along the straight line connecting that point on the efficient set with the risk-free point, $(0, r_f)$.

Examination of Figure 10.3 further suggests that not all of these straight lines are equally desirable. Consider, for example, the straight line connecting $(0, r_f)$ with B. Points along this line dominate those along the line connecting $(0, r_f)$ with A, since for any point on the latter straight line, there is a point on the line connecting $(0, r_f)$ with B that offers a higher expected return for the same risk. In similar fashion, any straight line connecting $(0, r_f)$ with a point on the efficient set will dominate any other such straight line that lies below it and is less steeply sloped. This implies that the highest straight line we can reach will be the one that passes through $(0, r_f)$ and is just tangent to the efficient set. This point of tangency is labeled point C in Figure 10.3, and the line connecting $(0, r_f)$ with C is referred to as the capital allocation line, or CAL. This line is also referred to in some discussions as the capital market line (CML).

It is important to note that we have now succeeded in breaking Portfolio Problem 4 into two parts. The first part consists of finding the efficient set of risky assets and then finding the point on that set that is just tangent to a straight line through the risk-free point. That single point can be thought of as the optimal portfolio of risky assets, since any portfolio the investor ultimately chooses will consist of a combination of that point with the risk-free asset. The second part then consists simply of finding the optimal point along the CAL, or the investor's preferred combination of the optimal portfolio of risky assets with the risk-free asset. Since we can think of the optimal portfolio of risky assets as if it were a single risky security, this second part of the problem is identical to Portfolio Problem 1, which we have already solved.

A word about the portfolio manager's information requirements is also in order here. Note, in particular, that finding the optimal portfolio of risky assets does not depend on any utility information about the individual investor, but only on the expected return, risk, and correlation characteristics of the risky assets plus the level of the risk-free rate, r_f. Any two investors would differ in their choice of an optimal portfolio of risky assets only if they faced different sets of risky asset opportunities, which could happen, for example, if some risky assets were available to one investor but not the other, or perhaps more commonly, if the investors differed in their assessments of expected returns, variances, and correlations. Specific information about investor utility comes in only in the second part of the problem, when we use the solution to Portfolio Problem 1 to find the investor's optimal point on the CAL. Thus, a portfolio manager could solve a good portion of the investor's overall portfolio problem in this context without having to resort to subjective measures of utility. The intention is not to downplay the difficulty of estimating expected returns, variances, and correlations for the risky securities, but this approach does at least limit the necessary information somewhat.

The last step we need is to establish a method for finding the optimal portfolio of risky securities, or point of tangency with the CAL. Looking back at Figure 10.3, we can see that the CAL is the steepest of the straight lines that passes through the risk-free point and still touches the efficient set. Thus, we can solve this part of the problem by finding the combination of risky securities that maximizes the slope of the CAL.

Suppose, then, that we have two risky assets, x and y. The optimal portfolio of risky assets will have the fraction F_x of the total risky portfolio invested in security x and the fraction $(1 - F_x)$ invested in security y.

This risky portfolio will have an expected return, $E(r_R^*)$, as given by Expression (10.9) and a standard deviation of returns, σ_R^*, as given by the square root of Expression (10.10). From Figure 10.3, we can see that the slope of the CAL can be written as $[E(r_R^*) - r_f]/\sigma_R^*$, so our problem can be written as

$$\max_{F_x} \frac{E(r_R^*) - r_f}{\sigma_R^*} = \frac{F_x E(r_x) + (1 - F_x)E(r_y) - r_f}{[F_x^2 \sigma_x^2 + (1 - F_x)^2 \sigma_y^2 + 2F_x(1 - F_x)\rho_{xy}\sigma_x\sigma_y]^{1/2}} \quad (10.32)$$

Setting the derivative of (10.32) with respect to F_x equal to zero and solving for F_x gives the solution for the proportion invested in security x in the optimal portfolio of risky assets (details involved in reaching the solution are given in the Appendix to this chapter, as follows:

$$F_x = \frac{[E(r_x) - r_f]\sigma_y^2 - [E(r_y) - r_f]\rho_{xy}\sigma_x\sigma_y}{[E(r_x) - r_f]\sigma_y^2 + [E(r_y) - r_f]\sigma_x^2 - \{[E(r_x) - r_f] + [E(r_y) - r_f]\}\rho_{xy}\sigma_x\sigma_y}$$

$$(10.33)$$

Equation (10.33) looks somewhat formidable, but it can be applied in relatively straightforward fashion, given the necessary inputs for the risky assets, x and y, and the risk-free asset. With these values, we can solve for F_x, the proportion of the *risky* portfolio invested in x and $(1 - F_x)$, the proportion of the *risky* portfolio invested in y. We can then use Equations (10.9) and (10.10) to calculate the expected return, $E(r_R^*)$, and variance, $(\sigma_R^*)^2$, of the optimal *risky* portfolio. Given these values, we can then use the solution to Portfolio Problem 1, as embodied in Equation (10.18), and calculate a_R^*, the optimal proportion of the *overall* portfolio to be invested in risky assets. The final portfolio proportions, then, consist of $(1 - a_R^*)$ of the overall portfolio invested in the risk-free asset, $a_R^* F_x$ of the overall portfolio invested in security x, and $a_R^*(1 - F_x)$ of the overall portfolio invested in security y. The implementation of this solution is further illustrated in Problems 5, 6, and 8 at the end of the chapter.

One catch here is that it is not so easy to come by good estimates of the initial inputs: the expected returns, variances, and correlations of the risky securities. A common approach is to estimate them as historical averages over some sample data period. This approach suffers from the difficulty, however, that the required inputs should really reflect investor forecasts, whereas the future isn't necessarily expected to be like the past.

A second approach, called scenario analysis, entails taking several broad categories of assets (for example, common stocks, long-term bonds, and Treasury bills) and forecasting how they will perform under various possible economic scenarios that might prevail over the investment horizon. If the analyst is then willing to attach probabilities of occurrence to the various scenarios, the necessary inputs can then be generated using the definitions in Section I of this chapter.

Given the inputs, the investor can engage in tactical asset allocation. Assuming, for example, that stocks and bonds are risky while Treasury bills are risk-free, how should the investor allocate his or her portfolio among these broad asset classes? The investor may have a long-term strategy for doing this, depending on his or her stage in the life cycle and long-term expectations about the relative performance of the asset classes. However, the investor may change tactics over any short period and reallocate the portfolio if one or another economic scenario is believed to have become more likely. Problem 7 at the end of this chapter provides some practice in exactly this type of analysis, using the solution to Portfolio Problem 4.

Before moving on to the next portfolio problem, it is worth pausing a moment to consider the analogue to Portfolio Problem 4 in which there are many risky securities. This generalization poses no particular conceptual difficulties, so we will not treat it as a separate problem. The analyst can find the efficient set of risky securities as in the analysis surrounding Portfolio Problem 3. Finding the point of tangency between this set and a straight line from the risk-free point then gives the optimal combination of risky assets. Once we have found this point, we can use the solution to Portfolio Problem 1 to find the optimal overall portfolio.

Portfolio Problem 4 has a number of applications. Since the optimal risky portfolio does not depend on investor preferences, for example, if all investors use the same estimates of security expected returns, variances, and correlations, they will all hold the same optimal combination of risky assets. Investors will differ only in the proportions in which they choose to combine this risky portfolio with the risk-free asset. In particular, as the number of risky assets becomes very large, investors' risky portfolios will become more like highly diversified index or market portfolios, whose composition approximates the set of all existing risky assets. Indeed, this concept is one of the basic insights of the capital asset pricing model, which we will discuss in more detail in the next chapter.

A variety of potential investing strategies arise from this insight. One is referred to as indexing, or passive investment, in which the investor makes no attempt to predict individual security returns or variances, but resigns himself to the fact that, in the absence of any superior forecasting ability, the analytics of portfolio theory will simply tell him to hold a broadly diversified portfolio anyway. The essential emphasis in this strategy, then, is on economy: The investor wishes to manage, as cheaply as possible, a portfolio that will closely track some broad market index.

While indexing has grown rapidly as a component of many portfolio strategies, however, most professional managers cannot resist the temptation to try to identify at least some securities that will outperform others. Another application of Portfolio Problem 4, then, is the optimal combination of an index portfolio with one or more individual securities that we believe to have superior performance potential. We will discuss this active-passive portfolio problem in more detail in Chapter 12.

III. SUMMARY

If we assume that all investors have a mean-variance utility function, with differing degrees of relative risk aversion, we can find any investor's optimal portfolio of securities under a variety of possible opportunities that the investor might face. To do so, we need to know the investor's forecasts of expected returns, variances, and correlations of the available securities in addition to the investor's degree of relative risk aversion.

In this chapter, we have seen four generic portfolio problems that can be solved in the mean variance framework and that provide a foundation for more complex issues and problems. These include equilibrium models of security pricing, which we will discuss in Chapter 11, and more advanced portfolio strategies, which we will discuss in Chapter 12.

The investment opportunities facing the investor in the four generic problems are as follows: (1) one risky and one risk-free asset; (2) two risky assets, with no risk-free asset available; (3) many risky assets, with no risk-free asset; and (4) two risky assets with a risk-free asset. Problem 1 illustrates how investors with varying degrees of risk aversion are willing to trade off expected return against risk in forming their portfolios. Problems 2 and 3 illustrate the benefits of diversification as both the correlations among securities and the number of securities in the portfolio vary. In the solutions to both problems, investors balance a hedging demand for securities with a speculative demand. The hedging demand concerns a security's capacity for reducing overall portfolio risk without regard for expected return, whereas the speculative demand concerns an investor's willingness to trade greater portfolio risk for higher expected return. Finally, in Problem 4, investors face two means for trading off risk and return: (1) they can vary the proportions in which two risky assets are held, thus working through the diversification possibilities the risky securities afford; or (2) they can vary the proportions between the risky portfolio and the risk-free asset, as in Problem 1. An important feature of the solution is that the choice of the optimal risky portfolio can be made independent of investors' risk aversion.

SUGGESTIONS FOR FURTHER READING

Additional reading on the mean-variance framework for portfolio analysis, assessing clients' degrees of risk aversion, and implementation problems stemming from errors in problem inputs can be found in the following:

1. Benninga, Simon, *Numerical Techniques in Finance.* Cambridge Mass.: MIT Press, 1989.

2. Bodie, Zvi, Alex Kane, and Alan J. Marcus, *Investments* (2nd ed.). Homewood, Ill.: Richard D. Irwin, 1993.

3. Chopra, Vijay K., and William T. Ziemba, "The Effect of Errors in Means, Variances and Covariances on Optimal Portfolio Choice," *Journal of Portfolio Management,* 19 (Winter 1993), pp. 6–11.

4. Frost, Peter A., and James A. Savarino, "For Better Performance: Constrain Portfolio Weights," *Journal of Portfolio Management,* 15 (Fall 1988), pp. 29–34.

5. Jorion, Philippe, "Portfolio Optimization in Practice," *Financial Analysts Journal,* 48 (January/February 1992), pp. 68–74.

6. Kritzman, Mark, "What Practitioners Need to Know About the Nobel Prize," *Financial Analysts Journal,* 47 (January/February 1991), pp. 10–12.

7. ———, "What Practitioners Need to Know About Optimization," *Financial Analysts Journal,* 48 (January/February 1992), pp. 10–13.

8. ———, "What Practitioners Need to Know About Time Diversification," *Financial Analysts Journal,* 50 (January/February 1994), pp. 14–18.

9. Lummer, Scott L., and Mark W. Riepe, "Convertible Bonds as an Asset Class: 1957–1992," *Journal of Fixed Income,* 3 (September 1993), pp. 47–56.

10. Michaud, Richard O., "The Markowitz Optimization Enigma: Is 'Optimized' Optimal?" *Financial Analysts Journal,* 45 (January/February 1989), pp. 31–42.

11. Riley, Jr., William B., and K. Victor Chow, "Asset Allocation and In-

dividual Risk Aversion," *Financial Analysts Journal,* 48 (November/December 1992), pp. 32–37.

12. Speidell, Lawrence S., Deborah H. Miller, and James R. Ullman, "Portfolio Optimization: A Primer," *Financial Analysts Journal,* 45 (January/February 1989), pp. 22–30.

13. Wainscott, Craig B., "The Stock-Bond Correlation and Its Implications for Asset Allocation," *Financial Analysts Journal,* 46 (July/August 1990), pp. 55–60.

PROBLEMS AND QUESTIONS

1. There are two securities in the economy, x and y. The correlation between returns on x and returns on y is $-.4$. Expected returns and standard deviations are as follows:

	EXPECTED RETURN	STANDARD DEVIATION
x	20%	20%
y	15%	25%

   a) Does security x dominate security y? Why? If it does, why would anyone invest in security y?
   b) What is the expected return and standard deviation of a portfolio consisting of 60% in x and 40% in y?
   c) Would any investor hold a portfolio in which y is sold short and the proceeds invested in x (for example, start with $100, sell $100 of y short and buy $200 of x)?

   Suppose your client wants the portfolio formed from these two securities with the lowest possible standard deviation.
   d) What is the portfolio weight for security x?
   e) What are the expected return and standard deviation of the portfolio?

2. a) Consider two securities, x and y. Both securities have identical standard deviations of return. The correlation, ρ_{xy} between their returns is .5. How should x and y be combined to form the minimum-variance portfolio?
   b) Explain why the minimum-variance portfolio in (a) contains no short positions. Would your answer be any different if the correlation between x and y were .95 or $-.95$?

c) Now consider two securities, A and B, with $\sigma_A = .7$, $\sigma_B = .04$, and $\rho_{AB} = .9$. How should A and B be combined so as to form the minimum-variance portfolio? Briefly explain why your answer in (c) differs from your answer in (a).

3. You are forming a portfolio consisting of two risky securities, A and B. Security A has an expected return of 15% and a standard deviation of 25%. Security B has an expected return of 30% and a standard deviation of 40%. Your risk aversion parameter, A, has a value of 2.

a) What is the composition of the minimum-variance combination of Securities A and B if the correlation between the returns on A and B is, successively, -1, 0, and $+1$?

b) What is your optimal portfolio combination of A and B if the correlation between the returns on A and B is, successively, -1, 0, and $+1$?

c) Briefly explain the differences between your answers to (a) and (b).

4. There are 30 securities in the economy. Each has $\sigma = 30\%$, expected return $= 20\%$, and correlation with all other securities of $\rho = .2$.

a) What are the expected return and σ of an equally weighted portfolio of these securities?

b) Would it help to reduce the portfolio σ if you could sell some of the securities short? Why or why not?

c) What would be the expected return and σ of a portfolio consisting of an infinite number of different securities with $E(r)$, σ, and ρ just like these?

5. Investors 1 and 2 allocate their portfolios among stocks, bonds, and cash. Both investors have utility functions of the form $U(r_p) = E(r_p) - \frac{1}{2}A_i\sigma_p^2$, but they differ as to the values of their risk aversion coefficients, A_i. Both investors allocate their portfolios optimally so as to maximize utility. The expected returns and standard deviations of return for the three asset classes are as follows:

ASSET CLASS	EXPECTED RETURN	STANDARD DEVIATION
Stocks	.15	.30
Bonds	.10	.16
Cash	.06	0

We also know that investor 1 allocates her portfolio as follows: 50% stock, 30% bonds, 20% cash. The standard deviation of returns on investor 1's overall portfolio is .1868. Investor 2, on the other hand, allocates his portfolio as follows: 30% stock, 18% bonds, 52% cash.

a) What is the expected return, $E(r_p)$, on investor 1's overall portfolio? What is investor 1's coefficient of risk aversion, A_1?

b) What is the expected return, $E(r_p)$, on investor 2's overall portfolio? What is the standard deviation of returns, σ_p, on investor 2's overall portfolio? What is investor 2's coefficient of risk aversion, A_2?

c) Given the information above, what must be the correlation of returns between stocks and bonds?

6. You are seeking to combine two securities, A and B, in an optimal fashion. The characteristics of A and B are as follows:

	SECURITY A	SECURITY B
Expected Return	10%	22%
Standard Deviation of Returns	15%	40%

The correlation of returns between securities A and B is $\rho_{AB} = .25$, and your coefficient of risk aversion is $A = 2.0$. There is also a risk-free asset, whose rate of return is 7%.

a) In what proportions should securities A and B be combined with the risk-free asset in your optimal overall portfolio?

b) Suppose, in contrast to (a), that you ignore the presence of the risk-free asset. How would you then combine securities A and B to form an optimal portfolio?

c) How would you combine securities A and B to form the minimum-variance portfolio?

d) Briefly explain how and why the portfolio proportions you calculated in (a), (b), and (c) differ from one another.

7. A portfolio manager is considering how to allocate the assets in a client's portfolio among stocks, long-term bonds, and stripped Treasury notes with exactly one year to maturity. The client's index of risk aversion is 5 (that is, $A = 5$). The portfolio manager envisions three possible economic scenarios that might unfold over the next year. In scenario 1, overall economic conditions will be weak and interest rates will fall. The portfolio manager feels that the probability of this scenario coming to pass is .1. In scenario 2, economic conditions will be reasonably strong, but interest rates will rise. The portfolio manager assigns a probability of 0.4 to this scenario. In scenario 3, economic conditions will be very favorable, and interest

rates will hold steady. The portfolio manager assigns a probability of .5 to this scenario. The portfolio manager also projects that, over the next year, the rates of return on stocks, bonds, and Treasury strips under each of the three scenarios will be as follows:

SCENARIO	BONDS	STOCKS	STRIPS
1	14%	− 20%	5%
2	− 4%	11%	5%
3	12%	23%	5%

a) Given the forecasts as described, how should the portfolio manager allocate the client's assets?
b) Now suppose that, after reading the latest James Grant Interest Rate Observer newsletter, the portfolio manager revises his probability estimates. He now places a probability of .5 on scenario 1, a probability of .4 on scenario 2, and a probability of .1 on scenario 3. The estimated rates of return on the different instruments under each of the three scenarios remain the same as listed. How should the portfolio manager allocate the assets in the client's portfolio now?

8. A financial analyst has recently argued that portfolio managers who rely on asset allocation techniques spend too much time trying to estimate expected returns on different classes of securities and not enough time on estimating the correlations between their returns. The correlations are important, he argues, because a change in correlation, even with no change in expected returns, can lead to significant changes in the optimal portfolio. In particular, he argues that as the correlation between stock and bond returns ranges from .2 to .6, the allocation to stocks remains fairly constant, but there are major asset shifts between cash and bonds.

See if you can illustrate this point with the following example: A portfolio manager is considering three categories of assets—stocks, bonds, and cash. The expected returns, $E(r)$, and standard deviations of returns, σ, for these asset classes are as follows:

	$E(r)$	σ
Stock	.14	.17
Bonds	.10	.09
Cash	.08	0

The average degree of risk aversion of the portfolio's clients is 4 (that is, $A = 4$).

a) What is the optimal portfolio composition if the correlation between stock and bond returns is .2?

b) What is the optimal portfolio composition if this correlation is .6?

c) How would you interpret your results in (a) and (b)? Are your answers to (a) and (b) consistent with the analyst's point? How would you explain what is happening as we move from the conditions in (a) to those of (b)?

9. **Spreadsheet Exercise:** A portfolio manager is trying to allocate a client's portfolio among various asset classes. There are six potential asset classes: stocks of U.S. large capitalization companies, stocks of U.S. small capitalization companies, U.S. corporate bonds, foreign stocks, foreign bonds, and cash. Expected returns, standard deviations of return, and correlations between the returns of different pairs of asset classes are as follows:

	US LARGE	US SMALL	US BONDS	FOREIGN STOCK	FOREIGN BONDS	CASH
Expected Return	.12	.13	.08	.12	.08	.06
Standard Deviation	.17	.21	.09	.20	.07	.005

CORRELATIONS

	US LARGE	US SMALL	US BONDS	FOREIGN STOCK	FOREIGN BONDS	CASH
US Large	1.0					
US Small	.9	1.0				
US Bonds	.3	.2	1.0			
Foreign Stock	.5	.4	.2	1.0		
Foreign Bonds	.4	.4	.7	.55	1.0	
Cash	.0	.0	.2	.0	.0	1.0

The portfolio manager has been informed that the client can be assumed to have a mean-variance utility function of the form $U(r_p) = E(r_p) - \frac{1}{2}A\sigma_p^2$, with a degree of risk aversion of 2.0 (that is, $A = 2$).

a) If the portfolio manager faces no constraints other than that the portfolio weights must add up to one, what weights should he choose for the six asset classes?

b) Suppose now that the client stipulates there should be no short positions in the portfolio. What portfolio weights should the portfolio manager choose in this case? How much is this constraint (that is, no short positions) costing the client in terms of the objective function?

c) Suppose, instead, that the client now allows short positions but refuses to own any foreign securities. What portfolio weights should the portfolio manager choose in this case? How much is this constraint (that is, no foreign securities) costing the client in terms of the objective function?

10. **Spreadsheet Exercise:** A portfolio manager is trying to allocate a client's portfolio among various asset classes. There are seven potential asset classes: convertible bonds, stocks of large capitalization companies, stocks of small capitalization companies, long-term Treasury bonds, Treasury bills, mortgage-backed securities, and cash. Expected returns, standard deviations of return, and correlations between the returns of different pairs of asset classes are as follows:

	CONVERTS	LARGE STOCK	SMALL STOCK	LONG-TERM TREASURY	T-BILLS	MORTGAGE-BACKED	REAL ESTATE
Expected Return	.102	.147	.198	.073	.061	.081	.106
Standard Deviation	.131	.208	.353	.104	.031	.112	.154

CORRELATIONS

	CONVERTS	LARGE STOCK	SMALL STOCK	LONG-TERM TREASURY	T-BILLS	MORTGAGE-BACKED	REAL ESTATE
Converts	1.0						
Large Stock	.9	1.0					
Small Stock	.86	.85	1.0				
Long-Term Treasury	.44	.26	.16	1.0			
T-bills	−.07	−.08	.1	.13	1.0		
Mortgage-Backed	.4	.31	.19	.9	.08	1.0	
Real Estate	.14	.03	.23	−.08	.19	−.03	1.0

The portfolio manager has been informed that the client can be assumed to have a mean-variance utility function of the form $U(r_p) = E(r_p) - \frac{1}{2}A\sigma_p^2$, with a degree of risk aversion of 4.0 (that is, $A = 4$).

a) If the portfolio manager faces no constraints other than that the portfolio weights must add up to one, what weights should he choose for the seven asset classes?

b) What are the weights for the seven asset classes in the minimum-variance portfolio? Briefly explain the major differences between the minimum-variance portfolio and the optimal portfolio you found in (a).

c) Suppose that, in addition to constraining the portfolio weights to sum to one, the client stipulates that no more than 40% of the portfolio should be allocated to large capitalization stocks, no more than 40% to small capitalization stocks, and no more than 10% to real estate. What is the optimal portfolio for the client in the face of these constraints? Do you think it is a good idea to impose constraints on the portfolio weights? Briefly explain. What criteria might be used in choosing these constraints?

Footnotes

[1] Throughout our analysis, we will ignore any transaction costs entailed by taking a short position, and we will assume that the seller in a short position has immediate use of the proceeds from the sale, which is not strictly true, since in fact the seller must keep the proceeds on deposit with the broker and must post margin as well. While our assumption greatly eases the analysis, since it allows short and long positions to be treated symmetrically, it should be recognized that it does make short positions appear somewhat more attractive than they really are.

[2] The axes are reversed in Figure 10.2 relative to Figure 10.1 because of the way the graphing feature works in spreadsheet programs.

Appendix to Chapter 10

I. SOLUTION TO PORTFOLIO PROBLEM 3

Before solving Portfolio Problem 3 itself, it will be useful to first find the minimum-variance portfolio when there are n risky securities. Given a vector of portfolio weights, $\mathbf{a}$, and a variance-covariance matrix, Σ, as defined in text Equation (10.30), we thus wish to find the value of $\mathbf{a}$ that minimizes $\mathbf{a}'\Sigma\mathbf{a}$, subject to the constraint that the portfolio weights sum to 1 (we can write this constraint as $\mathbf{a}'\mathbf{e} = 1$, where $\mathbf{e}$ is the $n \times 1$ unit column vector, each of whose entries is equal to one). To do this, we minimize the Lagrangian expression

$$L = \mathbf{a}'\Sigma\mathbf{a} - \lambda(\mathbf{a}'\mathbf{e} - 1) \tag{10A.1}$$

with respect to $\mathbf{a}$ and λ, which yields the following optimality conditions:

$$\frac{\partial L}{\partial \mathbf{a}} = 2\Sigma\mathbf{a} - \lambda\mathbf{e} = 0 \tag{10A.2}$$

$$\frac{\partial L}{\partial \lambda} = \mathbf{a}'\mathbf{e} - 1 = 0 \tag{10A.3}$$

Solving (10A.2) for $\mathbf{a}$,

$$\mathbf{a} = \frac{\lambda}{2}\Sigma^{-1}\mathbf{e} \tag{10A.4}$$

Premultiplying (10A.4) by $\mathbf{e}'$,

$$\mathbf{e}'\mathbf{a} = 1 = \frac{\lambda}{2}\mathbf{e}'\Sigma^{-1}\mathbf{e} \tag{10A.5}$$

which implies

$$\lambda = 2(e'\Sigma^{-1}e)^{-1} \tag{10A.6}$$

Then, substituting (10A.6) into (10A.4)

$$a = (e'\Sigma^{-1}e)^{-1}\Sigma^{-1}e \tag{10A.7}$$

To solve the complete portfolio problem, we now need to maximize the investor's utility, as given in text equation (10.27), subject to the constraint that the portfolio weights sum to one. In this case, the Lagrangian expression is

$$L = a'r - \frac{1}{2}Aa'\Sigma a - \lambda(a'e - 1) \tag{10A.8}$$

and the optimality conditions are

$$\frac{\partial L}{\partial a} = r - A\Sigma a - \lambda e = 0 \tag{10A.9}$$

$$\frac{\partial L}{\partial \lambda} = a'e - 1 = 0 \tag{10A.10}$$

Solving (10A.9) for a,

$$a = \frac{1}{A}\Sigma^{-1}r - \frac{\lambda}{A}\Sigma^{-1}e \tag{10A.11}$$

Premultiplying (10A.11) by e', using (10A.10), and solving for λ,

$$\lambda = (e'\Sigma^{-1}e)^{-1}e'\Sigma^{-1}r - A(e'\Sigma^{-1}e)^{-1} \tag{10A.12}$$

And finally, substituting (10A.12) into (10A.11),

$$a = \frac{1}{A}[\Sigma^{-1}r - (e'\Sigma^{-1}e)^{-1}e'\Sigma^{-1}r\Sigma^{-1}e] + (e'\Sigma^{-1}e)^{-1}\Sigma^{-1}e \tag{10A.13}$$

Note that the second term on the right-hand side of (10A.13) is identical to the value of a that yields the minimum-variance portfolio, as derived in Equation (10A.7). This term is independent of the investor's degree of risk-aversion and can be interpreted as the hedging demand for the set of risky assets. The first term, which does depend on A, embodies the investor's willingness to trade off expected return for risk by substituting

one security for another. It can be interpreted as the investor's speculative demand for the risky assets.

II. SOLUTION TO PORTFOLIO PROBLEM 4

Maximizing the slope of the CAL with respect to F_x requires that

$$\frac{d\left(\dfrac{E(r_R^*) - r_f}{\sigma_R^*}\right)}{dF_x} = -\left(\frac{1}{2}\right)[F_x E(r_x) + (1 - F_x)E(r_y) - r_f]$$

$$[2F_x\sigma_x^2 - 2(1 - F_x)\sigma_y^2 + 2(1 - 2F_x)\rho_{xy}\sigma_x\sigma_y](\sigma_R^*)^{-3}$$

$$+ [E(r_x) - E(r_y)](\sigma_R^*)^{-1} = 0 \tag{10A.14}$$

Multiplying through by $-(\sigma_R^*)^{-1}$, simplifying, and using the definition of
portfolio variance from (5.10),

$$[F_x E(r_x) + (1 - F_x)E(r_y) - r_f][F_x\sigma_x^2 - (1 - F_x)\sigma_y^2$$

$$+ (1 - 2F_x)\rho_{xy}\sigma_x\sigma_y]$$

$$= [E(r_x) - E(r_y)][F_x^2\sigma_x^2 + (1 - F_x)^2\sigma_y^2 \tag{10A.15}$$

$$+ 2F_x(1 - F_x)\rho_{xy}\sigma_x\sigma_y]$$

Finally, multiplying out both sides of (10A.15), collecting terms that contain F_x, and simplifying gives

$$F_x([E(r_x) - r_f]\sigma_y^2 + [E(r_y) - r_f]\sigma_x^2 - \{[E(r_x) - r_f]$$

$$+ [E(r_y) - r_f]\}\rho_{xy}\sigma_x\sigma_y) \tag{10A.16}$$

$$= \{[E(r_x) - r_f]\sigma_y^2 - [E(r_y) - r_f]\rho_{xy}\sigma_x\sigma_y\}$$

from which text Equation (10.33) follows.

11

Capital Market Equilibrium and the Pricing of Securities

I. IMPLICATIONS OF MARKET EQUILIBRIUM FOR SECURITY PRICING

In Chapter 10 we took a micro view of risk and return. That is, we took certain security characteristics (for example, expected returns, variances, and correlations) as given and then analyzed how an individual investor or professional portfolio manager might make portfolio choices in an optimal manner. Now we want to step back and take a wider view. In Chapter 10 we made some assumptions about how any given investor behaves (for example, maximization of a mean-variance utility function with constant relative risk aversion). Suppose we assume that all investors behave in the same general way (for example, they all try to maximize the same type of utility function, although there may be differences in their degrees of risk aversion). Given that securities markets must clear in equilibrium—that is, securities must be priced so that supply equals demand—what does our assumed investor behavior imply about security pricing? For example, what will the trade-off between expected return and risk look like when the capital market is in equilibrium?

In this chapter, we will examine two different models of capital market equilibrium, the capital asset pricing model (CAPM) and the arbitrage pricing theory (APT). These models make somewhat different assumptions about investors and the sets of opportunities they face and, as a consequence, each describes the trade-off between risk and return somewhat differently.

It should be emphasized at the outset that our primary purpose in this book is to develop quantitative tools for investment management

230

rather than capital market equilibrium models per se. Thus, no attempt has been made to offer a comprehensive treatment of these models. Rather, the objective of this chapter is to afford a brief overview of the implications of investors' portfolio selection for the market-wide pricing of securities and to develop some concepts, particularly the distinction between systematic and residual risk, that will be useful in Chapters 12 and 13.

II. THE CAPITAL ASSET PRICING MODEL

A. Derivation and Basic Properties of the Model

The model that flows most easily from our analysis in Chapter 10 is the capital asset pricing model. Let us recall first the assumptions we made, either explicitly or implicitly, in that chapter: (1) we assumed that investors choose portfolios so as to maximize a mean-variance utility function; (2) we assumed away all market frictions. That is, we excluded all taxes, transaction costs, and trading restrictions. Trading restrictions would encompass any indivisibilities in buying securities or restrictions on short sales of any security, including the risk-free asset. Let us now add a third major assumption: (3) we will assume that all investors have the same estimates of expected returns, variances, and correlations for all securities.

Consider investors' choice of an optimal risky portfolio under these three assumptions. We know from Portfolio Problem 4 in Chapter 10 that this choice is independent of the utility characteristics of any individual investor, so if all investors have the same estimates of the security risk and return characteristics, they will all reach the same solution to this portfolio problem. That is, they will all have the same optimal risky portfolio, and the only differences among them will stem from how they combine this risky portfolio with the risk-free security. Moreover, since securities markets must clear in equilibrium, this optimal risky portfolio must be the market portfolio of all risky securities.

To see what this scenario implies for the risk-return trade-off, consider the market portfolio, m, and any one risky security, x. From Portfolio Problem 4, if any investor were to combine security x with the market portfolio, then the optimal proportion, F_x, of the risky portfolio invested in asset x is given from (10.33) as follows:

$$F_x = \frac{[E(r_x) - r_f]\sigma_m^2 - [E(r_m) - r_f]\rho_{xm}\sigma_x\sigma_m}{[E(r_x) - r_f]\sigma_m^2 + [E(r_m) - r_f]\sigma_x^2 - \{[E(r_x) - r_f] + [E(r_m) - r_f]\}\rho_{xm}\sigma_x\sigma_m} \tag{11.1}$$

We know, however, that in equilibrium all investors hold only the market portfolio for their risky portfolio, so security x must be held only in the proportion in which it appears in the market portfolio. This condition means that $F_x = 0$ in equilibrium, which further implies that the numerator of (11.1) must be equal to zero. Imposing that condition and rearranging results in the following characterization of equilibrium security pricing,

$$E(r_x) = r_f + \frac{\rho_{xm}\sigma_x\sigma_m}{\sigma_m^2}[E(r_m) - r_f] \qquad (11.2)$$

Noting further that

$$\frac{\rho_{xm}\sigma_x\sigma_m}{\sigma_m^2} = \frac{\rho_{xm}\sigma_x}{\sigma_m} = \frac{\mathrm{cov}(r_x, r_m)}{\sigma_m^2}$$

is the definition of security x's beta, we can rewrite (11.2) in its familiar CAPM form as follows:

$$E(r_x) = r_f + \beta_x[E(r_m) - r_f] \qquad (11.3)$$

That is, Equation (11.3) tells us that, in equilibrium, a security will be priced so that its risk premium is proportional to the risk premium on the market portfolio and that the factor of proportionality is the security's beta, a measure of its systematic risk, which further implies that the risk-return tradeoff for individual securities or portfolios entails only their systematic risk. No investor is forced to bear unsystematic risk, so securities will not be priced to offer any additional reward for the unsystematic component of their total risk.

Whether or not the CAPM offers an empirically supportable description of security market returns has been the subject of considerable study and much controversy, the details of which we will not have space to cover in this book.[1] Regardless of whether or not the CAPM accurately describes security returns, however, we will find useful its distinction between the systematic risk of a security and its unsystematic, or residual, risk. Applications of this distinction to portfolio selection and performance evaluation can be found in Chapters 12 and 13.

B. An Application to Futures Contract Pricing

Market equilibrium models such as the CAPM can be combined with the types of arbitrage pricing relationships we have seen earlier in this book to generate new insights into the pricing of individual securities. In particular, we can apply the CAPM to the pricing of futures contracts, as previously discussed in Chapter 8.

Suppose, for example, that we have a commodity, i, whose spot price is S_{i0}. For simplicity, we will assume that the storage cost and convenience yield on this commodity are equal to zero (a non-dividend-paying stock would come close to providing an example of such a commodity), so the expected return from holding such a commodity comes entirely from expected price appreciation. For example, if $E(S_{i1})$ is the commodity price that is expected to prevail at the end of one period, we can write the expected, one-period return, $E(r_i)$, on commodity i as $E(r_i) = [E(r_i) - S_{i0}]/S_{i0}$.

Then, if we are willing to go a step further and stipulate that the expected return on i follows the CAPM, we can write

$$E(r_i) = \frac{E(S_{i1}) - S_{i0}}{S_{i0}} = r_f + \beta_i[E(r_m) - r_f] \tag{11.4}$$

where r_f is the one-period risk-free rate, β_i is the commodity's beta, and $E(r_m)$ is the one-period expected return on the market. Multiplying through by S_{i0} and rearranging, (11.4) can in turn be written as

$$E(S_{i1}) = S_{i0}(1 + r_f) + S_{i0}\beta_i[E(r_m) - r_f] \tag{11.5}$$

Then, using the basic spot-futures pricing relationship, as given in Equation (8.1) in Chapter 8, $S_{i0}(1 + r_f)$ must be equal to the futures price of commodity i, F_{i01}, for delivery one period from now. Thus, we can rewrite (11.5) as

$$F_{i01} = E(S_{i1}) - S_{i0}\beta_i[E(r_m) - r_f] \tag{11.6}$$

Given our additional assumptions about the pricing of commodity i, then, the futures price of i is equal to the expected future spot price minus a risk premium that is proportional to the commodity's systematic risk. Equation (11.6) relates the futures price to both investor expectations and, implicitly, the weighted average of investors' degrees of risk aversion (which is embodied in the risk premium on the market). In contrast, the no-arbitrage condition (8.1) tells us nothing about how futures prices are related to expected future spot prices, nor does it tell whether futures prices embody any sort of risk premium.

III. THE ARBITRAGE PRICING THEORY

A. Basic Results of the Theory

The arbitrage pricing theory, or APT, starts from a different vantage point by assuming that the random return on any security, i, during period t takes on the following form:

$$\tilde{r}_{it} = E(r_i) + b_{i1}\tilde{F}_{1t} + b_{i2}\tilde{F}_{2t} + \cdots + b_{in}\tilde{F}_{nt} + \tilde{e}_{it} \qquad (11.7)$$

where $F_1, \ldots, F_n$ represent a number of economic factors; $b_{i1}, \ldots, b_{in}$ represent security i's sensitivity to each of these factors; and $\tilde{e}_i$ represents a random residual return, which has an expected value of zero and which is uncorrelated with the residual return on any other security. The factors can be interpreted as surprises, or deviations from the expected values in n different economic variables. Possible examples of these variables might include inflation, the level of industrial production, the levels of long- and short-term interest rates, exchange rates, etc. Equation (11.7) thus states that, if there are no surprises in the economic variables (that is, each of the factors has a value of zero), the return on the security would be equal to its expected value, except for unsystematic, residual variations around that expected value. If there are any surprises, however, the return on security i will diverge systematically from its expectation, with the size of the divergence depending on security i's sensitivities to those surprises.

Given the returns-generating process specified in (11.7), the APT then goes on to assert that securities must be priced so that there is no room for arbitrage opportunities. An arbitrage opportunity is defined in this context as the availability of a well-diversified portfolio that requires no net investment, has an aggregate sensitivity of zero to each of the factors, and still has a positive expected return. Because such a portfolio has no sensitivity to any of the factors, it has no systematic risk. Because it is well diversified, it has no unsystematic risk, either. Thus, it represents an arbitrage opportunity because it allows an investor to generate a positive expected return with no risk and no net investment.

To illustrate such an arbitrage portfolio, consider the four securities characterized in Table 11.1. The example assumes that unexpected changes in the level of economic activity (as measured, say, by industrial production) and in long-term interest rates are the two systematic fac-

TABLE 11.1 Characteristics of four securities that afford an arbitrage opportunity

SECURITY	$E(r_i)$	b_{i1} INDUSTRIAL PRODUCTION SENSITIVITY	b_{i2} LONG-TERM INTEREST RATE SENSITIVITY
1	.12	0.5	2.0
2	.15	1.5	1.0
3	.22	3.0	3.0
4	.20	2.0	2.0

TABLE 11.2   Example of an arbitrage portfolio

SECURITY	WEIGHT w_i	$w_i E(r_i)$	$w_i b_{i1}$	$w_i b_{i2}$
1	− 0.4286	− 0.0514	− 0.2143	− 0.8572
2	− 1.2857	− 0.1929	− 1.9286	− 1.2857
3	− 1.2857	− 0.2829	− 3.8571	− 3.8571
4	3.0	0.60	6.00	6.00
Column Total	0	.0729	0	0

tors that affect security returns, and the table shows the sensitivities of each of the securities to both factors as well as their expected returns. However, the APT asserts that the expected returns given in Table 11.1 cannot possibly be equilibrium expected returns. The reason is shown in Table 11.2, where four portfolio weights have been found such that the portfolio requires no net investment (that is, the long position in security 4 is financed by the short positions in securities 1, 2, and 3), no net sensitivity to either of the two factors, and yet a positive expected return. If the residual risk could be diversified away (say, because we were adding this arbitrage portfolio to an already well diversified portfolio, or because the "securities" themselves represent diversified portfolios rather than individual securities), this scenario would represent a pure arbitrage opportunity. The presence of such an opportunity should in turn induce investors to trade, thus altering security prices and expected returns, until the opportunity no longer exists. The primary result of the APT is that, when all arbitrage opportunities have been eliminated, the expected return on any well-diversified portfolio must satisfy the following:

$$E(r_p) = \lambda_0 + \lambda_1 b_{p1} + \lambda_2 b_{p2} + \cdots + \lambda_n b_{pn} \qquad (11.8)$$

Furthermore, if we interpret λ_0 as a risk-free rate, since it represents the equilibrium return on a portfolio with no sensitivity to any factor, we can rewrite (11.8) as

$$E(r_p) = r_f + (\delta_1 - r_f) b_{p1} + (\delta_2 - r_f) b_{p2} + \cdots + (\delta_n - r_f) b_{pn} \quad (11.9)$$

where $\lambda_j = (\delta_j - r_f)$ now represents a risk premium that investors demand for bearing the systematic return variability caused by factor j, and δ_j represents the expected return on a portfolio that has a sensitivity coefficient equal to one for factor j and sensitivities of zero to all of the other factors.[2]

To illustrate, let us return to our numerical example. Suppose that the risk-free rate, r_f, is equal to 4%, that the industrial production risk premium, λ_1, is equal to 2%, and that the long-term interest rate risk premium, λ_2, is equal to 5%. In that case, it is easy to verify that the ex-

TABLE 11.3 Equilibrium returns on the four
securities given their sensitivities
to the two factors

SECURITY	$E(r_i)$	b_{i1}	b_{i2}
1	.15	0.5	2.0
2	.12	1.5	1.0
3	.25	3.0	3.0
4	.18	2.0	2.0

pected security returns shown in Table 11.3 conform to (11.9), and thus they are consistent with a market equilibrium in which all arbitrage opportunities have been eliminated. Given these expected returns, for example, the portfolio that is formed using the weights in Table 11.2 now has an expected return equal to zero, which is consistent with its requiring no net investment and posing no risk.

We can also create various kinds of specialized portfolios using these four securities. For example, if we set $w_1 = w_2 = 0$, $w_3 = -2$, and $w_4 = 3$, we create a portfolio with no sensitivity to either factor. Accordingly, its expected return is equal to 4%, the risk-free rate. Alternatively, if we set $w_1 = -1$, $w_2 = 2$, and $w_3 = w_4 = 0$, the result is a portfolio with no sensitivity to changes in interest rates, but a sensitivity of 2.5 to changes in economic activity. Accordingly, its expected return is equal to .04 + 2.5(.02), or 9%. While we can create any number of these specialized portfolios, however, we can no longer combine the four securities in such a way as to form an arbitrage portfolio.

B. Applying the APT to Portfolio Management

A primary potential use of the APT is in tailoring portfolios to meet particular client needs and risk preferences. Since the APT identifies more than one source of systematic risk, it provides some guidance as to how an investor might trade off one source of risk against another. Suppose, as in our previous example, there are two sources of systematic risk: changes in industrial production (factor 1) and changes in long-term interest rates (factor 2). We can find the trade-off between these two sources of risk by finding the portfolios that have the same expected return but different levels of exposure to each of the risk factors. For example, if we set production sensitivity, b_{p1}, equal to zero, the two-factor version of (11.9) tells us that interest rate sensitivity must be given by

$$b_{p2} = \frac{E(r_p) - r_f}{\delta_2 - r_f} \qquad (11.10)$$

Likewise, if we set interest rate sensitivity, b_{p2}, equal to zero, production sensitivity must be equal to

$$b_{p1} = \frac{E(r_p) - r_f}{\delta_1 - r_f} \qquad (11.11)$$

These values determine two points on a graph whose y- and x-axes are production and interest sensitivity, respectively. The set of all feasible portfolios having the same expected return is then given by the straight line joining these two points, and having a slope, or trade-off between the two factors, of

$$\frac{db_{p1}}{db_{p2}} = -\frac{\delta_2 - r_f}{\delta_1 - r_f} \qquad (11.12)$$

Several such equal-return lines are shown in Figure 11.1. Suppose now that we had been previously considering some index portfolio, I. If we knew the two factor sensitivities of the index portfolio, we could plot its position, as shown in Figure 11.1. What the graph then shows us is the set of feasible portfolios that would have the same expected return as the index portfolio but differing sensitivities to the two factors. Suppose, for example, that we have liabilities that are not very sensitive to changes in interest rates (floating rate liabilities, for example). In putting together a portfolio of assets, therefore, we may wish to choose a point such as P in Figure 11.1, which has more production risk than the

FIGURE 11.1 Tailoring portfolio factor sensitivity using the APT

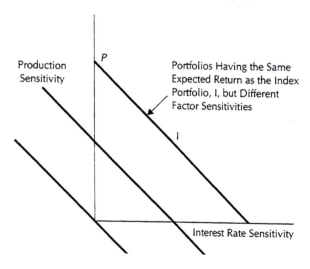

index portfolio, but no interest rate sensitivity. This approach is essentially a generalization of the passive, or index, portfolio strategy discussed in Chapter 10. The strategy is still passive, since there is no pretense of outperforming the basic APT asset pricing relationship. However, with more than one dimension to risk, this pricing relationship does allow us some leeway as to the preferred combination of factor sensitivities we wish to choose, consistent with a particular level of expected return.

While the APT is potentially quite useful along these dimensions, a major drawback is that the theory itself offers no guidance as to either the number or identity of the factors. We must know the parameters of Equation (11.9) in order to apply the APT to portfolio management problems, which means we must rely on an econometric judgment that these parameters have been properly estimated.

IV. SUMMARY

In contrast to Chapter 10, we have shifted our attention in this chapter to the capital market as a whole rather than the behavior of individuals within that market. By making certain assumptions about how all individuals behave within the market and imposing the condition that prices must be such that the market clears, we came up with two different equilibrium models of security pricing. These models are useful primarily in uncovering the determinants of security prices. They can provide some guidance, for example, about how much extra reward the market as a whole is offering for an additional unit of a particular risk. This knowledge can in turn give us a better understanding of the tradeoffs we face in constructing a portfolio.

The first model, the CAPM, concludes that assumed investor behavior will lead all investors to choose the market portfolio as their optimal risky portfolio. This conclusion implies that the risk-return tradeoff for securities or portfolios is entirely based on systematic, or market-related risk, as measured by beta.

The APT, by contrast, makes an assumption about the process that governs security returns. Specifically, security returns are a linear function of a number of economic factors plus an error term that is unrelated to that of any other security. This assumption allows unsystematic risk to be diversified away in large portfolios, and, as a result, the risk-return trade-off is based on a portfolio's exposure to the risk posed by these different economic factors. The notion that systematic risk may have a number of dimensions is potentially useful in constructing portfolios that conform to clients' specific preferences and investment objectives. Unfortunately, the theory does not guide us in identifying what these factors are.

SUGGESTIONS FOR FURTHER READING

Additional material comparing the CAPM and the APT and discussing their use, interpretation, and empirical validity can be found in the following:

1. Black, Fischer, "Estimating Expected Return," *Financial Analysts Journal* 49 (September/October 1993), pp. 36–38.

2. Bodie, Zvi, Alex Kane, and Alan J. Marcus *Investments* (2nd ed.). Homewood, Ill.: Richard D. Irwin, 1993.

3. Bower, Dorothy H., Richard S. Bower, and Dennis E. Logue, "A Primer on Arbitrage Pricing Theory," *Midland Corporate Finance Journal,* 2 (Fall 1984), pp. 31–40.

4. Grinold, Richard C., "Is Beta Dead Again?" *Financial Analysts Journal,* 49 (July/August 1993), pp. 28–34.

5. Keim, Donald B., "The CAPM and Equity Return Regularities," *Financial Analysts Journal,* 42 (May/June 1986), pp. 19–34.

6. Kritzman, Mark, "What Practitioners Need to Know About Factor Methods," *Financial Analysts Journal,* 49 (January/February 1993), pp. 12–15.

7. Roll, Richard, and Stephen A. Ross, "The Arbitrage Pricing Theory Approach to Strategic Portfolio Planning," *Financial Analysts Journal,* 40 (May/June 1984), pp. 14–26.

8. Sharpe, William F., "Factor Models, CAPMs and the APT," *Journal of Portfolio Management,* 11 (Fall 1984), pp. 21–25.

9. Treynor, Jack L., "In Defense of CAPM," *Financial Analysts Journal,* 49 (May/June 1993), pp. 11–13.

PROBLEMS AND QUESTIONS

1. Suppose the CAPM accurately describes security prices. You forecast that the correlation between the returns on your portfolio of risky securities and the return on the market portfolio is .5, that the standard deviation of returns on your risky portfolio is .4, and that the standard deviation of returns on the market portfolio is .25. How should you combine your risky portfolio with the risk-free asset to obtain a portfolio that has an overall beta of 1.2? How would your answer differ if the correlation between your own risky portfolio's return and that of the market were .8 (all other information staying the same)?

2. **Spreadsheet Exercise.** Again, suppose the CAPM accurately describes security prices. You are considering allocating your wealth among four risky securities:

SECURITY	$E(r_i)$	β_i
1	.098	.6
2	.130	1.0
3	.146	1.2
4	.194	1.8

a) How could you achieve a 15% expected return on your portfolio by investing some positive fraction of your wealth in each of these four assets? (Each of your four portfolio weights must be greater than zero and the four weights must sum to one.) What would be the beta of this portfolio?

b) Alternatively, you could invest your portfolio exclusively in either the market portfolio or the risk-free asset. For this approach, what set of portfolio weights will you need to obtain a 15% expected portfolio return? What is the beta of this portfolio?

c) Would you prefer to allocate your portfolio along the lines suggested in (a) or (b)? Briefly explain.

d) Now suppose that all other facts remain unchanged but that, based on security analysis you have conducted, you now expect the return on Security 3 to be 16% rather than 14.6%. Describe (that is, give a qualitative answer—no calculations) how you might try to put together an optimal portfolio under these circumstances.

3. You believe that the APT accurately describes security prices. There are two systematic risk factors: changes in industrial production and changes in long-term interest rates. The market demands a risk premium of 8% for unexpected changes in industrial production and a risk premium of 6% for unexpected changes in long-term interest rates. The risk-free rate is 6%, and the expected return on your portfolio is 13%.

a) If your current portfolio's sensitivity to unexpected changes in industrial production is 1.5, what must be its sensitivity to unexpected changes in interest rates?

b) Suppose you wish to revise your portfolio to maintain the same expected return but reduce your sensitivity to unexpected changes in industrial production to zero. If you do so, what will be your portfolio's sensitivity to unexpected changes in interest rates?

Footnotes

[1] For summaries of various elements in this controversy, see the articles by Black, Grinold, and Keim in the *Suggestions for Further Reading* section at the end of this chapter.

[2] For some purposes, it is important to note that, in the APT, (11.8) must govern the expected equilibrium returns on all well-diversified portfolios, but not necessarily on all individual securities. Most individual security returns must conform to (11.8), but a small number of individual securities' returns may not, since their deviations from (11.8) will become unimportant when they are added to a well-diversified portfolio. For our purposes, we will ignore this subtlety in the analysis that follows and assume that all individual securities' expected returns conform to (11.8). This issue is discussed further in Zvi Bodie, Alex Kane, and Alan J. Marcus, *Investments,* 2nd ed. (Homewood, Ill.: Richard D. Irwin, 1993).

12

Active Portfolio Strategies

If one adhered strictly to a market equilibrium model, such as those described in Chapter 11, this approach would suggest an indexing, or passive, investment strategy. Because securities would always be priced under such models to offer returns commensurate with their systematic risks, there would be no point in trying to tinker with the portfolio in an attempt to earn superior risk-adjusted returns. The portfolio manager would still have the job of tailoring the portfolio to suit the client's preferred risk profile, but any search for superior performance would be futile.

Hope springs eternal, however, and many portfolio managers do attempt to implement more active strategies, designed to achieve superior returns. In this chapter we will examine ways in which portfolio managers might attempt to take advantage of investment insights while still adhering to the principles of portfolio optimization that we saw in Chapter 10. First, we will look at ways in which managers might try to use ability to forecast the overall market return to tailor an indexed portfolio. This analysis also raises questions about how such market timing strategies might play out in a multiperiod context. Next, we will analyze how a manager might use superior information about individual security returns to "tilt" the portfolio in favor of "winner" securities while still retaining as much of the benefit of diversification as possible. We will also take a brief look at extensions of these two basic strategies, in which managers might try to take advantage of several types of forecasting ability at once. Finally, we will examine some ways in which portfolio managers might use futures and options in implementing active portfolio strategies.

242

I. MARKET TIMING

A. Single-Period Market Timing

To concentrate our attention on the portfolio manager's ability to forecast the market return, we will limit her to the market index as the only possible risky asset and allow her to combine this index portfolio with the risk-free asset. This choice is essentially the same one faced in Portfolio Problem 1 in Chapter 10. In contrast to Portfolio Problem 1, however, we will assume that the manager solving this problem has access to an analyst's forecast of the market return that may differ from the consensus forecast of other market analysts. Therefore, the manager may wish to time the market by adjusting the fraction of her portfolio that she allocates to the index portfolio over the period for which the manager's forecast market return differs from the consensus forecast. We will assume that the analyst's forecast is correlated with the true market return over a given period, but perhaps imperfectly so. Thus, the manager's problem is to decide whether and how to adjust this forecast in order to solve the portfolio problem in an optimal way.

Suppose the consensus market forecast is $E(r_m)$, and that the actual market return over the coming period is related to $E(r_m)$ by

$$\tilde{r}_m = E(r_m) + \tilde{e}_m \tag{12.1}$$

where $\tilde{e}_m$ is a random error term. Note also that the variance of the market return, σ_m^2, is equal to the variance of this error term, $\sigma^2(\tilde{e}_m)$.

The analyst tries to predict by how much the actual market return will differ from the consensus forecast by making a forecast, α_m, of the value of $\tilde{e}_m$. If we had time series of actual market returns for past periods and the portfolio analyst's forecasts for these same periods, we could get some idea of the analyst's forecasting track record by regressing the series of e_m values against the corresponding series of α_m values. Our regression model could be expressed as

$$\tilde{e}_m = a + b\tilde{\alpha}_m + \tilde{\varepsilon}_m \tag{12.2}$$

where a and b are the regression coefficients and $\tilde{\varepsilon}_m$ is the forecast error term, which has a mean value of zero and zero correlation with the forecast $\tilde{\alpha}_m$. Given an analyst's forecast for a specific period, then, we can use the regression model prediction, $a + b\alpha_m$, as our estimate of the difference between the actual market return and the consensus forecast. The portfolio manager thus uses the regression coefficients to adjust the analyst's forecasts for any biases that might be present. Note further that the regression coefficient, b, is an estimate of $\rho\sigma(e_m)/\sigma(\alpha_m)$, where ρ

is the correlation between the actual market return and the analyst's forecast. This correlation is a measure of the analyst's forecasting ability, since for values of ρ close to one, indicating near perfect forecasting ability, the estimate of the expected market return used in solving the portfolio problem will be close to the analyst's forecast, especially if the variability of the analyst's forecasts approximates the variability in the market returns. For values of ρ near zero, on the other hand, indicating an absence of forecasting ability, the value of b is near zero and the analyst's forecast is essentially ignored by the portfolio manager.

Given the slope of the regression model, we can also find the variance of the analyst's forecast error. From (12.2),

$$\sigma^2(e_m) = b^2\sigma^2(\alpha_m) + \sigma^2(\varepsilon_m) = \rho^2 \frac{\sigma^2(e_m)}{\sigma^2(\alpha_m)} \sigma^2(\alpha_m) + \sigma^2(\varepsilon_m) \quad (12.3)$$

from which it follows that

$$\sigma^2(\varepsilon_m) = (1 - \rho^2)\sigma^2(e_m) = (1 - \rho^2)\sigma_m^2 \quad (12.4)$$

The importance of the analyst's forecasting ability shows up clearly in (12.4) as well. With a complete lack of forecasting ability ($\rho = 0$), $\sigma^2(\varepsilon_m) = \sigma_m^2$. Thus, the portfolio manager achieves no reduction in risk by using the analyst's forecast. With perfect forecasting ability ($\rho = 1$), on the other hand, the analyst enables the portfolio manager to eliminate all risk.

The manager uses $[a + b\alpha_m + E(r_m)]$ as the estimate of expected market return. If the regression model is well specified, all of the uncertainty about the market return is captured by $\sigma^2(\varepsilon_m)$, so the manager uses (12.4) as the estimate of market return variance.[1] With these inputs, we can now solve the portfolio manager's problem. We will focus on the manager's choice of a portfolio beta. Since the portfolio beta, β_p, is equal to $a_R\beta_m = a_R$, it is equivalent to choosing the fraction of total funds to be allocated to the index portfolio. Thus, our portfolio problem can be written as

$$\max_{\beta_p} U(r_p) = E(r_p) - \frac{1}{2}A\sigma_p^2$$

$$= r_f + \beta_p[a + b\alpha_m + E(r_m) - r_f] - \frac{1}{2}A\beta_p^2(1 - \rho^2)\sigma_m^2 \quad (12.5)$$

Setting the first derivative with respect to β_p equal to zero and solving for β_p,

$$\beta_p = \frac{E(r_m) + a + b\alpha_m - r_f}{A(1 - \rho^2)\sigma_m^2}$$
(12.6)

If we contrast (12.6) with the solution to Portfolio Problem 1 (see Equation [10.18] in Chapter 10), we can see that the portfolio manager with market timing information adjusts the proportion invested in the market portfolio upward as the analyst's forecasts are more highly correlated with the true market return and as the adjusted market forecast, $a + b\alpha_m$, exceeds the consensus market return, $E(r_m)$.

To illustrate, suppose the consensus forecast is $E(r_m) = .15$, with $r_f = .07$, $A = 2$, and $\sigma_m^2 = .06$. With no market timing information, our best choice would be $\beta_p = (.15 - .07)/2(.06) = .667$. Suppose, on the other hand, that our analyst now forecasts a market return of .20, or a value for α_m of .05. In the past, this analyst has been somewhat overly optimistic, so we use $a = -.01$ and $b = .8$ to adjust this forecast downward to .18 (that is, $a + b\alpha_m = -.01 + .8[.05] = .03$, which gives a market return forecast of $.15 + .03 = .18$). In addition, we estimate that the correlation between forecast and actual market returns is .25. From (12.6), then, our optimal portfolio beta is .978, an increase of nearly 50% from the beta we would have chosen with no market timing information. If the correlation between our analyst's forecasts and the actual market return had been as high as .5, with all other parameters remaining the same, Equation (12.6) would advise us to increase our portfolio beta further to 1.22.

B. Some Multiperiod Issues

It should be recognized, before we move on, that market timing, or for that matter any active portfolio strategy, is inherently implemented in a multiperiod context. Such strategies are designed to take advantage of capital market conditions that may exist temporarily, but as these conditions change, portfolio rebalancing will be called for.

A natural approach to this rebalancing is to keep solving the single period portfolio problem over again, period by period. While this approach has the appeal of simplicity, it is not obvious on the surface that an investor with a long time horizon, maximizing a multiperiod utility function, would necessarily arrive at the same answer. It turns out, in fact, that the answer might be different and that multiperiod portfolio selection raises some new and difficult issues. While a full discussion of such issues is beyond the scope of this book, it is worthwhile at least to have a sense of the types of difficulties that may arise.

A fundamental problem is that, in a multiperiod context, it may no longer be appropriate to couch an investor's portfolio problem solely in terms of the expectation and standard deviation of portfolio returns. There can be an increasing distinction between investor wealth and the portfolio rate of return over multiple periods, and the standard deviation of returns may be an inappropriate measure of the risk that is most relevant to the investor.

To illustrate, consider an equity portfolio whose value follows a binomial process. The portfolio's initial value is 100, and each period the value will either increase by one-half or fall by one-third. If these two future states of the world are equally likely, the portfolio's expected return over a given period is $(.5)(50\%) + .5(-33.33\%) = 8.33\%$. For a single period, the standard deviation of returns is $[.5(50 - 8.33)^2 + .5(-33.33 - 8.33)^2]^{1/2} = 41.67\%$.

If we held this equity portfolio over four periods, instead of just one, and if its performance in any one period were independent of that in any other, we might view it as an equally-weighted portfolio of four uncorrelated securities, each with the same return distribution as the single-period equity portfolio. The four-period portfolio's yearly expected return would be 8.33%, and we could argue from the portfolio analogy that the yearly standard deviation is $[4 \times (.25)^2(41.67)^2]^{1/2} = 20.833\%$.[2] This result in turn suggests that there is a time diversification effect at work, whereby low returns in any one period are cancelled to some degree by high returns in others, producing lower risk if the portfolio is held over long periods.

The conclusion that risk falls as the number of periods increases is fallacious, however. Presumably the investor is truly interested in total wealth at the end of the investment horizon as opposed to per period return, and the standard deviation of terminal wealth tends to increase with time, even as the standard deviation of per period returns is decreasing.

To understand this concept, let us trace the possible wealth values at the end of each of the four periods for our numerical example. These values, with their probabilities of occurrence, are shown in Table 12.1. As the numbers in the table show, the mean or expected level of wealth rises with time, reflecting the compounding of returns, but so does the standard deviation of wealth. The latter fact is also indicated by the increasing dispersion of best and worst possible outcomes over time.

To analyze portfolio choices in this context, we first need to reassess our characterization of investor preferences. If investors are predominantly interested in terminal wealth in a multiperiod context rather than per period return, we should use a utility function that reflects this preference. One possibility is the logarithmic utility function, $U(W_T) = \ln W_T$, as introduced in Chapter 9.

TABLE 12.1 End-of-period wealth for equity portfolio following a binomial process

	PERIOD 0	PERIOD 1		PERIOD 2		PERIOD 3		PERIOD 4	
	WEALTH	WEALTH	PROBABILITY	WEALTH	PROBABILITY	WEALTH	PROBABILITY	WEALTH	PROBABILITY
								506.25	$\frac{1}{16}$
						337.5	$\frac{1}{8}$	225	$\frac{4}{16}$
				225	$\frac{1}{4}$			100	$\frac{6}{16}$
		150	$\frac{1}{2}$	100	$\frac{2}{4}$	150	$\frac{3}{8}$	44.44	$\frac{4}{16}$
	100	66.67	$\frac{1}{2}$	44.44	$\frac{1}{4}$	66.67	$\frac{3}{8}$	19.75	$\frac{1}{16}$
						29.63	$\frac{1}{8}$		
Mean		108.33		117.36		127.14		137.74	
Standard Deviation		41.67		66.15		91.03		118.20	

Using expected utility as our measure of investor satisfaction from an uncertain prospect, we can calculate the expected natural log of wealth for each year for the wealth levels and probabilities shown in Table 12.1. For all five periods, including the present, the result is $U(W_T) = 4.605$, indicating that the investor derives equal satisfaction from the equity portfolio regardless of the number of periods it is held. Had we been using a utility function based on the mean and standard deviation of per period portfolio return, we might have concluded from the constant mean return and decreasing standard deviation over time that the investor would derive greater utility from the equity portfolio the longer it is held. Had we been seeking to find the optimal allocation between, say, equities and a risk-free asset, we might also have concluded that the optimal portfolio would place a heavier weight on equities the longer it is held. With a logarithmic utility function, by contrast, such conclusions would be unwarranted.

The logarithmic utility function can also be used to illustrate the departures from optimality that may arise if an investor, who in fact has no market timing ability, nevertheless adopts a multiperiod market timing strategy. An investor who believes strongly in his timing ability will tend to adopt extreme portfolio proportions. Such an investor might move back and forth, for example, between a portfolio that is invested 100% in equities and one that is 100% invested in the risk-free asset, depending on whether he thinks the market return will be greater or less than that of the risk-free asset in a given period. If the investor has no particular forecasting skill, however, we could view these portfolio shifts as occurring randomly.

Suppose that such an investor in our four-period example adopts an all-equity portfolio for periods 1 and 3 and an all-risk-free portfolio for periods 2 and 4. The return on the risk-free asset is assumed to be 5%. Table 12.2 shows the possible wealth outcomes each period resulting from this strategy. For example, in periods 1 and 3, total wealth can either increase by half or decrease by a third from its beginning-of-period level, while in periods 2 and 4, beginning-of-period wealth must increase by 5%. Given these possible outcomes, the expected natural log of period 4 wealth is 4.703, which does exceed the expected utility of an all-equity strategy (4.605, found previously). However, it is less than the utility of an all-risk-free strategy [$\ln(100)(1.05)^4 = 4.800$]. Moreover, a property of the logarithmic utility function, given a stable stochastic process for the changes in equity value, is that the optimal allocation between equities and the risk-free security is the same each period.[3] If we differentiate the expected utility function and solve for the allocation that maximizes utility of first-period wealth, the result calls for approximately 20% of the portfolio to be invested in equities and 80% in the risk-free asset.

TABLE 12.2 End-of-period wealth for market timing strategy that adopts 100% equity portfolio in periods 1 and 3 and 100% risk-free portfolio in periods 2 and 4 (risk-free return = 5%)

PERIOD 0	PERIOD 1		PERIOD 2		PERIOD 3		PERIOD 4	
WEALTH	WEALTH	PROBABILITY	WEALTH	PROBABILITY	WEALTH	PROBABILITY	WEALTH	PROBABILITY
					236.25	$\frac{1}{4}$	248.06	$\frac{1}{4}$
	150	$\frac{1}{2}$	157.5	$\frac{1}{2}$	105	$\frac{2}{4}$	110.25	$\frac{2}{4}$
100	66.67	$\frac{1}{2}$	70	$\frac{1}{2}$	46.67	$\frac{1}{4}$	49	$\frac{1}{4}$

Tracing out the possible wealth levels in each of the four periods with this portfolio allocation and taking logarithms, the expected natural log of period 4 wealth is 4.811 (you are invited to work these steps out for yourself in Problem 1 at the end of the chapter). Thus, the market timing strategy sacrifices expected utility relative to the optimal strategy.

In summary, multiperiod portfolio analysis tends to shift our focus from per period returns to terminal wealth and also leads us to consider alternative utility functions to characterize investor preferences. The analysis quickly becomes quite complex, and many issues remain to be resolved. Having raised a warning flag, then, we will return in the remainder of the chapter to single-period portfolio problems.

II. ACTIVE-PASSIVE PORTFOLIO MANAGEMENT

A different portfolio problem arises if we have no special information on the market portfolio, but we do feel we have uncovered something special about a specific security, about a specific class of securities, or about the securities of a specific industry or sector. Suppose, for example, that we wish to allocate our portfolio among (1) a risk-free security; (2) an index or market portfolio, m, of risky securities; and (3) a single active risky security, A, which the portfolio manager expects to outperform the other risky securities.

Let us assume further that each individual security's returns take on the following form:

$$\tilde{r}_{it} = \alpha_i + r_f + \beta_i(\tilde{r}_{mt} - r_f) + \tilde{e}_{it} \tag{12.7}$$

That is, one component, $\alpha_i + r_f + \beta_i(\tilde{r}_{mt} - r_f)$, of security i's return in a given period, t, is assumed to be perfectly correlated (related in a linear fashion) with the return on the market portfolio, $\tilde{r}_{mt}$. In this component, β_i, the security's beta, is a measure of its systematic risk, since it reflects the security's sensitivity to the overall market return, while α_i reflects any superior expected return that the security may have. The second component, $\tilde{e}_{it}$, is a random residual return. We will assume that this residual return has an expected value of zero, so the expected return on security i is equal to $\alpha_i + r_f + \beta_i[E(r_m) - r_f]$. While the expected value of $\tilde{e}_{it}$ is assumed to be zero, its variance, $\sigma^2(e_i)$, is positive. We will further assume that $\tilde{e}_{it}$ is uncorrelated with either the market return or the residual return on any other asset. Thus, we can think of i's return as consisting of a systematic component, which reflects the extent to which i's returns vary with those of all other securities, and a unique or unsystematic component, which reflects the degree to which i's returns are unrelated to those of any other security.

Consider, then, our two choices for the risky portfolio: the market portfolio and the active security, A. The optimal combination of two risky assets in the presence of a risk-free asset is given by the solution to Portfolio Problem 4 (see Section II.D in Chapter 10). The market portfolio has an expected return, $E(r_m)$, variance of returns, σ_m^2, and no residual return (that is, the market cannot have a portion of its return that is uncorrelated with the market return). Security A's returns follow the form given in (12.7), so its expected return, $E(r_A)$, is equal to $\alpha_A + r_f + \beta_A[E(r_m) - r_f]$. Using the definitions in (10.7) and (10.8), A's variance of returns is $\sigma_A^2 = \beta_A^2\sigma_m^2 + \sigma^2(e_A)$, its covariance with the market return is $\mathrm{cov}(r_A, r_m) = \beta_A\sigma_m^2$, and its covariance with any other individual security, i, whose returns also follow (12.7), is $\mathrm{cov}(r_A, r_i) = \beta_A\beta_i\sigma_m^2$.

With these inputs, we can then use (10.33) from Chapter 10 to calculate the optimal fraction, F_A, of the risky portfolio to be invested in A, which, after simplifying, reduces to the following:

$$F_A = \frac{\alpha_A\sigma_m^2}{\alpha_A\sigma_m^2(1 - \beta_A) + [E(r_m) - r_f]\sigma^2(e_A)} \tag{12.8}$$

We can also express (12.8) in equivalent form if we divide both the numerator and denominator by $[E(r_m) - r_f]\sigma^2(e_A)$ as

$$F_A = \frac{w_0}{1 + (1 - \beta_A)w_0} \tag{12.9}$$

where

$$w_0 = \frac{\alpha_A/\sigma^2(e_A)}{\dfrac{E(r_m) - r_f}{\sigma_m^2}} \tag{12.10}$$

Note that w_0 is the value of F_A if the active security's beta is equal to one. In that case, we are making a reward-risk comparison between the index portfolio and the active security. The denominator of (12.10) reflects the risk premium (expected return over and above the risk-free rate) on the index portfolio relative to that portfolio's total risk. The numerator shows the superior expected return available from holding the active security and compares this return with the security's unique, or unsystematic risk, which is the additional risk to which we expose ourselves by holding the active asset in a proportion other than its proportion in the index portfolio. Since the index portfolio is assumed to be broadly diversified, it essentially eliminates unsystematic risk. However, we reintroduce this risk and thus sacrifice some of the benefits from diversification when we alter the proportion allocated to the active asset. Equation (12.10) thus says that we should be more willing to sacrifice diversification benefits when the additional expected return, as measured by α_A, is large relative to the additional risk, as measured by $\sigma^2(e_A)$. Finally, Equation (12.9) says that, as the active security's beta grows greater than one, we increase its weight in the overall risky portfolio relative to that called for in (12.10), while as the beta falls below one, we reduce its weight. The reason for this result is as follows: Because the active security's total risk is given by $\sigma_A^2 = \beta_A^2 \sigma_m^2 + \sigma^2(e_A)$, as beta increases, holding $\sigma^2(e_A)$ constant, the proportion of the active security's total variation that is explained by movements in the market increases. Thus, we can afford to hold more of that security and less of the index portfolio without unduly increasing our overall portfolio's unsystematic risk.

The final step in setting up our active-passive portfolio strategy is to consider the case in which there is more than one active security. It is shown in the Appendix to this chapter, that, like the active portfolio as a whole, each active asset should receive more weight in proportion to the ratio of its alpha to its residual risk relative to this ratio for the active portfolio as a whole. That is, with n active assets in all, the fraction, ω_k, of the *active* portfolio represented by active security k is given by

$$\omega_k = \frac{\dfrac{\alpha_k}{\sigma^2(e_k)}}{\displaystyle\sum_{i=1}^{n} \dfrac{\alpha_i}{\sigma^2(e_i)}} \tag{12.11}$$

Once the components of the active portfolio have been determined, the active portfolio can be combined with the index portfolio, exactly as described previously, to form the optimal overall portfolio.

At this point, a numerical example may be helpful in illustrating the various steps in implementing our portfolio strategy. Suppose your client has a risk aversion index, $A = 3$. She has chosen you to manage her portfolio, because she is aware that you are not only familiar with the benefits of diversification but are also a skillful security analyst. You set about constructing an optimal portfolio for her to comprise three active securities (1, 2, and 3), a market index portfolio, and a risk-free security. The market index portfolio has an expected return, $E(r_m) = .15$, and a standard deviation of returns, $\sigma_m = .20$. The return on the risk-free asset is .05, and the characteristics of the three potential active assets are as summarized in (1) of Table 12.3.

The remainder of Table 12.3 goes through the steps in choosing the optimal overall portfolio, beginning with the composition of the active portfolio, moving next to the allocation of the risky portfolio between the active and the index portfolio, and ending with the allocation of the final portfolio between the risky portfolio and the risk-free security.

TABLE 12.3   Example of active-passive portfolio choice

1. Active asset characteristics

SECURITY	α_k	β_k	$\sigma(e_k)$	$\alpha_k/\sigma^2(e_k)$	$\omega_k = \dfrac{\alpha_k/\sigma^2(e_k)}{\displaystyle\sum_{i=1}^{n} \alpha_i/\sigma^2(e_i)}$
1	.05	1.5	.4	$.05/(.4)^2 = .3125$	$.3125/.47917 = .6522$
2	.02	0.5	.2	$.02/(.2)^2 = .50$	$.50/.47917 = 1.0435$
3	− .03	1.0	.3	$− .03/(.3)^2 = \underline{−.3333}$	$− .3333/.47917 = \underline{−.6957}$
				Total .47917	1.000

2. Characteristics of the optimal active portfolio

$$\alpha_A = (.05)(.6522) + (.02)(1.0435) + (− .03)(− .6957) = .0744$$

$$\beta_A = (1.5)(.6522) + (.5)(1.0435) + (1)(− .6957) = .8044$$

$$\sigma^2(e_A) = (.4)^2(.6522)^2 + (.2)^2(1.0435)^2 + (.3)^2(− .6957)^2 = .1552$$

3. Composition of the optimal risky portfolio

$$W_0 = \dfrac{\dfrac{.0744}{.1552}}{\dfrac{.15 - .05}{(.2)^2}} = .1918$$

$$F_A = \dfrac{.1918}{1 + (1 - .8044)(.1918)} = .185$$

Optimal risky portfolio has

$$1 - F_A = .815 \text{ invested in index portfolio}$$

$$F_A\omega_1 = .121 \text{ invested in security 1}$$

$$F_A\omega_2 = .193 \text{ invested in security 2}$$

$$F_A\omega_3 = − .129 \text{ invested in security 3}$$

Table continued on following page

In this particular case, the final portfolio is relatively conservative, with the preponderance of the risky portfolio invested in the index. Nonetheless, there has been some attempt to mix in the active assets to gain additional return. Problems 2 to 5 at the end of the chapter illustrate a variety of features of the active-passive portfolio management strategy.

To determine how much better the investor has done than by simply following, say, a completely passive strategy requires some measurement of portfolio performance. We will turn to this issue in Chapter 13.

TABLE 12.3   Example of active-passive portfolio choice *Continued*

4. Characteristics of the optimal risky portfolio, R

$$\beta_r = F_A\beta_A + (1 - F_A) = .964$$

$$\alpha_r = F_A\alpha_A = .0138$$

$$E(r_R) - r_f = \alpha_R + \beta_R[E(r_m) - r_f] = .1102$$

$$\sigma_R^2 = \beta_R^2\sigma_m^2 + F_A^2\sigma^2(e_A) = (.964)^2(.2)^2 + (.185)^2(.1552) = .0425$$

5. Allocation of final portfolio between risky and risk-free securities

Proportion of overall portfolio held in risky assets:

$$a_R = \frac{E(r_R) - r_f}{A\sigma_R^2} = .864$$

Overall portfolio allocation:

Proportion invested in risk-free asset $= 1 - a_R = .136$

index portfolio $= a_R(1 - F_A) = .704$

Security 1 $= a_R F_A\omega_1 = .105$

Security 2 $= a_R F_A\omega_2 = .167$

Security 3 $= a_R F_A\omega_3 = -.111$

6. Characteristics of the final portfolio

$$E(r_p) = a_R E(r_R) + (1 - a_R)r_f = .1452$$

$$\sigma_p = a_R\sigma_R = .178$$

$$\alpha_p = a_R\alpha_R = .012$$

$$\beta_p = a_R\beta_R = .833$$

III. EXTENSIONS OF MARKET TIMING AND ACTIVE-PASSIVE MANAGEMENT

A fundamental result of the capital asset pricing model, as described in Chapter 11, is that, if all investors have the same views about assets' expected returns, variances, and covariances with one another, they will all hold the market portfolio as their portfolio of risky assets. By contrast, an investor following the portfolio strategies described in the preceding two sections holds different views from other investors. Under the market timing strategy, the investor uses an expected market return that differs from the consensus forecast to tilt the portfolio toward more or less exposure to the market portfolio than would be chosen by an investor with the same degree of risk aversion but consensus expectations. Similarly, an investor following the active-passive management strategy tilts the portfolio away from the passive, index portfolio and overweights those securities he believes will outperform the consensus forecast.

This basic technique can be extended to more complex portfolio management problems as well. That is, we can use some measures of consensus expected returns and a market equilibrium portfolio as benchmarks and then tilt in one or more directions away from that equilibrium portfolio according to both the extent to which our own beliefs differ from the consensus and the confidence we have in our beliefs. One obvious extension is simply to combine the market timing and active-passive management strategies. That is, the portfolio manager may have forecasts about both the market return and individual security returns. We could then implement the active-passive management solution with equations (12.9), (12.10) and (12.11), but using $[a + b\alpha_m + E(r_m)]$ as our forecast of the market return and $(1 - \rho^2)\sigma_m^2$ as our measure of the market variance. An example of such a combination strategy is given in Problem 6 at the end of this chapter.

A second extension has been developed at Goldman, Sachs & Co. for international asset allocation. The portfolio manager in this case chooses assets not only from a number of different classes (for example, equities, bonds, and currency forward contracts), but also from a number of different countries. With identical expectations, each investor would hold a global market portfolio, with all security classes from all countries represented in proportion to their total market value outstanding. Fischer Black has also shown that, under certain simplifying assumptions (for example, no taxes, inflation, or restrictions on capital flows), all investors will want to hedge the same fraction of their total currency risk.[4] He estimates this fraction to be about 80%. Thus, the equilibrium market portfolio is the value-weighted portfolio of all world securities, with about 80% of its currency risk hedged by forward contracts. The equilibrium, or consensus, expected returns on the different country–asset classes are those, given the covariance structure across assets, that would induce all investors espousing those expectations to hold the equilibrium market portfolio.

Given these consensus expectations, the portfolio manager can decide whether or not to adopt alternative views on any of the asset classes. Such alternative expectations could also be associated with standard deviations, reflecting the manager's degree of confidence in these views. An optimized portfolio could then be derived, as in the active-passive management problem. The greater the extent to which the manager adopts consensus views, the more closely the optimized portfolio will tend toward global diversification. If the manager does adopt some alternative views, however, the optimized portfolio will be tilted toward those country–asset classes that the manager expects to outperform the others on a risk-adjusted basis.[5]

A third extension, developed at Salomon Brothers, makes use of a risk attribute model, which is in the spirit of the arbitrage pricing theory.[6] Under this approach, the portfolio manager tries to identify undervalued stocks or sectors using some valuation criteria. Instead of simply constructing a portfolio of these securities using a mean-variance optimization procedure, however, the manager can control the portfolio's exposure to various APT factors. In the risk attribute model, these factors include economic growth, the credit cycle, the general level of stock prices, long- and short-term interest rates, inflation, and the relative value of the U.S. dollar. The manager could avoid undue exposure to any one factor, therefore, by constraining the factor exposures of the optimized portfolio to be equal to those of some benchmark portfolio such as the S&P 500. Alternatively, if the portfolio manager had views on movements in the factors for a given period that differed from consensus forecasts, the optimized portfolio could be tilted toward greater exposure to those factors whose movements he expected to increase portfolio returns. In this way the manager would be combining timing information (the forecasts of factor movements) with valuation forecasts for individual securities.

IV. USING FUTURES CONTRACTS IN ACTIVE PORTFOLIO MANAGEMENT STRATEGIES

A. Changing Exposure to Market Factors

Futures contracts can also prove useful in implementing a variety of active portfolio management strategies. Consider, for example, a manager whose risky portfolio is divided between equities and long-term bonds. The specific securities within these two classes have been chosen because, based on fundamental analysis, the portfolio manager believes they will outperform other securities. Now, however, the manager receives forecast information suggesting that the economy will be weaker than most investors expect in the upcoming period. The manager thus predicts that equities will perform more poorly than is commonly expected. Conversely, he believes that the weak economy will drive down interest rates and that bonds will perform better than is commonly expected. Accordingly, the manager would like to reduce the portfolio's exposure to stock prices and increase its exposure to interest rates. An obvious way to accomplish this result would be to liquidate some of the equity portion of the portfolio and buy longer-duration bonds, but the manager still has confidence in his individual security picks relative to other securities, so he would prefer not to disturb the securities composition of the portfolio.

The manager can accomplish both objectives by using futures contracts. The risky portfolio's current exposure to the general stock market index can be measured by its CAPM beta. If the current beta is β_R, the target beta is β_R^T, and the beta of a stock index futures contract is β_f, the number of index futures contracts, n_f^I, the manager should buy to adjust his portfolio beta is given by

$$n_f^I = \frac{(\beta_R^T - \beta_R)}{\beta_f} \frac{V_R}{V_f} \qquad (12.12)$$

where V_R and V_f are the values of the risky portfolio and the futures contract, respectively. Note that V_f is a measure of contract size. For example, the S&P 500 stock index futures contract has a magnitude of 500 times the value of the S&P index, so V_f would be equal to 500 times the quoted futures price. Note also in (12.12) that n_f^I will be negative if $\beta_R^T < \beta_R$, indicating a short position in index futures contracts. Another example of the use of futures to change market exposure is provided in Problem 7 at the end of the chapter.

In similar fashion, other exposure measures can be used to adjust the portfolio along different dimensions. In our example, the portfolio manager can control exposure to interest rate risk by using, say, the Treasury bond futures contract to adjust the portfolio's modified duration. Analogous to (12.12), the number of futures contracts, n_f^B, required to achieve a target duration, D_R^T, for the risky portfolio is

$$n_f^B = \frac{(D_R^T - D_R)}{D_f} \frac{V_R}{V_f} \qquad (12.13)$$

where D_R and D_f are the modified durations of the risky portfolio and the bond underlying the futures contract (measured as of the expiration of the contract) and V_R and V_f are the portfolio and contract values.

To illustrate, suppose our portfolio manager currently has 60% of a $100 million risky portfolio allocated to equities and 40% to long-term bonds. The equity portion of the portfolio has a beta of 1.5, while the bond portion has a modified duration of 6 years. The S&P 500 futures contract has a quoted price of 450 and a beta of 1.0, while the bond underlying the futures contract has an invoice price (including accrued interest) of .985 per dollar of face value and a modified duration of 9 years.[7] The S&P 500 contract has a size of 500 times the index, while the T-bond contract assumes $100,000 face value in underlying bonds. If the portfolio manager then wants to reduce the equity portfolio's beta to 0.75 and increase the bond portfolio's modified duration to 9 years, without disturbing the individual equity and bond securities in the portfolio, he can use (12.12) and (12.13) to determine the number of stock index and bond futures contracts as

$$n_f^I = \left(\frac{.75 - 1.5}{1} \right) \frac{60\text{MM}}{500 \times 450} = -200 \qquad (12.14)$$

$$n_f^B = \left(\frac{9 - 6}{9} \right) \frac{40\text{MM}}{98500} \cong +135 \qquad (12.15)$$

B. Incorporating Futures Positions in the Portfolio Optimization

In the preceding section, we analyzed how futures contracts could be used to facilitate movement toward the portfolio manager's optimal portfolio. The optimization itself was assumed to take place in the background, and the futures contracts only served as a vehicle for implementing the predetermined solution. There is no inherent reason, however, why the futures positions could not be incorporated in the portfolio optimization process.

To take a simplified example, suppose a manager has already chosen a portfolio of risky assets, with expected return $E(r_R)$ and standard deviation σ_R. Because the portfolio is internationally diversified, its returns are exposed to exchange rate fluctuations. The manager is trying to determine the optimal position in foreign currency futures contracts she should take to achieve an overall optimal portfolio. To keep the problem manageable, we will suppose that only one futures contract, perhaps on a composite currency such as the European Currency Unit (ECU), is being considered. We will also ignore for the time being the possible presence of a risk-free asset.

Because futures contracts require no net investment, we need not constrain our portfolio weights to a sum to one. Accordingly, we can assign a weight of one to our portfolio or risky assets, R, and our problem will be to choose a weight, a_f, representing the size of the foreign currency futures position relative to the value of the risky portfolio such that the combined portfolio will be optimized. If we let S_{x0} represent the spot exchange rate on the composite currency underlying the futures contract, $E(S_{x1})$ the expected exchange rate one period from now, and F_{x0} the current futures price on a one-period contract, we can define the expected return[8] on the futures contract as $[E(S_{x1}) - F_{x0}]/S_{x0}$. The expected return on the manager's total position, then, including both the risky portfolio and the futures position, is given by

$$E(r_p) = E(r_R) + a_f \frac{[E(S_{x1}) - F_{x0}]}{S_{x0}} \tag{12.16}$$

If σ_f and σ_R are the standard deviation of return on the currency futures contracts and the risky portfolio, respectively, while ρ_{Rf} is the correlation between the risky portfolio and futures contracts returns, the overall portfolio variance is given by

$$\sigma_p^2 = \sigma_R^2 + a_f^2 \sigma_f^2 + 2a_f \rho_{Rf} \sigma_R \sigma_f \tag{12.17}$$

With these inputs, we can write the portfolio optimization problem, which is just a slight variation on Portfolio Problem 2 from Chapter 10, as

$$\max_{a_f} U(r_p) = E(r_p) - \frac{1}{2} A \sigma_p^2$$

$$= E(r_R) + a_f \frac{[E(S_{x1}) - F_{x0}]}{S_{x0}} \tag{12.18}$$

$$+ \frac{1}{2} A(\sigma_R^2 + a_f^2 \sigma_f^2 + 2a_f \rho_{Rf} \sigma_R \sigma_f)$$

Setting the derivative of (12.18) with respect to a_f equal to zero and solving for a_f then gives the optimal futures position as

$$a_f^* = \frac{\dfrac{E(S_{x1}) - F_{x0}}{S_{x0}}}{A\sigma_f^2} - \frac{\rho_{Rf} \sigma_R}{\sigma_f} \tag{12.19}$$

As in the solution to Portfolio Problem 2, the second term in (12.19) is the hedging demand for futures contracts. It represents the size of the futures position relative to the risky portfolio value that minimizes overall portfolio variance. Note that the hedging demand can also be interpreted as the estimated coefficient in a regression of the risky portfolio's returns against the futures contract returns. This concept is the basis for the regression approach to hedging often described in discussions of futures contracts.[9]

More generally, however, investors will not necessarily wish to minimize variance but rather to maximize utility, so they will also consider the first term in (12.19), which represents the speculative demand for futures contracts, which in turn reflects the expected return on the futures contract relative to its risk plus the investor's degree of risk

aversion. The passive investor might wish to estimate the expected return on the futures contract using a market equilibrium model that reflects consensus expectations. If the investor believes that futures contracts are priced according to the CAPM, for example, as discussed in
Section II.B of Chapter 11, we could use Equation (11.6) to rewrite
(12.19) as

$$a_f^* = \frac{\beta_x[E(r_m) - r_f]}{A\sigma_f^2} - \frac{\rho_{Rf}\sigma_R}{\sigma_f} \qquad (12.20)$$

where β_x is the beta of the exchange rate relative to the market portfolio.[10] An example of the application of Equation (12.20) is provided in
Problem 8 at the end of the chapter. In (12.20), the investor's speculative
demand for currency futures contract is determined solely by her willingness to bear systematic risk. Alternatively, rather than use a market
equilibrium model to determine expected return, the investor could incorporate her own forecasts of future exchange rates and thus introduce
an additional market timing component, similar to that discussed in
Section I, into the overall portfolio optimization.

V. USING OPTIONS IN ACTIVE PORTFOLIO MANAGEMENT STRATEGIES

Options can be used in similar ways to futures contracts to tailor a portfolio's exposure to a variety of risk factors. Because options have asymmetric return distributions, they have the added feature that they can
be used to expand the available variety of portfolio return distributions.
However, because the mean-variance framework for portfolio analysis
assumes symmetrical return distributions, it is not well-equipped for in-
corporating options. Instead of discussing options in this framework,
therefore, we will simply describe some widely used option strategies
and their potential uses.

Two of the most popular strategies are writing covered calls and
buying protective puts. Writing covered calls refers to selling call options against the securities in a portfolio that one already owns. By doing so, the portfolio manager gains current income from the sale of the
call options but sacrifices at least some of the upside potential of the underlying securities, since they are likely to be called away if they perform well. In essence, this strategy truncates some of the upper tail of
the portfolio's return distribution. The manager might be willing to
make this trade if he thought the securities in the portfolio were unlikely to perform well in the near term, but at the same time he had con-

Value of Option
Position

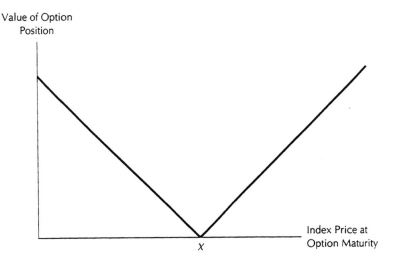

Index Price at
Option Maturity

X

FIGURE 12.1   Gross payoff at option maturity on a straddle (buying both index call and put options with same exercise price)

fidence in the securities' longer-run prospects and he didn't want to incur the expense of reallocating the portfolio.

Conversely, buying protective puts refers to buying put options against the securities in the portfolio.[11] This approach is a form of "portfolio insurance" in that it truncates the lower tail of the return distribution in exchange for an "insurance premium," which is the cost of purchasing the put options. Employing such a strategy with index put options, for example, would allow the portfolio manager to guard against a sudden downturn in the market while at the same time retaining the market's upside potential plus the individual securities' ability to perform well relative to the market, even if the market turns down. In the case of both strategies, of course, the portfolio manager is betting against investors on the other side of the option contracts, so the strategies will lead to superior performance only if the manager has made better guesses than these other investors.

It is also possible to use options to take a position on a security's volatility. Suppose, for example, that the portfolio manager buys both index call and put options with the same exercise price. This type of option position is called a straddle, and its payoff at maturity will be as depicted in Figure 12.1.[12] Note from the figure that the payoff from the option position increases with the amount by which the index value at maturity differs from the exercise price, regardless of whether that difference is positive or negative. In effect, by taking this option position, the portfolio manager is betting that the market index will be more volatile during the upcoming period than the average investor expects, but she is not taking any position on the direction in which the index will move.

Finally, it should be noted that many portfolio managers use synthetic options to implement portfolio strategies in an attempt to reduce costs. A protective put, for example, could be simulated by adjusting the proportions invested in the index portfolio and in cash so as to match an index put option's delta. The put option's delta is negative, so at any given time a proportion of the portfolio equal to the option's delta should be moved out of the index portfolio and into cash. As the index value declines, the option's delta becomes more negative, so the proportion invested in cash should be increased. As the index value increases, on the other hand, the proportion invested in cash should be decreased. Stock index futures contracts can also be used to make these adjustments in a portfolio's exposure to the index.[13]

VI. SUMMARY

In this chapter, we have examined a variety of active portfolio management strategies. The common thread connecting these strategies is that, in each case, the portfolio manager attempts to take advantage of return forecasts that differ from the consensus. At the same time, the portfolio manager is aware that the forecasts are subject to error, so while tilting the portfolio toward certain securities or security classes, the manager still wishes to maintain some degree of diversification.

One such strategy is market timing, in which the manager tries to make a better forecast than other investors of how the market as a whole will perform. The solution to this problem calls for increasing the portfolio's exposure to the market index (1) the higher is the forecast return but also (2) the more highly correlated the analyst's forecasts are with actual market returns. Caution must be exercised, however, both in formulating and implementing a market timing strategy in a multiperiod context.

Another strategy, active-passive management, balances the diversification benefits of an index portfolio against the desire to overweight individual securities that are forecast to be superior performers. The solution to this problem calls for increased overweighting of the individual securities to the extent that their predicted superior returns are large relative to their residual, or unsystematic, risks. These two types of strategies can also be combined, and the portfolio manager can take an active stance relative to some dimensions of portfolio return and a passive stance relative to others.

Futures and option contracts can be useful in implementing active portfolio strategies, as they afford a relatively easy way for the manager to alter the portfolio's return distribution in a variety of ways. Exposure to some risks can be increased at the same time that exposure to other risks is reduced. Options, in particular, can be used to truncate one side or the other of the portfolio's return distribution.

SUGGESTIONS FOR FURTHER READING

Additional reading on active portfolio management strategies can be found in the following:

1. Ambachtsheer, Keith P., "Where Are the Customers' Alphas?" *Journal of Portfolio Management,* 4 (Fall 1977), pp. 52–56.

2. Berry, Michael A., Edwin Burmeister, and Marjorie B. McElroy, "Sorting Out Risks Using Known APT Factors," *Financial Analysts Journal,* 44 (March/April 1988), pp. 29–42.

3. Black, Fischer, "Universal Hedging: Optimizing Currency Risk and Reward in International Equity Portfolios," *Financial Analysts Journal,* 45 (July/August 1989), pp. 16–22.

4. Black, Fischer, and Robert Litterman, "Asset Allocation: Combining Investor Views with Market Equilibrium," *Journal of Fixed Income,* 1 (September 1991), pp. 7–18.

5. Black, Fischer, and Robert Litterman, "Global Portfolio Optimization," *Financial Analysts Journal,* 48 (September/October 1992), pp. 28–43.

6. Bodie, Zvi, Alex Kane, and Alan J. Marcus, *Investments* (2nd ed.). Homewood, Ill.: Richard D. Irwin, 1993.

7. Bookstaber, Richard, "The Use of Options in Performance Structuring," *Journal of Portfolio Management,* 11 (Summer 1985), pp. 36–60.

8. Clarke, Roger G., "Asset Allocation Using Futures Markets," in *Active Asset Allocation* (rev. ed.), eds. Robert D. Arnott and Frank J. Fabozzi. Chicago: Probus Publishing Co., 1992.

9. Clarke, Roger G., and others, "Market Timing with Imperfect Information," *Financial Analysts Journal,* 45 (November/December 1989), pp. 27–36.

10. Hull, John, *Introduction to Futures and Options Markets.* Englewood Cliffs, N.J.: Prentice Hall, 1991.

11. Kritzman, Mark, "What Practitioners Need to Know About Hedging," *Financial Analysts Journal,* 49 (September/October 1993), pp. 22–26.

12. Kritzman, Mark, "What Practitioners Need to Know About Time Diversification," *Financial Analysts Journal,* 50 (January/February 1994), pp. 14–18.

13. Samuelson, Paul A., "Asset Allocation Could Be Dangerous to Your Health: Pitfalls in Across-Time Diversification." In *Active Asset Allocation,* eds. Robert D. Arnott and Frank J. Fabozzi, Chicago: Probus Publishing, 1992.

14. Sorensen, Eric H., and Chee Y. Thum, "The Use and Misuse of Value Investing," *Financial Analysts Journal,* 48 (March/April 1992), pp. 51–58.

15. Tilley, James A., and Gary D. Latainer, "A Synthetic Option Framework for Asset Allocation," *Financial Analysts Journal,* 41 (May/June 1985), pp. 32–43.

16. Treynor, Jack L., and Fischer Black, "How to Use Security Analysis to Improve Portfolio Selection," *Journal of Business,* 46 (January 1973), pp. 66–86.

17. Wolf, Jesse, "Calendar Spreads for Enhanced Index Fund Returns," *Financial Analysts Journal,* 46 (January/February 1990), pp. 66–73.

PROBLEMS AND QUESTIONS

1. **Spreadsheet Exercise.** Return to the numerical example in Section I.B of this chapter. Trace out the possible wealth levels for all four years obtained from the optimal strategy of allocating 20% of the portfolio to equities and 80% to the risk-free asset. Show that the expected utility of period 4 wealth from this strategy is 4.811.

2. You are an investment adviser with two clients, Rita Riskit and Tim Timid. Each of them has a utility function that can be expressed as $U = E(r_p) - \frac{1}{2}A\sigma_p^2$, but for Rita, $A = .5$, while for Tim, $A = 2$. You are trying to advise them about how to allocate their portfolios among three possible investments: (1) U.S. Treasury bills, (2) an index mutual fund whose holdings closely approximate the market portfolio of all risky assets, and (3) shares of stock in the Hi Flier Corporation. The expected returns, betas, and variances of total return for each of these investments are as follows:

	E(r)	$\sigma^2(r)$	β
Treasury bills	.06	0	0
Index fund	.14	.04	1.0
Hi Flier stock	.25	.20	2.0

You also know that each period's return on Hi Flier stock can be expressed as

$$\tilde{r}_{Ht} = a_H + r_f + \beta_H(\tilde{r}_{mt} - r_f) + \tilde{e}_{Ht}$$

where $\tilde{e}$ is a random residual return whose expected value is zero and whose correlation with the returns on any other asset is also zero.

a) What are the optimal portfolios of risky assets that you should recommend for Rita and Tim? Will you recommend a smaller proportion of Hi Flier stock for Tim because of his higher degree of risk aversion? Briefly explain.

b) What are the portfolio proportions for the optimal overall portfolios that you should recommend for Rita and Tim? Briefly explain how they differ.

3. A portfolio manager wishes to combine two active stocks, X and Y, with the market portfolio to form an optimal risky portfolio. The expected return on the market portfolio is 14% and its variance of returns is 0.14. The risk-free rate of return is 4%.

a) Suppose security X has an expected return of 20%, a variance of returns of 0.4, and a beta of 1.5 and that security Y has an expected return of 14%, a variance of returns of 0.16, and a beta of 1.0. Find the composition of the optimal risky portfolio.

b) Now suppose that the beta of security Y falls to 0.9. All other data remain the same. What is the composition of the optimal risky portfolio now?

c) Briefly explain the differences in your answers to (a) and (b).

4. Two portfolio managers, I. Pickem and Diane (Di) Versified, are putting together the risky portions of their clients' portfolios. Although neither manager is responsible for combining these risky portfolios with the risk-free asset, they both understand that the presence of a risk-free asset, whose return is currently 4% per year, will affect their choice of an optimal risky portfolio. In forming these risky portfolios, both managers have focused their attention on two stocks, Eureka Corp. and Boundless Horizons, which they expect

to outperform other securities on a risk-adjusted basis. The returns on both these stocks follow a process described by $\tilde{r}_{it} = \alpha_i + r_f + \beta_i(\tilde{r}_{mt} - r_f) + \tilde{e}_{it}$, where α_i and β_i are the stocks' alpha and beta, respectively; $\tilde{r}_{mt}$ is the return on the market index fund in period t; r_f is the risk-free rate of interest; and $\tilde{e}_{it}$ is a residual return, which is uncorrelated with both the market return and the return on the other stock. The expected value of $\tilde{e}_{it}$ is zero and its standard deviation is $\sigma(e)$. Both portfolio managers agree that the two stocks have the following expected returns, variances of total return, and betas:

STOCK	$E(r)$	$\sigma^2(r)$	β
Eureka	.16	.30	0.8
Boundless Horizons	.09	.09	0.4

a) Di Versified feels that one can take best advantage of these two stocks if they are combined with a passive index fund, whose characteristics closely resemble those of the market portfolio of all stocks. Currently, the expected return on this index fund is .14, and the variance of its returns is .14. Since the index fund tracks the overall market, its beta is 1.0. In what proportions should Ms. Versified combine the index fund, Eureka, and Boundless to form an optimal risky portfolio? What will be the expected return and standard deviation of returns for this portfolio?

b) I. Pickem, on the other hand, pooh-poohs the idea of diversification, and puts together a risky portfolio composed entirely of the two winner stocks, Eureka and Boundless. Given that he ignores the index fund, in what proportions should Mr. Pickem combine Eureka and Boundless to form an optimal risky portfolio? What will be the expected return and standard deviation of returns for this portfolio?

c) Explain the differences between these two portfolios.

5. Company Z's pension fund currently has $300 million in risky assets (that is, stocks, long-term bonds, real estate, etc.). The fund can also take long or short positions in the risk-free asset, whose current rate of return is .07, but that decision will be made after the composition of the risky portfolio has been determined. Rather than manage the risky assets in-house, Z's treasurer has decided to spread out this task evenly among three different money managers. Manager C makes no attempt to conceal the fact that he runs an index fund. That is, he runs a broadly diversified portfolio that is designed to

track the market index. Currently, the expected return on this market portfolio is .15 and the variance of the market return is .04. Managers A and B, on the other hand, are "closet indexers." That is, even though they claim to choose a portfolio of securities exhibiting superior performance, what they really do is to select a single security that they believe will perform well. They then combine that security with an index portfolio (having identical characteristics to manager C's portfolio) in a way that would be optimal if they were managing the entire pension fund. Manager A has identified security A as her superior performer, while manager B has identified security B. For either security, the return in any period t bears the following relationship to the overall market return:

$$\tilde{r}_{it} = \alpha_i + r_f + \beta_i(\tilde{r}_{mt} - r_f) + \tilde{e}_{it}$$

for i = A or B, where $\tilde{e}_{it}$ has an expected value of zero, a variance equal to $\sigma^2(e_i)$, and a correlation of zero with the residual returns on any other securities.

a) Security A has an expected return of .24, a β of 2.0, and a variance of total returns of .18. If manager A is given $100 million to manage, and she allocates it the same way she would if the $100 million were the entire pension portfolio of risky assets, what proportion will she invest in security A and what proportion will she invest in the index portfolio? What will be the α, β, expected return, and variance of total return for manager A's overall portfolio of risky assets?

b) Security B has an expected return of .15, a β of 0.5, and a variance of total returns of .09. If manager B is given $100 million to manage, and he allocates it the same way he would if the $100 million were the entire pension portfolio of risky assets, what proportion will he invest in security B and what proportion will he invest in the index portfolio? What will be the α, β, expected return, and variance of total return for manager B's overall portfolio of risky assets?

c) Company Z's overall pension portfolio is allocated as follows: one-third in manager A's portfolio, one-third in manager B's portfolio, and one-third in manager C's index portfolio. In the overall pension portfolio, what proportion is invested in the index portfolio (including the amounts that managers A and B have invested in the index portfolio), what proportion is invested in security A and what proportion is invested in security B? What is the α, β, expected return, and variance of total return for the overall pension portfolio?

d) Suppose instead that the pension fund were managed in-house on a centralized basis. In that event, a single manager would combine security A, security B, and the index portfolio in an optimal fashion. What would be the proportions for this optimal portfolio, and what would be the overall portfolio's α, β, expected return, and variance of total return?

e) A portfolio management expert has recently written:

> Suppose that you divide the equity portfolio among several balanced managers and possibly an index fund. Suppose also that each manager behaves as if he or she were managing the whole fund. Then the aggregate portfolio will be even more diversified than that of any single manager. In other words, the managers should be required to be less diversified than they would otherwise be; or equivalently, you need to reduce the fund's aggregate market exposure by selling index futures. Adding an index fund to a portfolio that is split among a number of balanced managers is likely to be even less appropriate than adding an index fund to a portfolio with a single active manager.

Comment briefly on this passage in light of your answers above.

6. A portfolio manager's security analysts have uncovered two securities, 1 and 2, that they feel will outperform the market on a risk-adjusted basis, regardless of what the market return actually turns out to be. The estimated characteristics of the two securities, including their alphas, betas, and residual variances are as follows:

k	α_k	β_k	$\sigma^2(e_k)$
1	.005	0.5	.04
2	.015	1.5	.04

The consensus forecast is that the market return in the upcoming period will be .15 and the variance of market returns around this forecast is .20. The risk-free interest rate is .06.

a) If the portfolio manager has no other information with which to predict the market return, how should she combine securities 1 and 2 with an index fund to form an optimal risky portfolio?

b) Suppose now that the manager finds another analyst who specializes in predicting the market return. For the upcoming period, the analyst predicts that the market return will be .19. The portfolio manager is somewhat skeptical and uses adjustment factors $a = 0$ and $b = .75$ to adjust the new analyst's market return forecast. However, she knows from past history that there is a correlation of 30% between the analyst's forecasts and actual market returns. Given this market forecast, what should be the composition of the manager's optimal portfolio of risky assets?

c) Suppose that all facts remain the same as in (a) and (b) except that the individual securities' betas are reversed (that is, now $\beta_1 = 1.5$, while $\beta_2 = 0.5$). How would this change affect the composition of the optimal portfolio of risky assets? (Assume that the portfolio manager continues to make use of the new analyst's market return forecast.)

d) Now return to the original beta estimates (that is, $\beta_1 = 0.5$, $\beta_2 = 1.5$), but suppose that the analyst's forecast of the market return is .11, rather than .19. All other facts, including the consensus forecast, market variance, and correlation between the analyst's forecast and actual market returns, remain as before. How would this change affect the composition of the optimal portfolio of risky assets?

e) Briefly explain the differences in your answers to (a) through (d).

7. You plan to put together a portfolio consisting solely of a market index fund and a risk-free asset. For simplicity, assume that none of the stocks in the index pays any dividend, so all of the return on the index fund is in the form of capital gains. The current level of the index is 500, and the consensus expectation is that, one year from now, the index will reach a level of 575. The risk-free rate of return is 5% per year and your risk-aversion coefficient is 2 (that is, $A = 2$). The variance of the index fund's returns is .10.

a) If you have no other information about the expected index fund return besides the consensus forecast, what is your optimal combination of the index fund and the risk-free asset?

b) Suppose that a futures contract is available on the same stock market index represented by the index fund. The current price on an index futures contract with a maturity of one year is 525. The correlation between movements in the futures price and in the level of the stock market index is 1.0. The variance of percentage changes in the futures price is .10. Is the futures contract priced so as to eliminate arbitrage opportunities? Is it priced consistently with the capital asset pricing model? Briefly explain both your answers.

c) Given the pricing of the futures contract, if you could combine the futures contract with the index fund and the risk-free asset, do you think you could achieve a better-performing or more desirable portfolio than the one you constructed in (a)? Note: Give a qualitative answer here; no calculations are necessary.

d) Suppose, in contrast to (a), that a market analyst tells you she expects the level of the market index to be 600 one year from now, rather than the 575 expected under the consensus forecast. You believe there is a correlation of 0.5 between this analyst's forecasts and the actual market return. In addition, you feel there is no need to adjust the analyst's forecast (that is, $a = 0$ and $b = 1$ would be the coefficients in a regression of the analyst's forecasts on actual market returns). If you were to make use of this analyst's forecast of the market return, what would be your optimal combination of the market index fund and the risk-free asset?

e) Suppose you moved from your optimal portfolio in (a) to your optimal portfolio in (d) using index futures contracts rather than buying or selling shares in the market index fund. Each index futures contract represents 500 times the level of the index futures price. Your portfolio value is 50 million dollars. How many index futures contracts will you need to buy or sell to adjust your portfolio? Would there be any advantage to adjusting your portfolio using index futures contracts rather than buying or selling shares in the index fund? Briefly explain.

8. A portfolio manager is holding an internationally diversified portfolio that is designed to track the world market portfolio. While the manager is satisfied to be a world market indexer, he is worried about exposing his clients to too much currency risk, so he is considering taking a position in currency futures contracts. Suppose there is a contract available that represents the value of a basket of foreign currencies relative to the U.S. dollar. The portfolio manager estimates that his own index portfolio has a standard deviation of returns of 40%, that the currencies underlying the futures contract have a composite standard deviation of 20%, and that the correlation between his own index portfolio returns and the returns on the futures contract is 25%. The manager also believes that currency futures contracts are priced consistently with the capital asset pricing model and that the expected risk premium on the world index portfolio is 10%.

a) What size futures position should the manager take relative to his index portfolio if he wants to minimize overall portfolio risk (assume that the manager is not considering putting any money into the risk-free asset)?

b) If the manager believes his average client has a risk aversion coefficient of $A = 3$, what is the size of the optimal futures position relative to his index portfolio? Explain how and why this optimal position differs from the risk-minimizing position you calculated in (a).

Footnotes

[1] In statistical terms, $a + b\alpha_m + E(r_m)$ and $(1 - \rho^2)\sigma_m^2$ are the market expected return and variance, respectively, conditional on the analyst's forecast. In contrast, σ_m^2 is the unconditional market variance.

[2] As pointed out in Zvi Bodie, Alex Kane, and Alan J. Marcus, *Investments,* 2nd ed. (Homewood, Ill.: Richard D. Irwin, 1993), Appendix C to Chapter 7, this standard deviation calculation is only an approximation, as it ignores the compounding of returns over time.

[3] See, for example, Paul A. Samuelson, "Asset Allocation Could Be Dangerous to Your Health: Pitfalls in Across-Time Diversification," in *Active Asset Allocation,* eds. Robert D. Arnott and Frank J. Fabozzi (Chicago: Probus Publishing, 1992).

[4] See Fischer Black, "Universal Hedging: Optimizing Currency Risk and Reward in International Equity Portfolios," *Financial Analysts Journal,* 45 (July/August 1989), pp. 16–22.

[5] Two articles by Fischer Black and Robert Litterman ("Asset Allocation: Combining Investor Views with Market Equilibrium," *Journal of Fixed Income,* 1 [September 1991], pp. 7–18; and "Global Portfolio Optimization," *Financial Analysts Journal,* 48 [September/October 1992], pp. 28–43) give examples of the construction of such optimized portfolios.

[6] See Eric H. Sorensen and Chee Y. Thum, "The Use and Misuse of Value Investing," *Financial Analysts Journal,* 48 (March/April 1992), pp. 51–58.

[7] Since any one of a number of bonds, differing rather widely in duration, can be delivered to satisfy the T-bond futures contract, the portfolio manager must be careful to use the price and duration of the cheapest-to-deliver bond. For further discussion, see John Hull, *Introduction to Futures and Options Markets* (Englewood Cliffs, N.J.: Prentice Hall, 1991).

[8] This definition of the futures contract expected return follows the practice of related literature. See, for example, Fischer Black and Robert Litterman, "Global Portfolio Optimization," *Financial Analysts Journal,* 48 (September/October 1992), pp. 28–43.

[9] See, for example, Chapter 4 in John Hull, *Introduction to Futures and Options Markets* (Englewood Cliffs, N.J.: Prentice Hall, 1991).

[10] Equation (12.20) should be viewed as illustrative only, since if a risk-free asset exists, as assumed by the CAPM, we should have solved the portfolio problem using a risk-free asset.

[11] Note from the put-call parity relationship that both covered call writing and protective put buying can be implemented in alternative ways. From Equation (5.12), for example, buying securities and selling calls

against them is equivalent to buying the riskless asset and selling puts against the securities. Similarly, buying the underlying securities and buying put options on them is equivalent to buying the riskless asset and buying calls on the securities.

[12] In a related position called a strangle, the put option has a lower exercise price than the call option, so there is a flat portion in the middle of the payoff diagram corresponding to stock prices between the two exercise prices in which the payoff is zero because neither option finishes in the money. Such a position would be useful if the portfolio manager thought the index price would move outside some specified band, to one side or the other. The portfolio manager could also sell calls and puts (short straddles or short strangles), in which case the portfolio would earn income from writing the options if index prices remained relatively stable, but the option positions would incur losses if index prices moved much in either direction.

[13] See Richard Bookstaber, "The Use of Options in Performance Structuring," *Journal of Portfolio Management,* 11 (Summer 1985), pp. 36–60; John Hull, *Introduction to Futures and Options Markets* (Englewood Cliffs, N.J.: Prentice Hall, 1991); and James A. Tilley and Gary D. Latainer, "A Synthetic Option Framework for Asset Allocation," *Financial Analysts Journal,* 41 (May/June 1985), pp. 32–43, for further discussion of these synthetic option strategies.

Appendix to Chapter 12

I. SOLVING THE ACTIVE-PASSIVE MANAGEMENT PROBLEM FOR MORE THAN ONE ACTIVE SECURITY

When there is more than one active security, (12.9) and (12.10) still give the optimal proportion invested in the active portfolio (relative to the index portfolio). It remains, then, to determine the best way to combine the individual active securities in the active portfolio.

Recall that (12.9) and (12.10) were determined in the first place by finding the portfolio of risky assets that maximizes the slope of the capital allocation line. In similar fashion, we wish to find the active security proportions that are consistent with maximizing the slope of the CAL. As we will see in Chapter 13, the slope of the CAL, or the expected risk premium on the optimal risky portfolio divided by that portfolio's standard deviation, is also referred to as the Sharpe measure of performance, S_p. In the analysis that follows, we will find it convenient to maximize the square of the Sharpe measure, or

$$S_p^2 = \frac{[E(r_p) - r_f]^2}{\sigma_p^2} = \frac{\{\alpha_p + \beta_p[E(r_m) - r_f]\}^2}{\beta_p^2 \sigma_m^2 + \sigma^2(e_p)}$$

$$= \frac{\left\{ \dfrac{\alpha_p}{\beta_p[E(r_m) - r_f]} + 1 \right\}^2}{\dfrac{\sigma_m^2}{[E(r_m) - r_f]^2} + \dfrac{\sigma^2(e_p)}{\beta_p^2[E(r_m) - r_f]^2}} \qquad (12A.1)$$

Recognizing that the first fraction in the denominator of (12A.1) is the reciprocal of the Sharpe measure, S_m, for the market portfolio, and that the market portfolio has no unsystematic risk, so that $\sigma^2(e_p) = F_A^2\sigma^2(e_A)$ and $\alpha_p = F_A\alpha_A$, we can rewrite (12A.1) as

$$S_p^2 = \frac{\left\{\dfrac{\alpha_p}{\beta_p[E(r_m) - r_f]} + 1\right\}^2}{\dfrac{1}{S_m^2} + \dfrac{\sigma^2(e_A)}{\alpha_A^2}\left\{\dfrac{\alpha_p}{\beta_p[E(r_m) - r_f]}\right\}^2} \qquad (12A.2)$$

Now note that, since the beta of the market portfolio is one, the beta of the risky portfolio is $\beta_p = F_A\beta_A + (1 - F_A)$. Thus we can write the fraction that appears in both the numerator and denominator of (12A.2) as

$$\frac{\alpha_p}{\beta_p[E(r_m) - r_f]} = \frac{F_A\alpha_A}{[F_A\beta_A + (1 - F_A)][E(r_m) - r_f]} \qquad (12A.3)$$

Then, substituting for F_A from text Equations (12.9) and (12.10) and simplifying,

$$\frac{\alpha_p}{\beta_p[E(r_m) - r_f]} = \frac{\dfrac{\alpha_A^2}{\sigma^2(e_A)}}{S_m^2} \qquad (12A.4)$$

Finally, substituting the right-hand side of (12A.4) into (12A.2) leads to

$$S_p^2 = S_m^2 + \frac{\alpha_A^2}{\sigma^2(e_A)} \qquad (12A.5)$$

Since the Sharpe measure for the market portfolio is given, (12A.5) tells us that the Sharpe measure for the overall risky portfolio will be maximized when the weights, ω_k, on the active assets are chosen so as to maximize $\alpha_A^2/\sigma^2(e_A)$. Furthermore, since the residual return components of the active assets are assumed to be uncorrelated with one another, we can write our problem as

$$\max_{\omega_k} \frac{\alpha_A^2}{\sigma^2(e_A)} = \frac{\left(\displaystyle\sum_{i=1}^{n} \omega_i\alpha_i\right)^2}{\displaystyle\sum_{i=1}^{n} \omega_i^2\sigma^2(e_i)} \qquad (12A.6)$$

Then, setting the derivative of (12A.6) with respect to ω_k equal to zero,

$$2\left(\sum_{i=1}^{n} \omega_i^2\sigma^2(e_i)\right)\left(\sum_{i=1}^{n} \omega_i\alpha_i\right)\alpha_k = 2\left(\sum_{i=1}^{n} \omega_i\alpha_i\right)^2\omega_k\sigma^2(e_k) \qquad (12A.7)$$

from which text Equation (12.11) follows.

13

Performance Evaluation and the Organization of Portfolio Management

This chapter concludes our discussion of portfolio analysis with two related topics. First, if we have hired a portfolio manager, we will want to have some standard for measuring that manager's performance. Second, any given portfolio manager may handle only one component of a larger overall portfolio. Thus, we will want to manage the investment management process, giving the proper instructions to each individual manager, so that the combined results are in line with our objectives and so that we can monitor the performance of each portfolio component in a meaningful way. In both cases, the principles of portfolio management that we have seen earlier offer some guidance as to how to go about these tasks.

I. PORTFOLIO PERFORMANCE MEASUREMENT

If portfolio managers follow active strategies, designed to outperform passive portfolios, their clients will want to evaluate whether or not superior performance has in fact been achieved. In general, accurate performance evaluation is very difficult, and we will see a number of potential pitfalls in this chapter. Nonetheless, portfolio theory affords some tools that we can use.

A. Performance Measures Based on Portfolio Theory

Four performance measures that have been suggested on the basis of portfolio theory are shown in Table 13.1. The first of these, the Sharpe measure, compares the expected risk premium on the managed portfolio with its standard deviation. It is essentially a reward-risk ratio measure and could be compared, for example, with the Sharpe measure for the market portfolio to see if the portfolio manager can expect to earn a return sufficient to compensate for any additional total risk that may have been undertaken. Since the Sharpe measure adjusts for total risk, it can be useful for assessing the performance of a portfolio that is less than fully diversified. Thus, any unsystematic risk the manager may have taken on will be reflected in the risk measure. A potential weakness of the Sharpe measure, however, is that the portfolio being evaluated may represent only one component of an investor's entire wealth. In that event, it is not clear that the total risk of this component portfolio is the most appropriate risk measure.

The Treynor measure, by contrast, compares the managed portfolio's expected risk premium with its beta, or systematic risk measure. Again, if we take the market portfolio as a benchmark, the Treynor mea-

TABLE 13.1   Portfolio performance measures

NOTATION:

$E(r_p)$, $E(r_m)$, r_f = Expected returns on the managed portfolio, market portfolio, and risk-free asset, respectively, over the evaluation period.

β_p = Beta of the managed portfolio over the evaluation period.

α_p = Alpha of the managed portfolio over the evaluation period.

$\sigma(r_p)$, $\sigma(e_p)$ = Standard deviation of managed portfolio total returns and residual return, respectively, over the evaluation period; residual return for time t is equal to $r_{pt} - r_{ft} - \beta_p(r_{mt} - r_{ft})$.

PERFORMANCE MEASURES

NAME	DEFINITION
Sharpe	$\dfrac{E(r_p) - r_f}{\sigma(r_p)}$
Treynor	$\dfrac{E(r_p) - r_f}{\beta_p}$
Jensen	$\alpha_p = E(r_p) - r_f - \beta_p[E(r_m) - r_f]$
Appraisal Ratio	$\dfrac{\alpha_p}{\sigma(e_p)}$

Note: For after-the-fact portfolio evaluation, average realized returns can be substituted for expected returns in each of the performance measurements.

sure for the market would simply be its expected risk premium, since its beta is equal to one. Comparison with a managed portfolio would then suggest whether or not the manager could expect to earn a risk premium at least commensurate with a systematic risk level that may be higher or lower than that of the market portfolio. The Treynor measure is best suited for evaluating the performance of either a well-diversified portfolio or of a portfolio that will be a component of a well-diversified portfolio, since it does not consider any unsystematic risk to which the portfolio might be exposed.

The Jensen measure uses the portfolio's alpha as the yardstick of its ability to outperform the market. The term $\beta_p[E(r_m) - r_f]$ measures the portfolio risk premium that we would expect based on the capital asset pricing model, so alpha measures the portfolio's ability to earn a higher expected risk premium. In contrast to the Sharpe and Treynor measures, the Jensen measure carries its own benchmark with it: the expected risk premium relative to the market that is commensurate with the portfolio's systematic risk level. Like the Treynor measure, the Jensen measure considers only systematic risk and does not take unsystematic risk into account.

Finally, the appraisal ratio is taken from the solution to the active-passive portfolio management problem, which gives heavier portfolio weights to securities whose alphas are large relative to their residual risk. Accordingly, the appraisal ratio can be useful for comparing the expected performance of two active portfolios, either of which could be combined with a passive portfolio. Since it takes no account of systematic risk, however, it is not well-suited for comparing the performance of a highly diversified portfolio with that of a relatively undiversified portfolio.

A crucial point to note about all four of these measures is that all of them are forward-looking. That is, they deal with prospective rates of return and return variability. This approach makes sense, because the essence of portfolio theory is to formulate the best possible decisions in the face of uncertainty, or before the ultimate outcome is known. Under these circumstances, the best we can hope for is a manager who makes good before-the-fact decisions. Since a good before-the-fact decision might not turn out as well as we expect, and since we don't want to penalize a manager who made good decisions but wound up having bad luck, it is logical to assess portfolio performance using forward-looking measures of the mean and standard deviation of returns. Problems 1 to 6 at the end of the chapter allow you to do exactly this, as they provide assumed characteristics of portfolio return distributions.

Unfortunately, we cannot simply assume values for the needed expected returns, variances, and covariances in practice. At the same time, trying to estimate these values is a very subjective process. To make matters worse, we may be largely at the mercy of the manager to provide measures of portfolio expected return and risk. Thus, the one who is being evaluated is providing the key inputs to the evaluation process, and the values of these inputs cannot be objectively verified. As a result, before-the-fact performance assessment is nearly impossible to implement, and instead, portfolio performance is nearly always measured on an after-the-fact basis.

B. Difficulties with After-the-Fact Performance Assessment

As suggested previously, after-the-fact evaluation suffers from its own set of difficulties. One of these is the problem of achieving statistical power. Without statistical power, we cannot have great confidence that we are not penalizing managers who made good decisions but had bad luck, or conversely, rewarding managers who made misguided decisions before the fact but wound up having good luck. Hall of Fame pitcher Vernon (Lefty) Gomez once captured the essence of this issue by remarking, "I'd rather be lucky than good."

Unfortunately, it is difficult to achieve the kind of statistical power needed to say with confidence that we are not making either of the two types of errors described in the preceding paragraph. It is easy to calculate any of the measures in Table 13.1 using after-the-fact data, or sample statistics, as opposed to the actual parameters of return distributions. It is less easy to establish that performance has been either superior or inferior in a statistically significant way. For example, we could take realized monthly portfolio returns over some sample period; use the average return as our measure of expected return; calculate sample variances, covariances, and betas; and compare our portfolio's realized performance with that of a benchmark over the same period. The Jensen measure is especially popular for after-the-fact performance measurement, since alpha can be conveniently estimated as the intercept term in a regression of the managed portfolio's historical risk premiums against the market portfolio's historical risk premiums. The intercept term's t-statistic can in turn be used to assess the statistical significance of any estimated superior performance. If the risk-adjusted portfolio performance exceeds that of the benchmark in a statistically significant way, we can conclude with reasonable reliability that the manager has outperformed the benchmark over this period in a way that is unlikely to be attributable purely to luck.

To illustrate, suppose we have two years' worth of past monthly returns for Treasury bills with one month remaining to maturity, a market index portfolio, and a managed portfolio, as shown in Table 13.2. The portfolio manager has earned a higher average monthly return than the

TABLE 13.2 Monthly returns over two-year period for one-month treasury bills, market portfolio, and managed portfolio

	r_f	r_m	r_p
Year 1 Returns	0.007	−0.018	0.0045
	0.005	−0.045	0
	0.005	0.166	0.0211
	0.008	−0.117	−0.0045
	0.006	−0.083	−0.0029
	0.007	−0.076	−0.0013
	0.006	−0.013	0.0041
	0.008	−0.027	0.0045
	0.008	−0.037	0.0035
	0.006	−0.021	0.0033
	0.006	0.002	0.0056
	0.006	−0.009	0.0045
Year 1 Average Return	0.0065	−0.0231667	0.00353333
Year 1 Standard Deviation	0.00104083	0.06621409	0.00617661
Year 2 Returns	0.005	−0.01	−0.025
	0.004	0.031	0.058
	0.006	0.064	0.122
	0.005	−0.033	−0.071
	0.005	−0.014	−0.033
	0.005	−0.066	−0.137
	0.004	0.046	0.088
	0.004	0.051	0.098
	0.004	0.049	0.094
	0.004	0.024	0.044
	0.004	0.067	0.13
	0.006	0.125	0.244
Year 2 Average Return	0.00466667	0.02783333	0.051
Year 2 Standard Deviation	0.00074536	0.04942137	0.09879103

market in each of the two years and has done so with a lower standard deviation in year 1 but a higher standard deviation in year 2. To determine whether the manager has outperformed the market in a statistically significant, risk-adjusted manner, we can estimate the Jensen alpha measure by regressing the managed portfolio's monthly risk premiums against the market portfolio's monthly risk premiums. This regression results in the following estimated coefficients (t-statistics are shown in parentheses below the coefficients):

$$r_p - r_f = .0243 + .799(r_m - r_f)$$
$$(2.13) \quad (4.51)$$
$$r^2 = .481$$

(13.1)

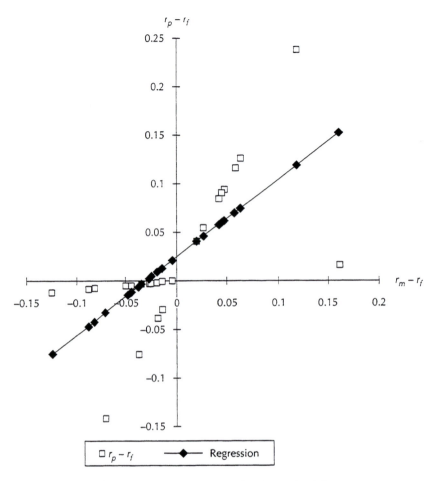

FIGURE 13.1 Performance measurement using Jensen's alpha

We would conclude that the manager has chosen a portfolio with a beta of approximately .8 and that the managed portfolio has outperformed the market, on average, by about 2.4% per month, adjusted for risk (you can verify these regression results in Problem 8 at the end of the chapter). The regression line is illustrated relative to the actual portfolio risk premiums in Figure 13.1. The slope of the regression line is the managed portfolio's estimated beta, while the intercept on the vertical axis is the estimated alpha. Moreover, since the t-statistic exceeds 2.0, we can infer that there is only about a 5% chance that the manager achieved this superior performance purely by chance.

In this example, the manager's superior performance is quite pronounced. In other situations, however, it may be more difficult to detect superior performance with confidence. For example, Grinblatt and Titman have estimated that, given the variability of security market returns, average superior portfolio performance of 200 basis points per year may not be statistically significant even if there are 10 years' worth of monthly portfolio returns with which to perform the evaluation.[1] Since many clients are unwilling to give a portfolio manager ten years or more in which to demonstrate superior performance, the problem of statistical power is a rather severe impediment to accurate performance evaluation.

A second problem with after-the-fact performance measurement is that of benchmark portfolio choice. Ideally, the benchmark portfolio might represent the choice that would be made by a portfolio manager with good sense and a knowledge of basic financial principles but no special ability to forecast security returns. Thus, if conditions in securities markets are poor generally, our own portfolio may do poorly but we should not expect it to do worse than the benchmark portfolio on a risk-adjusted basis. In applications of the capital asset pricing model, for example, the market portfolio is often considered the appropriate benchmark.

However, as argued by Roll, a major implication of the CAPM is that the market portfolio is mean-variance efficient.[2] That is, the market portfolio must lie on the efficient set (as, for example, point C does in Figure 10.3. Thus, he argues, any empirical test of the CAPM is really a joint test of the validity of the pricing model and the mean-variance efficiency of the market portfolio. Unfortunately, given the huge variety of assets traded in world capital markets, it is very difficult to find an accurate proxy for the true market portfolio. Not only does this problem make empirical testing of the CAPM very difficult, but it also implies that, if we are using a CAPM-based performance measure, such as Jensen's alpha, the market benchmark that we use may not actually turn out to be mean-variance efficient. As Roll goes on to show, using an inefficient benchmark portfolio for performance assessment can lead to erroneous inferences. That is, managers who have actually underperformed the market may be judged to have been superior performers, and vice versa. Moreover, these performance judgments can be very sensitive to the benchmark portfolio that is employed.

The development of the arbitrage pricing theory has further fueled controversy over benchmark choice, with APT proponents arguing that the appropriate benchmark should be multidimensional so as to reflect all of the common factors that determine security returns. A variation of this approach has been developed by Sharpe, in which he suggests that an asset class factor model, reflecting a portfolio's exposure to the return variation on the major asset classes, is an appropriate benchmark.[3] Such a benchmark reflects a money manager's investment style (for example, growth, income, value, etc.). To estimate the benchmark, Sharpe regresses the returns on a managed portfolio against the returns on twelve prespecified passive portfolios that are intended to capture the major asset classes. The estimated regression coefficients then define a multidimensional benchmark portfolio with the same style as the managed portfolio, and the returns on the two can be compared to see if the managed portfolio exhibits superior performance.

A third difficulty with after-the-fact performance evaluation is the detection of market timing ability. Performance measures such as those described previously implicitly assume that characteristics of security and portfolio return distributions, such as means, variances, covariances, and betas, are stable over the assessment period. However, as we saw in our discussion of the market-timing problem in the preceding chapter, a market-timing manager will deliberately change the portfolio's risk-return profile from period to period, which makes it difficult for an observer to select the period over which performance should be measured.

Consider, for example, a situation in which the Sharpe measure of performance for the market portfolio tends to have a historical average of .5. However, our portfolio manager believes that the market will perform worse than average over the next year and better than average over the following year. Accordingly, he chooses a portfolio with a lower-than-normal beta and hence a lower-than-normal standard deviation for the first year; analogously, he chooses a portfolio with higher-than-normal risk for the second year. After the fact, suppose the annualized quarterly risk premiums for the portfolio during the first year are −2%, 8%, −3%, and 9%, respectively, which works out to an average risk premium of 3% with a standard deviation of 5.52%, and a Sharpe measure of .543. Suppose further that, in the second year, the portfolio earns annualized quarterly risk premiums of −10%, 36%, −12%, and 38%, respectively, which works out to an average risk premium of 13% with a standard deviation of 24.02%, implying a Sharpe measure of .541. In each of the two years, then, the manager has outperformed the market portfolio. We should be pleased. However, suppose we measured the manager's performance using all eight quarters of data. In that case, the average risk premium works out to 8% with a standard deviation of 18.13%. These values in turn imply a Sharpe measure of .441, which suggests that the manager has underperformed the market. The problem is that the Sharpe measure implicitly assumes such underlying parameters as expected return and standard deviation, which we are estimating using realized returns, to be constant over the period of measurement. In this case, by contrast, the underlying parameters are quite explicitly not constant over a two-year measurement period because of the portfolio manager's strategy.

This problem is not peculiar to the Sharpe measure, as similar difficulties can arise with measures such as Jensen's alpha. Grinblatt and Titman have presented an example of a manager who practices the market timing technique as discussed in Section I of Chapter 12.[4] This manager holds only the index portfolio plus the risk-free asset, so the only way to outperform the market is to vary the portfolio beta to take advantage of anticipated market swings. Specifically, the manager chooses a low beta when timing information suggests the market will perform poorly and a high beta when she thinks it will perform well.

This situation is depicted in Figure 13.2. Suppose that in one period the manager expects the market risk premium to be relatively low. She therefore chooses a low beta portfolio by increasing the proportion allocated to the risk-free asset and reducing the fraction allocated to the index. The realized portfolio risk premiums for this case will plot along the line labeled Low Beta Portfolio in Figure 13.2. Suppose, for example, that after the fact the combination of realized portfolio and index risk premium is given by point A. In the next period, however, the manager expects a relatively high index risk premium, so she reduces the portfolio proportion allocated to the risk-free asset in order to increase portfolio beta, which implies that realized portfolio risk premiums will plot along the line labeled High Beta Portfolio.[5] After the fact, suppose the combination of realized portfolio and index risk premium is given by point B.

Overall, the manager has done exactly what clients might desire. She has protected against losses in the weak market environment, and

FIGURE 13.2 Failure of traditional performance measures to detect market timing ability

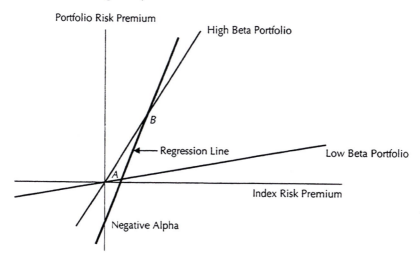

she has tailored the portfolio to take advantage of the strong market environment. She has achieved a higher combined portfolio return across the two periods than if she had simply held beta fixed at some intermediate level for both periods. However, if we plotted a regression line between the two realized risk premium points, A and B, it would have a negative intercept on the portfolio risk premium axis, as shown by the thicker line in Figure 13.2. Since the regression intercept represents our estimate of Jensen's alpha measure, we would judge after the fact that this successful market timing manager had underperformed the index portfolio. Again, as in the previous example, the problem is that the regression model assumes constant parameters across the entire time period, whereas the manager has quite explicitly altered the portfolio beta between the two subperiods.

C. Regression-Based Measures of Timing Ability

Considerable effort has been devoted to finding alternative performance measures that address the third of the difficulties just described, that of detecting market timing ability. Two such measures that are based on regression analysis of the managed portfolio's realized returns have been proposed by Treynor and Mazuy and by Henriksson and Merton.[6]

The Treynor-Mazuy measure adds a quadratic term to the standard Jensen regression specification, as follows:

$$r_p - r_f = a + b(r_m - r_f) + c(r_m - r_f)^2 + e_p \qquad (13.2)$$

Note that in this equation the sensitivity of the portfolio's risk premium to changes in the market risk premium is given by

$$\frac{d(r_p - r_f)}{d(r_m - r_f)} = b + c(r_m - r_f) \qquad (13.3)$$

In (13.3), the coefficient b represents the estimated portfolio beta for a portfolio manager with no special timing ability. In addition, if the coefficient c is positive, we infer that the portfolio's sensitivity to the index grows larger as the index risk premium increases. Since this is exactly what we would expect the portfolio beta to do when the manager has timing ability, a positive and statistically significant estimate of the regression coefficient c is Treynor and Mazuy's indicator of superior market timing ability.

In a somewhat similar vein, Henriksson and Merton propose the regression specification, as follows:

$$r_p - r_f = a + b(r_m - r_f) + cD(r_m - r_f) + e_p \qquad (13.4)$$

where D is a dummy variable that takes on a value of 1 when $r_m > r_f$ and zero otherwise. The idea behind this specification stems from Merton's insight that successful timing ability acts like an option on the index portfolio.[7] In (13.4), for example, if we work with returns rather than underlying values, the term $D(r_m - r_f)$ acts like the payoff (over and above the risk-free rate) on a call option on the market index with a strike price equal to r_f. If the estimated coefficient c is significantly greater than zero, therefore, this approach is equivalent to the portfolio manager's having taken a long position in these calls, thus demonstrating superior timing ability. Problem 8 at the end of the chapter illustrates the use of these two-regression-based measures of timing ability.

D. The Positive Period Weighting Measure

The Treynor-Mazuy and Henriksson-Merton timing measures are limited, however, by implicit restrictions on investor utility and on the joint return distributions of individual securities and the market portfolio. Grinblatt and Titman have developed another measure that is subject to somewhat less restrictive assumptions, yet is capable of detecting both market timing and individual security selection ability.[8] This measure is calculated by taking some number, T, of past periods and constructing a series of weights, one for each period, such that: (a) each weight is nonnegative; (b) the weights sum to 1; and (c) when the weights are applied to the series of risk premiums on the benchmark portfolio for the T periods, the weighted average benchmark risk premium is zero. If the same weights, applied to the managed portfolio risk premiums over these T periods, produce a positive average risk premium, Grinblatt and Titman show that this result can be interpreted as evidence of superior performance. In effect, the weights can be interpreted as the marginal utilities for the T periods of an investor who holds the benchmark portfolio. If the benchmark is perceived as optimal, the portfolio optimality condition dictates that marginal utility times the benchmark risk premium should be zero for each period. However, if we apply the same weights to a different portfolio and obtain a positive average risk premium, this result indicates that adding a small amount of the alternative portfolio to the investor's existing portfolio would increase his utility. Thus we can interpret a positive average risk premium calculated with these marginal utility weights as evidence that the managed portfolio is superior to the benchmark.

E. Performance Measures that Use the Managed Portfolio's Composition

A salient feature of all of the portfolio performance measures discussed so far is that none require knowledge of the actual portfolio composition. Rather, they rely only on overall portfolio and benchmark characteristics such as average return, standard deviation, beta, and residual standard deviation. If the managed portfolio's composition is known, on the other hand, we can make use of that information to devise additional performance measures and even to try to identify the sources of superior performance.

One type of performance measure stems from the insight that, if a portfolio manager has superior ability, there should be a positive covariance between the returns on securities or classes of securities on the one hand and their weighting in the managed portfolio on the other. That is, if the manager can predict over what period a given security will have an abnormally high return, she will assign a higher portfolio weight to the security for that period than for other periods. Viewed from a different angle, if a manager has superior ability, securities should perform better when they have a heavy weight in his portfolio than when they do not. Performance measures that rely on estimating a covariance between realized security returns and portfolio weights have been devised by Cornell, Copeland and Mayers, and Grinblatt and Titman.[9]

Another method for assessing performance that makes use of portfolio weights is performance attribution analysis. This method consists of comparing the managed portfolio with a benchmark portfolio along several dimensions, one at a time. Suppose, for example, that you choose as your benchmark a portfolio that allocates 50% of its total value to an index portfolio of stocks, 40% to an index portfolio of bonds, and the remaining 10% to Treasury bills. Suppose further that the stock index return is 16% over the measurement period, the bond index return is 8%, and the T-bill return is 5%. The total return on the benchmark portfolio is thus 11.7%. Your portfolio manager, on the other hand, allocates 60% of your portfolio to stocks (not the same mix as the stock index portfolio), 35% to bonds (again, not the same mix as the bond index portfolio), and 5% to T-bills. The return on the stock portion of your portfolio over the same measurement period turns out to be 18%, the return on your bond portfolio is 9%, and the return on T-bills is 5%. Your total portfolio return is thus 14.2%, so you have outperformed the benchmark by 250 basis points. You would now like to know how much of this superior performance you can attribute to various decisions the portfolio manager made.

First, we can attribute some of the portfolio's superior performance to the manager's asset allocation decision. Your manager allocated 60%

of the portfolio to stocks and 35% to bonds. Had the benchmark portfolio used your manager's weights, it could have earned $(.6)(16) + (.35)(8) + (.10)(5) = 12.65\%$, instead of 11.7%, so 95 basis points in extra return can be attributed to asset allocation. That is, we can assert that the manager had some insight into the relative performance of stocks and bonds generally, independent of the individual stocks and bonds that were chosen.

Second, your manager engaged in active security selection. If you had used the weights from the benchmark portfolio but applied these to the portfolio manager's choices of stocks and bonds, your portfolio would have earned $(.5)(18) + (.4)(9) + (.1)(5) = 13.1\%$, compared to the benchmark's 11.7%. Holding the allocation among security classes constant, we can thus attribute 140 basis points in extra return to security selection.

Between these two performance components, we have explained $95 + 140 = 235$ of the total 250 basis points in extra return on the managed portfolio. The remaining 15 basis points can be attributed to the interaction of asset allocation and security selection. Specifically, we can calculate the interaction effect by multiplying the difference in the portfolio weights between the manager's and the benchmark portfolio times the difference in return for each security class and summing across security classes. In the case at hand, this interaction effect thus accounts for $(.1)(2) + (-.05)(1) + (-.05)(0) = 0.15\%$.

Many variations on this basic version of performance attribution analysis are also possible. For instance, the comparisons in the example just given are not adjusted for risk, but if we had betas for the different asset classes, we could attempt to discern whether the managed portfolio earned a return that was enough better than the benchmark's to justify any additional risk that may have been assumed. Problem 9 at the end of this chapter offers an example of this sort of risk-adjusted performance attribution. For international portfolios, the analysis can also be expanded to assess the contribution of any currency exposure management that may have been undertaken.

II. THE ORGANIZATION OF MONEY MANAGEMENT

It should be clear by now that the principles of portfolio theory, whose applications we have seen throughout Part 2 of this book, afford no magic gateway to unlimited riches. Rather, much of what portfolio theory tells us can be viewed as a means for organizing our guesses about security performance in a logically coherent framework. In a similar vein, portfolio theory also offers some tips on how to organize the money management function itself. Specifically, our discussion of the various generic portfolio problems, active strategies, and performance measure-

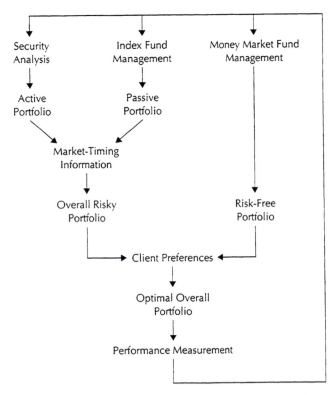

FIGURE 13.3   Money management organization based on portfolio theory

ment would suggest a setup something like that depicted in Figure 13.3. Three separate portfolios, the active, passive and risk-free, or money market, portfolios can be managed pretty much in isolation from one another. From Equation (12.11), for example, the composition of the active portfolio is independent of the market and index and risk-free returns provided the active securities' alphas and residual variances are independent of the index and risk-free return levels. Thus we could focus all individual security analysis activities on the active portfolio, concentrating instead on transactions and management economy for the passive and money market portfolios. Then market-timing information could be used in combining the active and passive portfolios to form the overall risky portfolio, and information about client preferences could be used in combining the risky and risk-free portfolios to form the overall optimal portfolio. We could then apply the performance measures discussed in this chapter to the portfolio's after-the-fact returns, and the results of this analysis would then react back and affect the next round of portfolio management decisions. This form of organization will not, of course, eradicate the difficulties inherent in forecasting returns or assessing performance. Nevertheless, it can help to focus whatever portfolio management skills we may have at our disposal on those areas where they can potentially add the most value.

III. SUMMARY

In this chapter, we have examined the problems of portfolio performance measurement and organizing the portfolio management process. While these are both difficult problems, the principles of portfolio theory that we have seen in earlier chapters can help us to approach these tasks in ways that are at least logical and coherent.

The Sharpe, Treynor, Jensen, and appraisal ratio measures, for example, all rely on the theory's principles to measure a managed portfolio's risk-adjusted performance relative to some benchmark. This task is made difficult, however, by the fact that the portfolio manager makes decisions before the fact, whereas we are almost inevitably forced to evaluate these decisions based on after-the-fact returns.

Specifically, after-the-fact performance measurement is plagued by the problem of achieving sufficient statistical power reliably to distinguish between skill and luck. Additional difficulties include the choice of an appropriate benchmark portfolio and the detection of market timing ability.

Alternative performance measures based on regression techniques or on weighting the portfolio's returns over different time periods offer some potential for reducing these difficulties. In addition, knowledge of the managed portfolio's composition is a useful input to performance assessment. In particular, it allows us to use performance attribution analysis to separate and measure the contributions to performance made by various components of the manager's overall portfolio decision.

Portfolio theory can also help in setting up a portfolio management system. It suggests, for example, the elements of the overall process, such as active security selection or index fund management, that can be usefully decentralized.

SUGGESTIONS FOR FURTHER READING

Further discussion of alternative portfolio performance measures and their use can be found in the following:

1. Ankrim, Ernest M., "Risk-Adjusted Performance Attribution," *Financial Analysts Journal*, 48 (March/April 1992), pp. 75–82.

2. Ankrim, Ernest M., and Chris R. Hensel, "Multicurrency Performance Attribution," *Financial Analysts Journal,* 50 (March/April 1994), pp. 29–33.

3. Bailey, Jeffery V., "Evaluating Benchmark Quality," *Financial Analysts Journal,* 48 (May/June 1992), pp. 33–39.

4. Goode, Stephen, and Peter J. Higgs, "Target Active Returns and Attribution Analysis," *Financial Analysts Journal,* 49 (May/June 1993), pp. 77–80.

5. Grinblatt, Mark, and Sheridan Titman, "Performance Evaluation," Working Paper, March 27, 1994.

6. Reilly, Frank K., G. Wenchi Kao, and David J. Wright, "Alternative Bond Market Indexes," *Financial Analysts Journal,* 48 (May/June 1992), pp. 44–58.

7. Sharpe, William F., "Asset Allocation: Management Style and Performance Measurement," *Journal of Portfolio Management,* 18 (Winter 1992), pp. 7–19.

8. Treynor, Jack, and Kay Mazuy, "Can Mutual Funds Outguess the Market?" *Harvard Business Review,* 44 (July 1966), pp. 131–36.

9. Zimmerman, Heinz, and Claudia Zogg-Wetter, "On Detecting Selection and Timing Ability: The Case of Stock Market Indexes," *Financial Analysts Journal,* 48 (January/February 1992), pp. 80–83.

PROBLEMS AND QUESTIONS

1. It is 1986. You are a progressive mutual fund portfolio manager, and you have decided to introduce international diversification into your portfolio of stocks. You estimate that the expected yearly returns and standard deviations of return on domestic stocks, foreign stocks, and cash are as follows:

	$E(r)$	σ
Domestic Stocks	.15	.20
Foreign Stocks	.17	.35
Cash	.05	0

a) You also estimate that the correlation between the returns on domestic and foreign stocks is zero. If the assets above are the only three asset classes under consideration, how should you divide the risky portion of your portfolio between domestic and foreign stocks?

b) International diversification is somewhat novel, and your fund's Board of Directors wants you to justify your portfolio strategy. How could you quantify the increase in performance that you could expect from combining domestic and foreign stocks versus the expected performance of a risky portfolio that consisted exclusively of domestic stocks? Briefly explain your measure of expected performance.

c) It is now 1996. You have awakened, Rip Van Winkle-like, from a ten-year slumber and have decided to re-examine your portfolio strategy. You estimate that the expected returns and standard deviations of return on all asset classes are the same as those given previously, but you also estimate that, because of increased global integration of product and financial markets, the correlation between the returns of foreign and domestic stocks is now .6 (instead of zero, as in [a]). Given this change in correlation, what is the optimal allocation of your risky portfolio between domestic and foreign stocks in 1996?

d) Given your optimal portfolio in 1996, by how much is your risky portfolio expected to outperform a risky portfolio consisting exclusively of domestic stocks? Use the same portfolio performance measure that you used in (b).

e) Briefly explain the difference between your answers to (a) and (b), on the one hand, and your answers to (c) and (d) on the other. In particular, why do you think an increase in the global integration of product and financial markets might increase the correlation between domestic and foreign stock returns? How does this relationship in turn affect the optimal allocation between domestic and foreign stocks and the potential gain from international diversification?

2. Calculate all four measures of performance for the risky portion of the active-passive portfolio constructed in Table 12.1. Compute the same four measures for the market portfolio (from the example, $E[r_m] = .15$, $\sigma_m = .2$, and $r_f = .05$). What do you conclude from comparing these measures?

3. Two portfolio managers, Pete Plunger and Darlene Diversifier, are putting together the risky portion of their portfolios. They are considering two risky assets: (1) a market index fund, with an expected return of .15 and a standard deviation of returns of .20; and (2) stock in the Zowie Corporation, which has an expected return of .23, a standard deviation of returns of .30, and a beta of 0.5. In any given period

t, the return on Zowie's stock, $\tilde{R}_{Zt}$, is consistent with the following relationship:

$$\tilde{r}_{Zt} = \alpha_Z + r_f + \beta_Z(\tilde{r}_{mt} - r_f) + \tilde{e}_{Zt}$$

where α_Z and β_Z are Zowie's alpha and beta, respectively; $\tilde{r}_{mt}$ is the return on the market index fund in period t; r_f is the risk-free rate of interest; and $\tilde{e}_{Zt}$ is a residual return, which is uncorrelated with the market return. The expected value of $\tilde{e}_{Zt}$ is zero and its standard deviation is $\sigma(e)$. The current risk-free rate is .05.

a) Pete neglected to take any finance courses in school and does not understand the concept of diversification. He decides to invest 100% of his portfolio in Zowie stock. Calculate the Sharpe and Treynor performance measures for Pete's portfolio.

b) Darlene, on the other hand, has read this book and understands the benefit of diversification extremely well. She also understands that, even though she is not personally responsible for combining the risky portfolio with the risk-free asset, the presence of the risk-free asset will affect her choice of an optimal risky portfolio. How should Darlene allocate her portfolio between the market index fund and Zowie stock?

c) Calculate the Sharpe and Treynor measures for Darlene's optimal risky portfolio.

d) Which of the two measures do you think is more appropriate for comparing the relative performance of Pete's and Darlene's portfolios? Briefly explain the reasons for your choice.

4. Al and Betty are two portfolio managers. Each follows a strategy of trying to identify a winner stock through fundamental security analysis and then combining this winner stock with the market index. The market index has an expected return of .14 and a variance of returns of .14. The risk-free rate of return is .04.

a) Al has identified security A as his winner. Security A has an expected return of .205, a variance of returns of .36, and a beta of 1.5. What is the composition of Al's optimal portfolio of risky securities?

b) Betty has identified security B as her winner. Security B has an expected return of .105, a variance of returns of .08, and a beta of 0.5. What is the composition of Betty's optimal portfolio of risky securities?

c) Calculate the appraisal ratio for Al's and Betty's optimal *active* portfolios. Calculate the Sharpe measures for Al's and Betty's optimal *risky* portfolio.

d) How would you explain the similarities and differences between Al's and Betty's portfolios in terms of portfolio composition and expected performance?

5. You are trying to choose between two portfolio managers to manage your pension fund. Manager A will combine a market index fund with active security A. Manager B will combine a market index fund with active security B. Both managers are also aware that a risk-free asset is available, although you are hiring them only to put together an optimal portfolio of risky stocks. (The decision on how much of the risk-free security to combine with this risky portfolio will be made separately.) The returns on both securities A and B follow a process described by

$$\tilde{r}_{it} = \alpha_i + r_f + \beta_i(\tilde{r}_{mt} - r_f) + \tilde{e}_{it}$$

for $i = A$ or B, where $\tilde{e}_{it}$ has an expected value of zero, a variance equal to $\sigma^2(e_i)$, and a correlation of zero with the market return or the residual returns on any other securities. Other characteristics of securities A and B, the market index fund, and the risk-free security are as follows:

SECURITY	$E(r)$	$\sigma^2(r)$	β
Security A	.12	.065	0.5
Security B	.22	.265	1.5
Market Index Fund	.15	.10	1.0
Risk-Free Asset	.05	0	0

a) Calculate an appraisal ratio for security A. What is manager A's optimal combination of the index fund with security A?
b) Calculate an appraisal ratio for security B. What is manager B's optimal combination of the index fund with security B?
c) Calculate both the Sharpe and Treynor measures of expected performance for the optimal risky portfolios put together by managers A and B.
d) If you could hire only one portfolio manager, which one should you hire? Briefly explain your answer by explaining whether the Sharpe measure, Treynor measure, or the appraisal ratio affords the best measure of performance in this case and why.

6. Return to Problem 5 in Chapter 12. Calculate the Sharpe measure for the decentralized pension portfolio [your answer to c) of Problem 5] and compare it with the Sharpe measure for the centralized portfolio [your answer to d) of Problem 5]. What does your answer tell you about the ideal organization of the portfolio management function?

7. You have a two-year investment horizon. The consensus forecast is that the return on the market portfolio will be .15 per year in each of

the two years. The yearly variance of the market return is .08, and the one-year risk-free rate is .05. The yield curve is flat. Your coefficient of risk aversion, A, is equal to 2.

a) With no additional information, how should you allocate your portfolio if your only two investment choices are a market index fund and the risk-free asset?

b) Now suppose that you hire a market analyst whom you believe to have market timing ability. You believe that the correlation between the analyst's forecasts of the market return and the actual market return is .6. You also feel that it is unnecessary to adjust the analyst's forecasts [that is, you set $a = 0$, $b = 1$ in the notation of Equation (12.2)]. The analyst forecasts that the market return for the first year will be .20. How should you allocate your portfolio for the first year, given the analyst's forecast?

c) After a year has gone by, the analyst forecasts that the market return for the second year will be only .10. How should you allocate your portfolio for the second year, given the analyst's forecast?

d) Suppose that, after the fact, the analyst's forecasts turn out to be correct. That is, the market return turns out to have been .20 in the first year and .10 in the second year. How would you suggest measuring the extent to which the analyst has added value to your portfolio? Calculate your measure(s) to illustrate your argument.

8. a) **Spreadsheet Exercise.** Using the data in Table 13.2, verify the regression results reported in Equation (13.1).

b) For the same data, estimate Treynor Mazuy (Equation 13.2) and Henriksson-Merton (Equation 13.4) regressions. What do you conclude about the manager's timing ability?

c) Now run the following regression:

$$r_p - r_f = a + b(r_m - r_f) + cD + e_p$$

where D is the dummy variable taking a value of 1 when the risk premium on the market portfolio is positive and zero otherwise (note that this regression is similar to the Merton-Henrikkson regression, but the dummy variable is not multiplied by the market risk premium). What do you conclude from your results about the portfolio manager's market timing ability?

d) Delete the observation for the third month of the first year (that is, the one in which the market return is 16.6% and the managed portfolio's return is 2.11%. Rerun the Treynor-Mazuy and Merton-Henrikkson regressions using the remaining 23 observations. What do you conclude from your results?

9. The market portfolio consists of sectors of stocks (technology stocks, utilities, etc). A portfolio manager might hope to outperform the market both by weighting the various sectors differently from the market portfolio and by emphasizing some stocks more than others within sectors. Suppose we are faced with a manager who has used this approach and who claims that his chosen portfolio can be expected to outperform the market benchmark. We wish to evaluate the manager's claim before the fact (that is, on an expected rather than a realized return basis) using performance attribution analysis.

One commonly used system for performance attribution analysis decomposes the difference between the manager's expected portfolio return and the benchmark expected return into three components: (1) the *allocation effect* is calculated by taking differences between the weights on each sector in the manager's portfolio and the sectoral weights in the benchmark portfolio, multiplying these differences by the expected benchmark return for each sector, and adding them up; (2) the *selection effect* is calculated by taking the differences between manager's expected return for each sector and the expected sectoral returns for the benchmark and adding up these differences, weighting them by the sectoral weights for the benchmark portfolio; (3) the *interaction effect* is calculated by taking the differences in sectoral expected return for the manager's and the benchmark portfolio, multiplying each by the corresponding difference in portfolio weights, and summing these products.

We have the following information about the sectoral weights and sectoral betas for the manager's and the benchmark portfolios and the sectoral expected returns for the manager's portfolio:

SECTOR	MANAGER'S PORTFOLIO			BENCHMARK PORTFOLIO	
	WGT	β	$E(r)$	WGT	β
Technology	.30	1.6	.16	.15	1.4
Producer Durables	.10	1.5	.15	.05	1.2
Consumer Discretionary	.40	1.4	.14	.20	1.1
Utilities	.05	0.8	.10	.10	0.6
Other Stocks	.15	0.9	.12	.50	0.9

We also know that the current risk-free rate, r_f, is 4% and the expected risk premium, $E(r_m) - r_f$, on the overall market benchmark portfolio is 8%.

a) Using the definitions above, calculate the allocation, selection, and interaction effects for the manager's portfolio. How can you interpret each of these effects in terms of what each tells us about the manager's expected performance?

b) An alternative system for performance attribution analysis adjusts each of the three effects, as calculated in (a), in the following ways:

(1) Adjust the allocation effect by multiplying the sectoral weighting differences by the corresponding benchmark sectoral betas, add these up, and multiply the sum by the expected risk premium on the market; then subtract the adjustment factor from the allocation effect computed in (a).

(2) Adjust the selection effect by multiplying differences in sectoral betas between the manager's and the benchmark portfolio by the corresponding benchmark sectoral weights, add these up, and multiply the sum by the expected risk premium on the market; then subtract the adjustment factor from the selection effect computed in (a).

(3) Adjust the interaction effect by multiplying differences in sectoral betas between the manager's and the benchmark portfolio by the corresponding differences in sectoral weights, add these up, and multiply the sum by the expected risk premium on the market; then subtract the adjustment factor from the selection effect computed in (a).

Explain what you think would be accomplished by this adjustment procedure. Do you think it would be a good idea to make these adjustments to your performance attribution analysis? Why or why not?

c) Using the procedure described in (b), calculate adjusted allocation, selection, and interaction effects for the manager's portfolio. How can you interpret each of these adjusted effects in terms of what each tells us about the manager's expected performance?

Footnotes

[1] See Mark Grinblatt and Sheridan Titman, "A Study of Monthly Mutual Fund Returns and Performance Evaluation Techniques," *Journal of Financial and Quantitative Analysis,* 29 (September 1994), pp. 419–44.

[2] See Richard Roll, "A Critique of the Asset Pricing Theory's Tests, Part I: On Past and Potential Testability of the Theory," *Journal of Financial Economics,* 4 (March 1977), pp. 129–76; and Richard Roll, "Ambiguity When Performance Is Measured by the Securities Market Line," *Journal of Finance,* 33 (September 1978), pp. 1051–69.

[3] See William F. Sharpe, "Asset Allocation: Management Style and Performance Measurement," *Journal of Portfolio Management,* 18 (Winter 1992), pp. 7–19.

[4] See Mark Grinblatt and Sheridan Titman, "Portfolio Performance Evaluation: Old Issues and New Insights," *Review of Financial Studies,* 2, no. 3 (1989), 393–421.

[5] Note that, because the portfolio manager is constrained to combinations of the index portfolio and the risk-free asset, both the high beta and low beta portfolio lines pass through the origin. Thus, before the fact, it is actually impossible for the portfolio manager to exhibit a positive Jensen's alpha measure with either portfolio.

[6] See Jack Treynor and Kay Mazuy, "Can Mutual Funds Outguess the Market?" *Harvard Business Review,* 44 (July 1966), pp. 131–36; and Roy D. Henriksson and Robert C. Merton, "On Market Timing and Investment Performance II: Statistical Procedures for Evaluating Forecasting Skills," *Journal of Business,* 54 (October 1981), pp. 513–33.

[7] See Robert C. Merton, "On Market Timing and Investment Performance I: An Equilibrium Theory of Value for Market Forecasts," *Journal of Business,* 54 (July 1981), pp. 361–406.

[8] See Mark Grinblatt and Sheridan Titman, "Portfolio Performance Evaluation: Old Issues and New Insights," *Review of Financial Studies,* 2, no. 3 (1989), 393–421.

[9] See Bradford Cornell, "Asymmetric Information and Portfolio Performance Measurement," *Journal of Financial Economics,* 7 (December 1979), pp. 381–90; Thomas Copeland and David Mayers, "The Value Line Enigma (1965–1978): A Case Study of Performance Evaluation Issues," *Journal of Financial Economics,* 10 (November 1982), pp. 289–321; and Mark Grinblatt and Sheridan Titman, "Performance Measurement Without Benchmarks: An Examination of Mutual Fund Returns," *Journal of Business,* 66 (January 1993), pp. 47–68. A useful survey article, comparing and contrasting the different performance measures, is Mark Grinblatt and Sheridan Titman, "Performance Evaluation," Working Paper, March 27, 1994.

Index